THE PRESERVATION KITCHEN

The Craft of
Making and Cooking with
Pickles, Preserves, and
Aigre-doux

Paul Virant

WITH KATE LEAHY

TEN SPEED PRESS
Berkeley

TABLE OF CONTENTS

Capturing the Year in a Jar

The soul of my kitchen isn't in my kitchen at all. It hovers one floor above, contained within a narrow storage room lined with aluminum shelves. Even on the brightest days, the sunlight that filters through a small east-facing window is dim, hardly adequate. It doesn't seem to matter. Packed with jars of pickles, jams, sauerkrauts, and other experiments in preserving, these shelves radiate with possibility.

When I need inspiration, I head upstairs and take inventory. Each visit provides me with a snapshot of the growing seasons. Early spring yields light-green baby artichokes, white turnips, and jars of lemon preserves. Army-green ramps and asparagus soon follow trailed by glossy pints of strawberry jam. Summer starts out slowly, a few pickled green beans, some snappy snow peas, a batch of giardiniera. By the end of September, however, the shelves bulge, emanating primary colors as carrots, dill pickles, peppers, eggplant, peaches, porcini, cherries, summer squash, and tomatoes—lots and lots of tomatoes—compete for attention. Then comes autumn, a subdued time when ruby-hued cranberries and winter squashes quietly signal an end to the harvest.

By the time winter blankets the neighborhood with snow, we have started dipping into our flavor arsenal, fortifying gravy with fiery cherry bomb peppers saved from July and dressing up cheese plates with sweet-sour grapes. Winter months are slow days for canning, but the process never completely stops. As soon as the New Year arrives, the mailbox fills with fragrant lemons and mandarins from generous friends in California, and we get to work.

When my family and I opened Vie in the fall of 2004, I knew I was going to serve local produce year-round. This idea doesn't sound that radical now. But even just a few years ago, there were far fewer local family farms supplying Chicago restaurants than there are today. Among those, only a handful managed to extend the Great Lakes' all-too-short growing season beyond summer. And we had other challenges. When we opened, Vie was a novelty in Western Springs, a historic suburb a half hour west of Chicago on the Metra commuter rail. It's a quiet village of tree-lined streets and comfortable homes surrounding a main street with small-town essentials: butcher shop, bakery, diner, produce stand, hardware store, and ice cream parlor. We were the first serious restaurant to put down roots, and the first to acquire a liquor license. (Western Springs had been dry since Prohibition.) The whole project was enough of a gamble that I knew I couldn't stay in business if I drafted a menu devoted solely to beets—one of the few local items available year-round—even if the menu tasted delicious. I started preserving a few summer staples to extend the seasons. But that was well before I realized how many flavors I could capture in a jar.

I grew up eating pickles. My grandmothers, both from Missouri, were avid canners, their summer meals often punctuated with a plate of tart dill-marinated tomatoes served straight from the refrigerator. Several years (and several restaurant stints) later, I grasped what my grandmothers always knew: vinegar draws out flavor. I decided that pickles had a place on a restaurant table.

In the pre-Vie days, while working around town for other chefs, I started making my own pickles. The experiment soon gravitated to homemade sauerkraut as vats of vegetables fermented on the counter. Soon I was reading everything I could find on preserving. Especially memorable were the archaic methods outlined in old American cookery books, which always went heavy on vinegar, spices, and sugar. Then I met Christine Ferber, the famed Alsatian jam maker whom many in France call—no exaggeration—the fairy godmother of jams and jellies. After taking her preserving class at Chicago's French Pastry School, I became hooked on the world of *aigre-doux*, a French sweet-sour style of condiment that seemed to go with everything, from cheese to roasted meat. This inevitably led to more experiments.

CHRISTINE FERBER

Pastry chef Christine Ferber's preserves are so popular in France that food lovers make annual pilgrimages to her shop in Niedermorschwihr, the Alsatian village where she also grew up. Her standards are famously high: she uses only pristine produce, avoiding fruit picked after a rain (too soggy) or after baking in the hot sun (too soft). Yet what inspired me most about Christine's preserve making is her knack for combining flavors, from cherries and strawberries simmered in Pinot Noir to raspberries cooked with elderflowers. Our paths crossed several years ago in Chicago. She was invited by the French Pastry School to teach a preserving class, and I signed up. That's when I first heard about macerating fruit for at least a day before finishing a jam. It's also the class that piqued my interest in aigre-doux. Through the years, I've adapted some of her recipes to suit my needs. All recipes in this book inspired by Christine are credited in the introductory note.

Local farmers turned my part-time canning habit into a full-blown commitment. I started getting to know an entrepreneurial network of Midwesterners who worked year-round to grow local produce, insulating crops with hoop houses, greenhouses, and even compost piles so that chard, beets, arugula, parsnips, and sunchokes could flourish even when outside temperatures hovered well below freezing. Small farms in southern Wisconsin began to come together through community-supported agriculture programs, while stretches of central Illinois highway, once bordered by oceans of corn and soybeans only, transformed into land that supported goats, sheep, tomatoes, peppers, and lettuces. Michigan and Indiana farms beckoned with more produce, especially juicy organic berries and stone fruits. Through the back door came boxes of peak-season, Midwestern-grown produce that outperformed anything shipped from California. This produce deserved to be savored, and saved.

In the early days, I started slowly, a few cases of tomatoes and a couple of jams. But as I packed away jars of locally grown San Marzano tomatoes, more ideas came flooding in. How about fermenting Brussels sprouts, for instance? Or what about puréeing black walnuts with maple syrup for a nut butter? For about two years, our kitchen went through what I call our "experimental preserving extravaganza" period. Not everything was a success. A baby leek and carrot aigre-doux failed to win fans (leeks are generally better fresh or lightly pickled). Fermented tomatoes, meanwhile, polarized the kitchen—I liked them, and still make them on occasion. Others did not like their pungent tang. Gradually, the murkier experiments were pushed aside in favor of the winners, of which there were plenty. As our canning inventory accumulated, spreading from the second-story storage room into the basement of one of my employees, it became clear that this habit had evolved into an obsession, just as much about flavor as about principle. I had become a so-called jarring chef.

Our menus at Vie have developed alongside our seasonal preserves, and they are intrinsically linked together. The bond is reflected in this book. In Part One: In the Jar, I share recipes for preserves that take advantage of peak-season ingredients. In Part Two: At the Table, I demonstrate how to use these preserves in meals ranging from weeknight dishes to celebratory occasions. Organized around the seasons, these menus mix fresh produce with preserved ingredients, unlocking the culinary potential that occurs when we stretch growing seasons. Tying both sections of the book together is one simple adage: I eat what I can and what I can't, I can.

Principles of Safe Preserving

A Brief History

Canning looks pretty old-fashioned. Hot jars filled with jam or pickles, capped with a two-piece lid, are dropped gently into a pot. Once boiled, these sealed, shelf-stable items line a pantry shelf to be used throughout the year. But home canning as we know it is a relatively modern practice. Before the development of the self-sealing Mason jar in the 1850s, and even after, canning was, thanks to Napoleon and his experiments in feeding an army, a military endeavor. In the nineteenth century, homemakers were more likely to preserve and store produce in vats of heavily salted, sweetened, and spiced vinegar brines, then store these containers in cool pantries for months. *Housekeeping in Old Virginia*, a collection of regional recipes published in 1879, included recipes for brines containing two pounds of sugar for every gallon of vinegar. It was a brine "strong enough to bear an egg"—and acidic enough to keep just about anything from spoiling. Some recipes in this household manual recommended soaking vegetables in brine for at least six months before eating them. What's amazing about the collection of recipes in *Housekeeping* is the range of foods that were preserved this way: lemons, cabbage, green tomatoes, and melon rinds all received the strong-brine treatment.

While reusable Mason jars with their dependable two-piece lids ushered in a handier way to preserve food, other principles of preserving—how it keeps food from spoiling—remained a mystery. In 1915, USDA scientists had a breakthrough: they identified the bacterium that causes botulism poisoning. Eventually scientists established the safety pillars of canning: acidity, heat, and a sealed, airless (anaerobic) environment would ensure shelf-stability.

Yet some debate continues between American food scientists and home cooks about safe canning practices. The open-kettle method, in which hot food is poured into a hot jar, closed with a cap, and left on the counter to seal itself, is one of the biggest points of debate. While this method was common years ago, American food scientists do not endorse it today. Even though the jar may seal, the food still runs the risk of spoilage because the jar was never sterilized in boiling water. When my coauthor, Kate, and I took an acidified foods canning class through the University of Wisconsin extension program, one woman shared her grandmother's practice of packing hot tomato sauce into jars, capping the jars with lids, and storing them above the stove until she needed to use them. Every once and a while, a jar exploded because of residual microbial activity. The mess alone would be reason enough to avoid this method. However, many prominent European jam makers endorse this process, and it is common to find recipes for marmalades that don't require water-bath processing once the marmalade is packed in jars. I can understand the argument—a marmalade is pretty stable on its own; fruit is high in acid and sugar itself acts as a preservative. Even so, I always boil jars of jams in water for at least 10 minutes, the point at which I can be sure that the jar, the lid, and the contents are sterilized.

As the popularity of canning and preserving once again expands, contradictory information continues to circulate. Meanwhile, warnings from jargon-prone government guides can scare a newcomer away from even trying. You don't need an advanced degree or access to a sterile lab to can safely. However, you do need to understand a few facts.

The Science

Entire university departments are dedicated to understanding the complex relationships between food and spoilers. My intention here is not to cover the minutiae but rather to provide background on basic canning science. After reading this section, you will understand why a fruit jam is processed in a boiling water bath and low-acid garlic conserva is processed in a pressure canner. (And by "processed," I'm referring to the time the jars spend in a pot of boiling water or in a pressure canner.) You will also know why I process larger jars longer than smaller jars.

Preserving science comes down to destroying microorganisms, mainly molds, yeasts, and bacteria. Not all molds and yeasts in food are bad, as anyone who has enjoyed a piece of blue cheese or sourdough bread can attest. In some instances, bacteria is an essential part of the process, like in sauerkraut production. In general, however, preserving food requires limiting microbial activity as much as possible. It is no fun opening a jar of jam to find that a family of mold has colonized the surface. (This can happen when a jar is not properly sterilized. If you find mold on the surface of a preserve, throw out the jar.)

The combination of heat, acidity, and an airtight seal is crucial to the safety of the contents in a jar. Yeasts, molds, and most bacteria generally have low tolerances to heat, and heating food at the boiling point of water destroys most of these organisms. Most of these spoilers also need oxygen to survive, and an airtight seal cuts off this lifeline. Consequently, boiling a jar filled with preserves in a water bath destroys microorganisms, sterilizes the food in the jar, and forces air out of the jar, enabling the lid to seal as it cools.

An airtight seal keeps oxygen and new microbes out, but it also can create the perfect habitat for the dangerous bacterium *clostridium botulinum*. In an anaerobic environment, the spores of *clostridium botulinum* flourish. These spores give off a toxin that, if consumed, leads to botulism poisoning, a serious and sometimes fatal illness. That's where acid comes in. *Clostridium botulinum* is sensitive to acid. If the environment within the jar is acidic, botulism spores cannot survive. The only other way to destroy botulism is to process jars at temperatures well above the boiling point of water. Since water boils at higher temperatures under pressure, foods that are not acidic enough to stave off botulism need to be processed in a pressure canner. Most of the preserving recipes in this book are acidic enough to use a boiling water bath for processing. For the

few low-acid preserves in the book, I've included instructions in Pressure-Canned Preserves, page 121.

pH

A pH of 4.6 is the dividing line between acidic foods that can be processed in a water bath and low-acid foods that must be pressure-canned. Every preserve with a pH of 4.5 or lower can be processed safely in a water bath. (On a pH scale, 1 is a strong acid, 14 is a strong base, and 7 is neutral.) Most fruits, and consequently most jams, are naturally acidic, but most vegetables are not. A lemon has an average pH of 2.2 while a carrot clocks in at about 6. While lemons cooked into marmalade are acidic enough on their own, carrots need vinegar to lower their pH below 4.6. Essentially, they need to be pickled. If you wanted to pack carrots in water, you would have to process the jars in a pressure canner because the jar would not be acidic enough to inhibit botulism spore growth. (And what's the point? A jar of carrots in water is hardly an improvement on fresh carrots.) Yet not all fruit is acidic enough to preserve as is: figs are borderline, and so are some tomatoes. (For more on acidity and tomatoes, see page 46.) All of my recipes have been tested for pH. While minor changes to the recipes, like using a different herb or spice, will not change the overall acidity level, I urge you not to play around with the quantity or variety of vinegar, alcohol, or lemon juice called for because it could compromise the product's pH level.

TESTING PH

When I develop a new canning recipe, I sacrifice one finished jar from the batch to test pH. If the jar has a pH below 4.6, the recipe meets the safety requirements for water-bath processing and I can be confident that the rest of the jars can be safely consumed. You do not need to test the acidity of each batch of preserves you make from this book, but if you plan on developing your own preserving recipes, you should double-check your work to ensure your new creations are safe to eat, particularly with pickles. When testing the pH of a batch of pickles, you are measuring the equilibrium pH—the acidity level of the vegetable after it has been processed in brine and allowed to sit on the shelf for at least two days. By this point, the vegetable should have soaked up enough vinegar to be acidic even when taken out of the brine.

I use a pH meter for the task. Sold by science-supply companies, these meters require an investment of a few hundred dollars. If you are planning to sell preserves, you also may consider sending samples to a third-party lab that assesses pH. Before testing, calibrate the pH meter. The meter should come with a few vials of pH buffer solutions: an acid (4.0 pH), a neutral (7.0 pH), and a base (10.0 pH). To calibrate, dip the tip of the meter into each solution to ensure that it is reading the pH levels accurately. Next, drain away the brine from the pickled vegetables and put the vegetables in a blender. Purée the vegetables with just enough distilled water to make a slurry (a thin purée). Dip the calibrated pH meter into the slurry and record the reading.

The Set-Up

Working in a restaurant kitchen, I have one big advantage over a home cook. My stove's large burners not only accommodate large pots easily but also bring water to a boil quickly. Even while processing the jars, the water will come to a boil quickly without any help from a lid. But a restaurant kitchen has disadvantages. Canning is never the only activity going on, so claiming a space on the stove isn't easy. Finding a work space is another issue. You need a spot to fill clean jars and another area to keep the jars as they cool. With canning, every kitchen space comes with its own challenges, and it can take a little time to work out a system that's effective for you.

To get started, you will need:

CLEAN JARS WITH LIDS AND BANDS

I use Mason jars (Ball or Kerr—both brands are owned by the same company) because they are relatively inexpensive, easy to find (just about every hardware store carries them in several sizes and shapes), and extra jar lids and bands are easy to come by. You can use a jar indefinitely until it chips or cracks. Bands can be used over until they show signs of rust. But you should cap jars with new lids every time. The bottom rim of the lid has a rubber sealing compound. After one use, its sealing properties are compromised. I also avoid old lids bought years ago, even if they haven't been used. The rubber on older lids may have hardened, which also compromises sealing capabilities.

A LARGE POT

You can buy a pot marketed specifically for canning, but it isn't necessary. More important is finding a pot tall enough to accommodate the jars. Because you need to cover the jars with at least an inch of water to adequately boil them, most pots at home aren't tall enough, particularly for quart jars (though many are fine for half-pint jars). If you're shopping for a pot that will accommodate quart jars, bring a jar with you to ensure that you have a few inches of space from the top of the jar to the rim of the pot. In general, a 33-quart/31-liter pot, quite large by home kitchen standards, will hold nine quart jars.

A RACK THAT FITS INTO THE BOTTOM OF THE POT

A rack cushions the jars as they process, preventing glass from hitting the bottom of the pot and cracking. If you buy a pot specifically for canning, chances are it will come with a rack. However, I prefer a round cooling rack, the kind used for cakes. Or you can make your own rack from extra jar bands: tie the bands together until they form a circle that covers the bottom of the pot.

OTHER TOOLS

I use a pair of regular kitchen tongs as well as a jar lifter, a nifty contraption with rubber-lined prongs that grasps a jar as you pull it out of hot water. A wide-mouth funnel can be helpful when filling messy preserves into jars, but it isn't essential. To make sure you are leaving enough headspace—the gap between the contents and the rim of the jar—it's handy to have a ruler for measuring. I also like to have a separate small pot ready for warming lids. Some people like to use a stick with a magnet on the end for drawing out hot lids from water. They're fun, but my hands are tough enough to handle a little hot metal. A working kitchen timer, however, is non-negotiable. Get one. For checking the temperature of jams or brines, I recommend acquiring an inexpensive handheld digital thermometer.

Water-Bath Processing

The recipes in this book contain concise instructions on how to process jars in a water bath. Here I've described the process in more detail. Before diving into the canning recipes in this book, I recommend reviewing the following steps.

Fit a rack in a large pot, fill the pot with water, and bring the water to a simmer. It should be hot but not boiling. Otherwise you might burn yourself when putting the jars in the pot. If your stove brings water to a boil slowly, you may want to invest in an electric kettle, which boils water rapidly without taking up burner space. An electric kettle also provides an easy way to keep hot water on hand in case you need to add more to the pot after adding the jars.

Next, scald the jars. Using tongs, plunge the jars into the simmering water. I let the jars sit in the pot while I'm gathering the rest of the ingredients, then pull them out right before I'm ready to fill them. This ensures that the jars are hot before I put them back into the pot, which prevents cracking. You do not need to sterilize the jars because all of the preserves in this book are processed for at least 10 minutes, the minimum amount of time needed to sterilize the jars, lids, and contents.

Meanwhile, soak clean lids in hot but not boiling water to soften the rubber seal. I often throw the rings in, too, although if you have sensitive hands this will make it harder to screw the rings on the jars later. This isn't about sterilizing the equipment either, but rather ensuring that everything is relatively the same temperature before processing.

If making a preserve with a brine, bring the brine to a brisk simmer. It should be about 180°F when poured into the jars. At this point, you should have all of the ingredients—a finished jam, blanched or raw vegetables, spices—ready to pack in the jar.

Take the jars out of the water and line them on a counter. Go about filling the jars with spices and garlic, if needed. Then fill the jars with the main ingredients. If making a preserve with a brine, transfer the hot brine to a heat-proof pitcher and pour it into the jars. For a quart jar, leave 1 inch of room from the rim of the jar to the contents. For smaller jars, a $^1/_2$-inch space will do, though for very small jars of jam, $^1/_4$ inch of space is sufficient. Too much or too little room between the rim of the jar and the contents can compromise sealing.

Wipe the rims with a clean, damp towel or paper towel, ensuring that there aren't any bits of food on the rim of the jar that might inhibit sealing. Place the warmed lids on top of each jar. Holding the lid on the rim of the jar with one hand, screw on the bands with the other hand. You want to screw the bands just until what canners like to call "fingertip tight"—snug enough that the lid will stay in place, but not so tight that you can't unscrew the band using the tips of your fingers. The point here is to ensure the jar will be able to expel air as it processes, enabling the lid to vacuum seal. If it's too tight, it will prevent air from releasing. If you screw on the band snugly and then give it a quarter turn in the opposite direction, you should be fine.

Using the jar lifter, lower each jar gently into the pot. You may need to add more water to ensure that the jars are covered by at least 1 inch. Next, bring the pot to a boil (you may want to cover the pot with a lid). Once the water reaches a boil, start the timer for the processing time indicated in the recipe. Processing times aren't arbitrary: they are based on how long it takes for the contents inside a jar to reach and hold a boiling point for enough time to kill spoilers. (Larger jars and denser vegetables or fruits will have longer processing times.) While the jars are processing you can keep the lid on the pot or take it off—it doesn't matter as long as the water stays boiling.

PRINCIPLES OF SAFE PRESERVING

Once the jars are processed, turn off the heat and let the jars sit in the water for a minute or two. If you take the jars out of the water immediately, temperature change from the pot to the counter can cause hot brine to bubble up through the top of the jar, wedge a seed or spice into the lid, and disrupt the seal. Using the jar lifter, gently pull each jar from the hot water and set it down to cool. As the jars cool (or even as soon as you pull them out of the water), you might hear a popping sound—this is the sound of the lids sealing. I usually know within a few minutes if I have any sealing issues with jars; I just tap the top and see if the lid has formed a tight suction. Yet most guides suggest waiting a few hours before removing the bands and testing the seal, for good reason: when the jar is hot, the rubber seal is still soft and could shift if prodded. If the jar has sealed correctly, you should be able to remove the band and pick the jar up by the lid without incidence.

If your jars don't seal, a few things might have gone wrong. Your lids may be old. A bit of food may have wedged itself between the lid and the jar. The rim could have had a small chip or crack. Or the jars were not covered completely by water while boiling. If this happens, the preserve is still edible—you can keep it in the refrigerator and eat it within a few weeks. Or you can reprocess: Set out hot, clean jars and new lids. Bring the preserve to a boil, pack it back into the jars, and process for the same amount of time as before.

Once the jars have been checked for a good seal, I remove the bands. They can hide a faulty seal, or they can rust. (If I'm transporting preserves, however, I screw the bands back on.) Finally, I label and date the jars and add them to the pantry.

PROCESSING JARS IN THE OVEN

Europeans have always taken a slightly different approach to canning than Americans. This book follows the FDA- and USDA-approved processing procedures, in which jars are boiled in a water bath or pressure-canned for a set amount of time. French jam maker Christine Ferber uses a different technique: she processes filled jars in the oven until the aigre-doux liquid begins to bubble up through the lid. The idea behind this method is that a filled jar left in the oven long enough with eventually reach an internal temperature hot enough to kill spoilers. There are benefits to using the oven for processing: it's gentle on the fruit, allowing it to retain its shape. It's also easier—just put the jars on a large sheet tray and place in a preheated 215°F oven for about 1 hour. The downside is that it is less precise. While water always boils at 212°F at sea level, oven temperatures vary widely and hot dry air doesn't transfer heat as quickly as hot water or steam. I've experimented with the process, and I've liked the results—especially with the blueberry aigre-doux (page 91). But I'm still waiting on the canning authorities to give this method a closer study.

CANNING AT ALTITUDE

For people living at elevations of 1,000 feet and above, it's essential to modify the canning process. It comes down to pressure and temperature. While water always boils at 212°F at sea level, it boils at lower temperatures at higher altitudes because higher altitudes have lower atmospheric pressure. Ask anyone who has tried hard-boiling eggs at 7,000 feet: even after 12 minutes in boiling water, the eggs come out with strange, soft whites.

To adjust for altitude:

WATER-BATH PROCESSING:
Add 5 minutes for 1,000 to 3,000 feet above sea level, 10 minutes for 3,001 to 6,000 feet above sea level, 15 minutes for 6,001 to 8,000 feet above sea level, and 20 minutes for 8,001 to 10,000 feet above sea level.

PRESSURE-CANNING:
Look up the pressure needed at your specific altitude. The USDA advises that 11 pounds of pressure be used at 2,000 feet, 11.5 pounds of pressure at 3,000 feet, 12 pounds of pressure at 4,000 feet, and so on.

Measuring Ingredients: Using Weight, Volume, and Percentages

Each preserving recipe provides ingredient quantities in volume, weight (ounces or pounds and grams), and percentages.

WEIGHT MEASUREMENTS

Weight measurements offer more accuracy than volume measurements. The weight of a cup of sugar varies depending on the brand of sugar and the cook measuring it, but a pound of sugar will always be the same amount. Beyond accuracy, scales make life easier. For a reasonable amount of money—about fifty bucks—you can own a digital scale that transitions easily between grams and ounces. The scale also has the all-important "tare" button, which will bring the weight on the scale back to zero. So I can set a bowl on the scale, reset the scale to zero, then pour an ingredient directly into a bowl on the scale until it hits the correct weight, all without going through the trouble of digging out measuring cups. If measuring multiple ingredients into the bowl, I simply push tare in between additions. Yet digital scales have a drawback. Unless you spend a lot of money for a high-precision model, most scales can't distinguish between five thyme sprigs and 10 thyme sprigs. I stick with volume measurements for small increments.

VOLUME MEASUREMENTS

With all the joy that a digital scale can provide, many of us are still attached to measuring cups. So I've also included volume measurements in the recipes. While they can be used on their own, volume measurements are best if used in tandem with weight measurements. If you're not sure what a pound of a certain ingredient looks like, volume can provide a guideline. And as I mentioned with weight measurements, I use volume measurements with ingredients like spices and herbs that are hard to weigh on a home kitchen scale.

PERCENTS

The percents calculated in each recipe are based on the weight measurements. In all but a few cases where indicated, they add up to 100 percent. Essentially, the percents are like ratios. They give you the freedom to scale a recipe to fit the quantity of produce on hand. A classic vinaigrette is three parts oil and one part vinegar, whether you're making one cup of vinaigrette or ten cups. Likewise, if you have two pounds of gooseberries for jam instead of the four pounds called for in the recipe, you can decrease the ingredient quantities as long as the percentages of the ingredients used—75.5 percent gooseberries, 23 percent sugar, 1.5 percent lemon juice—stay the same. The one exception is with spices and herbs. Since it's hard to weigh them accurately, the recipes do not include percentages for spices or herbs. Frankly, I find it is easier to add a spoonful of black peppercorns to each jar than calculate a new total quantity. If you double the recipe, you still add a teaspoon to each jar; you just need more jars.

A Few Words on Salt and Vinegar

While quality produce, spices, and sugar are important parts of my preserving pantry, the two ingredients that I rely on the most are salt and vinegar. Without salt, we wouldn't have a key ingredient for sauerkraut. Without vinegar, we wouldn't have pickled vegetables.

SALT

We tested the recipes in this book using kosher salt. Some people prefer pickling salt for its clarity when dissolved in brine, but I choose kosher because I use it in the kitchen for nearly everything else. You may substitute other salts in recipes that rely on salt for flavor, such as most pickles and aigre-doux recipes. Since salt is not crucial for preservation in these cases, you can adjust the quantity to suit your taste. For recipes that require salt for preservation, however, the variety and quantity do matter. When making sauerkraut, you need a specific amount of salt in the brine to encourage beneficial fermentation and discourage spoilers. If you do decide to use an alternative salt, use weight, not volume, to determine what you need.

VINEGAR

I use Champagne vinegar almost exclusively when I make pickles. I like its sharp flavor and clean finish. Other light wine vinegars can be used in its place, with this caution: before you use any vinegar, check the acidity level on the label. When pickling, a vinegar with less than 5 percent acidity will compromise the overall pH of the pickle and may render it unsafe for water-bath canning. The champagne vinegar that I use runs 6 percent, so I strongly recommend using champagne vinegar or a vinegar of the same strength. Avoid homemade vinegars unless you can be certain of their acidity levels.

PART ONE

In the Jar

PICKLES, RELISHES, AND OTHER ACIDIFIED PRESERVES

Pickles are the foundation of our canning program at Vie. From early spring ramps to late fall celery root, every season brings us something that we can pack away in a jar filled with brine. Some experiments, like pickled fennel, have been slam dunks, the vinegar and spices bringing out new characteristics in the vegetable. Other batches were less enlightening. Porous chanterelles, we learned, do not hold up well in vinegar.

Our pickle experiments would be a lot less meaningful if we only served the occasional spear of pickled asparagus, but this is hardly the case. Having a variety of pickles on hand challenges me to use them in ways I hadn't thought of before. A jar of sweet-pickled cherry tomatoes can be eaten alone. But purée a jar and you have the base of a sweet, tangy vinaigrette. And just as a squeeze of lemon juice can bring out the flavors in a simple dish, a splash of leftover pickling brine added to a soup, sauce, braise, or roast has a similar brightening effect. In fact, I often dress fresh vegetables with their pickled counterparts and a splash of brine. Carrots, beets, asparagus, turnips, and green beans are especially good prepared this way.

Food scientists categorize pickles as acidified foods. They don't have enough acid on their own, so they need the addition of acid (most often from vinegar) to render them safe for water-bath canning. With pickles, the brine penetrates the vegetable, drawing out some of its water and replacing it with vinegar. This is why when you use a pH meter to test acidity, you drain away the brine and purée the vegetable with distilled water to best measure how acidic the vegetable has become.

When developing pickle recipes, I err on the side of having more brine than I need. That way, if I need additional brine to fill in air pockets in the jar, I have enough on hand. The probable outcome of this is that you will often have leftover brine. This isn't a bad thing: leftover brine from a batch of asparagus pickles can easily be added to a fresh pot of brine for fennel. Or make a jar of refrigerator-pickled onions—just pour the hot brine over sliced onions and let them marinate in the refrigerator.

THE ALL-PURPOSE CRÈME FRAÎCHE SAUCE

After spending the better part of a decade sorting out what to do with jars of pickles, I've come across something that I can only call the crème fraîche effect. Mix a generous spoonful of crème fraîche into sliced pickled vegetables with a splash of brine and you have a sauce, vinaigrette, or dip.

Try warming sliced pickled asparagus in a pan with a spoonful of brine. Stir in a dollop of crème fraîche, and then use it as sauce over a fried egg and watercress. Or purée a jar of pickled cherry tomatoes and mix in crème fraîche for a creamy condiment for crostini. The same trick works with countless other pickles, from green beans to celery root.

BASE RECIPE: CRÈME FRAÎCHE

Although we could buy crème fraîche, I find that it is much more economical to make it ourselves. At Vie, we always have a batch on hand to garnish smoked sturgeon or swirl into a sauce.

makes 4 to 5 cups

4 cups heavy cream
1 cup buttermilk

1. In a tall pitcher or storage container, whisk the cream and buttermilk together. Cover the pitcher with a layer of cheesecloth and leave it at room temperature for 2 days, or until the cream has thickened. Refrigerate the crème fraîche until needed. Before using, give it a good whisk.

PICKLED BABY ARTICHOKES

The artichokes I receive in February and March may not be local, but they are so refreshing that it would be hard to imagine spring menus without them. We save the best specimens—the tender baby artichokes that have yet to develop a hint of purple choke—for this pickle. I will eat them straight out of the jar, or I'll crisp them in a pan with some olive oil and serve them as an appetizer or side dish.

There are two parts to the recipe: braising and processing in jars. First, I trim the artichokes and braise them gently with wine and onions. After the artichokes are cooked, they are delicious to eat straight from the pan. To preserve them, I take it one step further, making a brine from the braising liquid and packing the artichokes in jars for processing. With artichokes, I prefer a milder pickle to ensure that the vegetable's naturally sweet flavor isn't eclipsed by vinegar. These artichokes have a higher pH than most pickles, but they still fall below 4.6 pH, the maximum pH for water-bath canning.

After cleaning, you will have about 5 pounds of artichokes for pickling.

makes 8 pints

POACHING

INGREDIENT	VOLUME	OUNCES	GRAMS
Lemons	1 1/2	—	—
Baby artichokes	40–50	9 pounds, 8 ounces	4300 grams
Sweet onion, preferably candy or Vidalia, sliced	1	8 ounces	250 grams
Thyme sprigs	6	—	—
Water	8 cups	64 ounces	1814 grams
White wine	1/2 cup	4 ounces	114 grams
Kosher salt	2 teaspoons	1/3 ounce	10 grams

1. Fill a bowl with cold water and squeeze half a lemon into it. Pluck off the coarse outer leaves of the artichokes, stopping when you reach the lighter green, tender inner leaves. Working with one artichoke at a time, trim the tips of the leaves by about 1/2 inch, then trim the end of the stem. Using a paring knife, strip away the skin of the stem, leaving as much of the stem intact as possible. Halve the artichokes. If you see any hint of a purple, prickly choke, gently scrape it out with the tip of a spoon. Otherwise, leave the center intact. Soak the artichoke halves in the lemon water while you clean the rest.

2. Drain the artichokes and transfer to a large, wide pot or Dutch oven. Coat the artichokes in the juice of the remaining lemon and add the lemon rinds to the pot. Mix in the onion and thyme, cover with the water and wine, and sprinkle with salt. Cover with a parchment paper lid (see page 20). Bring the pot to a brisk simmer over medium-high heat, then decrease to a gentle simmer and cook until tender (the tip of a paring knife slides

easily into its heart), about 30 minutes. Let cool to room temperature. Strain 4 cups of the poaching liquid and reserve for the pickling brine. Reserve the onions and artichokes for pickling. (The vegetables will weigh just shy of 4½ pounds after straining.)

PICKLING

INGREDIENT	VOLUME	OUNCES	GRAMS	PERCENT
Poaching liquid	4 cups	32 ounces	907 grams	21.25%
Champagne vinegar	3 cups	24 ounces	680 grams	15.85%
Water	3 cups	24 ounces	680 grams	15.85%
Kosher salt	½ teaspoon	less than ⅛ ounce	2 grams	.05%
Poached artichokes with onion slices	14 cups	4 pounds, 7 ounces	2012 grams	47%

{continued}

1. In a medium pot, bring the poaching liquid, vinegar, water, and salt to a boil. Keep hot.

2. Scald 8 pint jars in a large pot of simmering water fitted with a rack—you will use this pot to process the jars. Right before filling, put the jars on the counter. Divide the artichokes and onion slices among the jars, using about 10 artichoke halves per jar. Meanwhile, soak the lids in a pan of hot water to soften the rubber seal.

3. Transfer the brine to a heat-proof pitcher and pour over the artichokes, leaving a $1/2$-inch space from the rim of the jar. Check the jars for air pockets, adding more brine if necessary to fill in gaps. Wipe the rims with a clean towel, seal with the lids, then screw on the bands until snug but not tight.

4. Place the jars in the pot with the rack and add enough water to cover the jars by about 1 inch. Bring the water to a boil and process the jars for 15 minutes (start the timer when the water reaches a boil). Turn off the heat and leave the jars in the water for a few minutes. Remove the jars from the water and let cool completely.

MAKING A PARCHMENT PAPER LID

When braising, there are times when a conventional pan lid is too constraining. It can lock in too much liquid, preventing needed evaporation while ingredients steam. Other times, cooking without a lid encourages too much moisture loss. To find the middle ground, some chefs use a lid made out of parchment paper.

Here's how to do it: Fold a sheet of parchment in half twice. We use full sheets of parchment at Vie, but at home a half sheet—about 12 by 16 inches—will be enough to cover most pots. Hold it over the top of the pot to ensure that the rectangle is longer than the radius of the pot. Fold the rectangle into a triangle so that the tip of the triangle is in the center of the piece of parchment. Continue to fold the parchment until you have a narrow triangle, about 1 inch thick. Slice off the tip of the triangle (this will form a hole in the center that will allow steam to escape). Hold the triangle in the center of the pot to gauge how much you'll need to trim off the ends to make a circle that fits inside of the pot. Trim the end and unfold the parchment. You should have a round that fits inside the pot, directly on the bubbling liquid.

PICKLED ASPARAGUS

I love serving pickled asparagus spears with fresh ones. Slices of pickled asparagus dressed in crème fraîche make an excellent accent for smoky grilled asparagus, a regular feature on my spring menus.

You can use either thick or thin asparagus spears. If using thick spears, peel them before blanching. I use quart jars to maximize the length of each spear, though you can cut spears in half and pack them in pint jars. If you have a lot of good-quality stem trimmings, include it in the total weight of asparagus and tuck them in the jars with the spear tops.

To ensure you have enough asparagus for the recipe, start with about 5 pounds.

makes about 4 quarts

INGREDIENT	VOLUME	OUNCES	GRAMS	PERCENT
Champagne vinegar	6¹/₂ cups	52 ounces	1474 grams	36%
Water	3¹/₂ cups	28 ounces	794 grams	19%
Kosher salt	3 tablespoons	1 ounce	28 grams	.6%
Sugar	2 tablespoons	⁵/₈ ounce	20 grams	.4%
Dill seed	4 teaspoons	—	—	—
Dill sprigs	8	—	—	—
Garlic cloves	4 whole cloves, halved	—	—	—
Asparagus, trimmed	16 cups	4 pounds	1814 grams	44%

1. In a pot, bring the vinegar, water, salt, and sugar to a boil. Keep hot. In a dry sauté pan over medium heat, toast the dill seed until fragrant, about 1 minute.

2. Scald 4 quart jars in a large pot of simmering water fitted with a rack—you will use this pot to process the jars. Right before filling, put the jars on the counter. In each jar, place 1 teaspoon dill seed, 2 dill sprigs, and 2 garlic clove halves. Meanwhile, soak the lids in a pan of hot water to soften the rubber seal.

3. In a large pot of boiling, salted water, blanch the asparagus for 1 minute. Drain the asparagus and divide among the jars.

4. Transfer the brine to a heat-proof pitcher and pour over the asparagus, leaving about a 1-inch space from the rim of the jar. Check the jars for air pockets, adding more brine if necessary. Seal with lids and screw on the bands until snug but not tight.

5. Place the jars in the pot with the rack and add enough water to cover by about 1 inch. Bring the water to a boil and process the jars for 20 minutes (start the timer when the water reaches a boil). Turn off the heat and leave the jars in the water for a few minutes. Remove the jars from the water and let cool completely.

At the Table: GRILLED AND PICKLED ASPARAGUS WITH PROSCIUTTO AND FRIED EGGS (PAGE 141)

LEMON-PICKLED TURNIPS

Called hakuri or salad turnips, these small white root vegetables are crisp like a radish. A few years ago I sampled them in a whole new light: raw, shredded, and dressed with lemon. The brightening effect of the lemon on the earthy, sweet turnip inspired this simple, sharp pickle. I serve these turnips two ways: with a splash of brine and olive oil, or tossed in a warm sauce of rendered lardons and sherry vinegar.

makes 5 pints

INGREDIENT	VOLUME	OUNCES	GRAMS	PERCENT
White turnips, greens removed	8 cups, sliced	2¹/₂ pounds	1135 grams	46%
Kosher salt	1 tablespoon plus ¹/₂ teaspoon	¹/₂ ounce	15 grams	.6%
Lemons, zested and juiced	3	3 ounces	85 grams	3.4%
Water	3¹/₄ cups	26 ounces	737 grams	29.8%
Champagne vinegar	1³/₄ cups	14 ounces	397 grams	16%
Sugar	¹/₂ cup plus 1 teaspoon	3³/₄ ounces	105 grams	4.2%
Coriander seeds	4 teaspoons	—	—	—

1. Trim off the root ends and tops of the turnips. Halve and slice the turnips about ¹/₄-inch thick. Mix the turnips in a large colander with the salt. Set aside to drain for 1 hour.

2. Grate the lemon zest into a small pot. Halve the lemons and squeeze the juice over the zest. Pour in the water, vinegar, and sugar. In a dry sauté pan over medium heat, toast the coriander seeds until fragrant. Coarsely crush the coriander and add it to the pot.

3. Scald 5 pint jars in a large pot of simmering water fitted with a rack—you will use this pot to process the jars. Right before filling, put the jars on the counter. Pack the jars with the turnips, using about 8 ounces per jar. Meanwhile, soak the lids in a pan of hot water to soften the rubber seal.

4. Bring the brine to a boil. Transfer to a heat-proof pitcher and pour over the turnips, leaving a ¹/₂-inch space from the rim of the jar. Check the jars for air pockets, adding more brine if necessary to fill in gaps. Wipe the rims with a clean towel, seal with the lids, then screw on the bands until snug but not tight.

5. Place the jars in the pot with the rack and add enough water to cover the jars by about 1 inch. Bring the water to a boil and process the jars for 15 minutes (start the timer when the water reaches a boil). Turn off the heat and leave the jars in the water for a few minutes. Remove the jars from the water and let cool completely.

At the Table: LEMON-PICKLED TURNIPS WITH BABY LEEKS AND PICKED HERBS (PAGE 134)

PICKLED RAMPS

Ramps taste like onions juiced on chlorophyll. I first started picking ramps while attending college in West Virginia, where ramp season, the first true signal of spring, has always been a big deal for home cooks. Although the Ozarks are well known for ramps, some fear that the population of wild ramps has been threatened by over harvesting. Currently, Midwestern fields and forests still offer large, dependable crops. I turn to a handful of suppliers, like former Vie cook Abra Berens, who runs Bare Knuckle Farm in Northport, Michigan, with her husband, Jess Piskor. This recipe was brought to me by another former cook, Stacy Kunesh. Stacy's sweeter brine brought a nice balance to the jar.

The weight of the ramps in this recipe is based on trimmed ramps. To ensure you have enough for the recipe, start with 3 pounds before trimming.

makes 4 pints

INGREDIENT	VOLUME	OUNCES	GRAMS	PERCENT
Champagne vinegar	2 cups plus 7 fluid ounces	23 ounces	680 grams	32.5%
Water	scant 1 1/2 cups	11 1/2 ounces	326 grams	16.4%
Sugar	scant 2 cups	11 1/2 ounces	326 grams	16.4%
Kosher salt	4 teaspoons	1/2 ounce	15 grams	.7%
Garlic cloves	4	—	—	—
Red pepper flakes	1 teaspoon	—	—	—
Ramps, roots removed	about 10 cups	2 1/2 pounds	1134 grams	34%

1. In a medium pot, bring the vinegar, water, sugar, and salt to a boil. Keep hot.

2. Scald 4 pint jars in a large pot of simmering water fitted with a rack—you will use this pot to process the jars. Right before filling, put the jars on the counter. In each jar, place 1 garlic clove and 1/4 teaspoon red pepper flakes. Meanwhile, soak the lids in a pan of hot water to soften the rubber seal.

3. In a large pot of boiling, salted water, blanch the ramps for 1 minute. Drain and pack into the jars. Transfer the brine into a pitcher and pour into the jars, leaving a 1/2-inch space from the rim of the jar. Check the jars for air pockets, adding more brine if necessary. Seal with lids and screw on the bands until snug but not tight.

4. Place the jars in the pot with the rack and add enough water to cover by about 1 inch. Bring the water to a boil and process the jars for 10 minutes (start the timer when the water reaches a boil). Turn off the heat and leave the jars in the water for a few minutes. Remove the jars from the water and let cool completely.

At the Table: RAINBOW TROUT WITH CREAMED RAMPS AND MORELS (PAGE 159); PICKLED RAMP MARTINI (PAGE 209)

SMOKED AND PICKLED SPRING ONIONS

With small, firm, knobby ends and grassy green stalks, spring onions are the lighter, brighter onion alternative to the mature bulbs used all winter. They also readily absorb smoke flavor. To get the onions smoking, I set up the top rack of our well-used smoker (see The Draw of Smoke, page 197). But with spring's iffy weather, a stovetop smoker, described in the instructions below, can be more reliable. The purpose of smoking the onions is strictly for flavor, not texture. If you're not in the mood to rig a smoker, grill the onions over a wood fire instead. They'll blister and caramelize, which will change the texture, but they'll also develop a similar smoky flair. If spring onions are hard to come by, use green onions.

makes 3 pints

INGREDIENT	VOLUME	OUNCES	GRAMS	PERCENT
Spring onions, root ends trimmed	6 to 8 cups	1 1/2 pounds	680 grams	52%
Grapeseed oil, for coating the onions	—	—	—	—
Champagne vinegar	1 1/4 cups	10 ounces	284 grams	21.7%
Water	1 1/4 cups	10 ounces	284 grams	21.7%
Honey	3 tablespoons	2 ounces	57 grams	4.5%
Kosher salt	1/2 teaspoon	less than 1/8 ounce	2 grams	.1%
Thyme sprigs	6	—	—	—

1. Line a deep disposable aluminum pan large enough to cover two burners with aluminum foil. Pile 1/2 cup of wood chips (hickory or applewood) on one end of the pan and cover with a fitted perforated pan or a wire rack. Coat the spring onions lightly in grapeseed oil and place on the perforated pan or rack. Put the pan over a pair of front and back burners with the wood-chip end over the front burner. Cover the smoker with aluminum foil and cut a small slit in the end opposite the wood chips to allow smoke to escape. Ensuring that the ventilation fan is on, turn the front burner to medium. Once smoke begins to escape through the hole in the aluminum foil, decrease the heat and gently smoke until the onions have softened slightly and have yellowed, about 12 minutes.

2. In a pot, bring the vinegar, water, honey, and salt to a boil. Keep hot.

3. Scald 3 pint jars in a large pot of simmering water fitted with a rack—you will use this pot to process the jars. Right before filling, put the jars on the counter. Place 2 sprigs of thyme in each jar, then pack the jars with the smoked onions, tucking the long stalks into the jar. Meanwhile, soak the lids in a pan of hot water to soften the rubber seal.

4. Transfer the brine to a heat-proof pitcher and pour over the onions, leaving a 1/2-inch space from the rim of the jar. Check the jars for air pockets, adding more brine if necessary to fill in gaps. Wipe the rims with a clean towel, seal with the lids, then screw on the bands until snug but not tight.

5. Place the jars in the pot with the rack and add enough water to cover the jars by about 1 inch. Bring the water to a boil and process the jars for 10 minutes (start the timer when the water reaches a boil). Turn off the heat and leave the jars in the water for a few minutes. Remove the jars from the water and let cool completely.

At the Table: SMOKED SPRING ONION RELISH (PAGE 230)

PICKLED CANDY ONIONS

Though they look similar to conventional yellow onions, candy onions are mild enough to slice and serve raw over a salad. When pickled, their sweetness counters the acidity of the vinegar, which makes them a tangy accompaniment for roasted chicken sausage. For a crisp texture, I salt the onion slices first to draw out excess water. You can also use Vidalia or Maui onions.

makes 6 pints

INGREDIENT	VOLUME	OUNCES	GRAMS	PERCENT
Candy onions, sliced	12 cups	3 1/2 pounds	1587 grams	51%
Kosher salt	1/4 cup	2 ounces	57 grams	1.7%
Champagne vinegar	3 3/4 cups	30 ounces	850 grams	27%
Water	2 cups plus 2 tablespoons	15 ounces	425 grams	14%
Sugar	1 cup	7 ounces	198 grams	6.3%

1. In a large colander or perforated pan, mix the onions and salt together. Set aside to drain for 1 hour.

2. Scald 6 pint jars in a large pot of simmering water fitted with a rack—you will use this pot to process the jars. Meanwhile, soak the lids in a pan of hot water to soften the rubber seal. Right before filling, put the jars on the counter. Pat the onions dry briefly (don't wipe away all of the salt) and pack into the jars.

3. In a pot, bring the vinegar, water, and sugar to a boil. Transfer the brine to a heat-proof pitcher and pour over the onions, leaving a 1/2-inch space from the rim of the jar. Check the jars for air pockets, adding more brine if necessary to fill in gaps. Wipe the rims with a clean towel, seal with the lids, then screw on the bands until snug but not tight.

4. Place the jars in the pot with the rack and add enough water to cover by about 1 inch. Bring the water to a boil and process the jars for 15 minutes (start the timer when the water reaches a boil). Turn off the heat and leave the jars in the water for a few minutes. Remove the jars from the water and let cool completely.

At the Table: BEEF CHILI (PAGE 265)

PICKLED CARROTS

When carrots are pickled they retain their crunch but take on the tang of vinegar, making them excellent on salads, in sandwiches, and with roasted root vegetables. At Chicago's Green City Market, I cave for the first baby carrots of the year. But the largest selection arrives—along with everything else—in the summer, when short, round Thumbelinas compete with slender purple and yellow varieties for my attention. By fall, the Thumbelinas are gone, but not the large deep-orange carrots, which have a pronounced sweet flavor.

Ideally, you would find carrots about four inches long, which would fit perfectly in pint jars. Realistically, you can also buy longer carrots and slice them in half on a diagonal so both halves fit into the jar. For very thick carrots, slice them in half lengthwise. If the greens look pristine, you can opt to leave an inch or so attached to the top. With the tip of a paring knife, scrape away any residual dirt left around the base of the stem. Tuck the greens into the pickling liquid when capping the jars. If the greens are less than perfect, however, remove them—it's not worth the hassle.

For this recipe, start with about 3½ pounds of unpeeled carrots.

makes 6 pints

INGREDIENT	VOLUME	OUNCES	GRAMS	PERCENT
Water	4 cups	32 ounces	907 grams	30.25%
Champagne vinegar	2¼ cups	18 ounces	515 grams	17%
Sugar	½ cup plus 1 tablespoon	3¾ ounces	105 grams	3.5%
Kosher salt	3 tablespoons	1 ounce	28 grams	1%
Coriander seeds	2 teaspoons	—	—	—
Fennel seeds	2 teaspoons	—	—	—
Black peppercorns	1 teaspoon	—	—	—
Red pepper flakes	1 teaspoon	—	—	—
Baby carrots, peeled and trimmed (about 4 inches long)	12 cups	3 pounds, 3 ounces	1445 grams	48.25%

1. In a pot, bring the water, vinegar, sugar, and salt to a boil. Keep hot. In a dry sauté pan over medium heat, toast the coriander and fennel seeds, black peppercorns, and red pepper flakes.

2. Scald 6 pint jars in a large pot of simmering water fitted with a rack—you will use this pot to process the jars. Right before filling, put the jars on the counter. Divide the spices among the jars, using about 1 teaspoon per jar. Soak the lids in a pan of hot water to soften the rubber seal.

3. Meanwhile, in a pot of boiling, salted water, blanch the carrots for 2 minutes. Drain and pack into the jars.

4. Transfer the brine to a heat-proof pitcher and pour over the carrots, leaving a $^1/_2$-inch space from the rim of the jar. Check the jars for air pockets, adding more brine if necessary to fill in gaps. Wipe the rims with a clean towel, seal with the lids, then screw on the bands until snug but not tight.

5. Place the jars in the pot with the rack and add enough water to cover the jars by about 1 inch. Bring the water to a boil and process the jars for 10 minutes (start the timer when the water reaches a boil). Turn off the heat and leave the jars in the water for a few minutes. Remove the jars from the water and let cool completely.

At the Table: ROASTED ROOT VEGETABLE SALAD WITH PICKLED CARROTS, AGED CHEDDAR, AND APPLES (PAGE 257); PORK RILLETTES (PAGE 274)

THE OBLIQUE CUT

Vegetables can vary dramatically in size and shape. If the baby carrots you've obtained are more like teenage carrots, they won't fit inside a Mason jar without being pared down. To rein in size inconsistencies, I use the oblique cut—a technique of slicing vegetables at an angle that gives the cut a uniform, attractive shape and size. Because the vegetables are cut at an angle, it also is easier to pack more pieces into a jar than if the vegetables are cut bluntly. This cut is just as useful for roasting vegetables as it is for pickling, since it increases the vegetable's cut surface area. To slice a carrot into "obliques"—kitchen slang for this cut—lay the peeled carrot on a cutting board parallel to the edge of the counter. Hold the root end of the carrot with one hand. With the knife in the other hand, slice the vegetable at an angle. With the supporting hand, rotate the carrot a quarter turn, then slice it again at the same angle. Repeat until the vegetable is completely sliced.

PICKLED CELERY

A kitchen workhorse, celery is easy to take for granted. But it undergoes a transformation when pickled, offering an acidic, crunchy accent to tuna salad or a platter of cured meat. When mixed with crème fraîche, the celery becomes a tangy condiment for pan-seared chicken (page 237). The best reason to pickle celery is when you can find a superlative, relatively local crop. I'm hooked on crisp, green stalks that grow around Holland, Michigan. The region has been recognized for celery since they started cultivating the crop in the nineteenth century. If friends are heading toward Holland, I have been known to ask them to come back with a few cases for me.

For this recipe, you will need to start with about two pounds of celery, which is either one large bunch or two smaller bunches. When cutting the stalks into 4-inch pieces, I halve large pieces lengthwise and leave small pieces whole. I try to use as much of the celery as I can, including the tender heart—which is the best part of the vegetable. Even so, trimmings are inevitable. This recipe yields about eight ounces of trimmings, which I save for stock.

makes 4 pints

INGREDIENT	VOLUME	OUNCES	GRAMS	PERCENT
Champagne vinegar	3¼ cups	26 ounces	737 grams	39.7%
Water	1¾ cups	14 ounces	397 grams	21.4%
Sugar	3 tablespoons	1 ounce	28 grams	1.5%
Kosher salt	4 teaspoons	½ ounce	15 grams	.8%
Black peppercorns	1½ teaspoons	—	—	—
Coriander seeds	1½ teaspoons	—	—	—
Fennel seeds	1½ teaspoons	—	—	—
Celery, trimmed to 4-inch pieces	40 to 60 pieces	1½ pounds	680 grams	36.6%

1. In a pot, bring the vinegar, water, sugar, and salt to a boil. Keep hot. In a dry sauté pan over medium heat, toast the peppercorns, coriander seeds, and fennel seeds.

2. Scald 4 pint jars in a large pot of simmering water fitted with a rack—you will use this pot to process the jars. Right before filling, put the jars on the counter. Divide the spices among the jars, using about 1 teaspoon per jar, then pack with celery, using 10 to 15 stalks per jar. Meanwhile, soak the lids in a pan of hot water to soften the rubber seal.

3. Transfer the brine into a heat-proof pitcher and pour over the celery, leaving a ½-inch space from the rim of the jar. Check the jars for air pockets, adding more brine if necessary to fill in gaps. Wipe the rims with a clean towel, seal with the lids, then screw on the bands until snug but not tight.

4. Place the jars in the pot with the rack and add enough water to cover by about 1 inch. Bring the water to a boil and process the jars for 15 minutes (start the timer when the water reaches a boil). Turn off the heat and leave the jars in the water for a few minutes. Remove the jars from the water and let cool completely.

At the Table: PAN-SEARED CHICKEN WITH CELERY SAUCE AND TOMATO JAM–ROASTED POTATOES (PAGE 237); SMOKED STURGEON WITH RUTABAGA SAUERKRAUT LATKES AND CRÈME FRAÎCHE (PAGE 271)

CHOW CHOW

It's nearly impossible to make it through summer without eating piles of freshly husked corn. What we can't eat fresh we pack in vinegar with onions, peppers, and mustard seeds. Chow chow is an old-fashioned term used since at least the nineteenth century for a relish made with any combination of chopped peppers, onions, cabbage, green onions, and mustard seeds. A spoonful dresses up a warming bowl of chili in the winter (page 265), but I've also served it as an amuse-bouche with a few rings of calamari. This relish is also great with a classic shore lunch, a Great Lakes tradition of fish fried in a skillet with potatoes, bacon, and onions.

makes 5 pints

INGREDIENT	VOLUME	OUNCES	GRAMS	PERCENT
Corn, cut off the cob	8 cups kernels (about 8 ears of corn)	3 pounds	1360 grams	48.25%
Sweet onion (such as candy or Vidalia), diced	1	7 ounces	198 grams	7%
Sweet pepper, such as a red bell pepper, diced	about 1/2 pepper, seeded and diced	4 ounces	113 grams	4%
Brown sugar	1/2 cup, packed	2 ounces	57 grams	2.1%
Kosher salt	4 teaspoons	1/2 ounce	15 grams	.5%
Black mustard seeds	1 1/2 tablespoons	—	—	—
Yellow mustard seeds	1 1/2 tablespoons	—	—	—
Sweet paprika	2 teaspoons	—	—	—
Black pepper, ground	1 1/2 teaspoons	—	—	—
Water	3 cups	24 ounces	680 grams	24.15%
Champagne vinegar	1 3/4 cups	14 ounces	397 grams	14%

1. In a large pot over medium-high heat, mix together the corn, onion, sweet pepper, sugar, salt, mustard seeds, paprika, and black pepper. Pour in the water and vinegar and bring to a boil. Decrease to a simmer and cook for 10 minutes. Keep hot.

{continued}

2. Scald 5 pint jars in a large pot of simmering water fitted with a rack—you will use this pot to process the jars. Right before filling, put the jars on the counter. Meanwhile, soak the lids in a pan of hot water to soften the rubber seal.

3. Ladle the relish into the jars, ensuring that there is enough liquid to cover the vegetables in each jar. Leave a $^1/_2$-inch space from the rim of the jar and check for air pockets, adding more relish or liquid if necessary to fill in gaps. Wipe the rims with a clean towel, seal with the lids, then screw on the bands until snug but not tight.

4. Place the jars in the pot with the rack and add enough water to cover the jars by about 1 inch. Bring the water to a boil and process the jars for 15 minutes (start the timer when the water reaches a boil). Turn off the heat and leave the jars in the water for a few minutes. Remove the jars from the water and let cool completely.

At the Table: BEEF CHILI (PAGE 265)

DILL PICKLES

A world away from bread-and-butter varieties, this sharp pickle enlivens the burger we serve at Vie. I also mix slices of it with fresh cucumbers for a simple salad. A word on choosing the cucumber for the job: look for small, firm vegetables. You can go as small as a cornichon and have good results (just count on adding more cucumbers to each jar), but I avoid anything longer than 4 inches.

To prepare the cucumber for pickling, trim off the blossom end. It holds enzymes—proteins that can cause cucumbers to go soft. I like my dill pickles tart. If you happen to prefer a sweeter pickle, add an ounce of sugar (about 2 tablespoons) to the brine.

makes 5 quarts

INGREDIENT	VOLUME	OUNCES	GRAMS	PERCENT
Water	5$^1/_2$ cups	44 ounces	1247 grams	30.6%
Champagne vinegar	3$^1/_2$ cups	28 ounces	794 grams	19.35%
Kosher salt	2 tablespoons	$^3/_4$ ounce	20 grams	.5%
Sugar	1 tablespoon	$^1/_3$ ounce	10 grams	.25%
Dill seeds	5 teaspoons	—	—	—
Dill sprigs	10	—	—	—
Garlic cloves	5	—	—	—
Pickling cucumbers, blossom end trimmed	about 25 (4-inch)	4 pounds, 8 ounces	2016 grams	49.3%

1. In a pot, bring the water, vinegar, salt, and sugar to a boil. Keep hot. In a dry sauté pan over medium heat, toast the dill seeds until fragrant, about 1 minute.

2. Scald 5 quart jars in a large pot of simmering water fitted with a rack—you will use this pot to process the jars. Right before filling, put the jars on the counter. Into each jar add 1 teaspoon dill seeds, 2 sprigs dill, and 1 garlic clove. Pack the cucumbers into the jars, using about 5 per jar. Meanwhile, soak the lids in a pan of hot water to soften the rubber seal.

3. Transfer the brine to a heat-proof pitcher and pour over the cucumbers, leaving a 1-inch space from the rim of the jar. Check the jars for air pockets, adding more brine if necessary to fill in gaps. Wipe the rims with a clean towel, seal with the lids, then screw on the bands until snug but not tight.

4. Place the jars in the pot with the rack and add enough water to cover by about 1 inch. Bring the water to a boil and process the jars for 30 minutes (start the timer when the water reaches a boil). Turn off the heat and leave the jars in the water for a few minutes. Remove the jars from the water and let cool completely.

At the Table: WOOD-GRILLED BURGERS WITH BEEF BACON (PAGE 175); PORK RILLETTES (PAGE 274); DUCK FAT–POACHED WHITEFISH WITH DILL PICKLE VINAIGRETTE AND BRAISED SAUERKRAUT (PAGE 284)

EGGPLANT-TOMATO RELISH

I rely on this tangy relish for escabeche (page 195) but it's equally successful as a sauce for roasted chicken or grilled sausage. One key part of making the preserve is drawing out the eggplant's water with salt, which encourages it to soak up more vinegar.

makes 4 pints

INGREDIENT	VOLUME	OUNCES	GRAMS	PERCENT
Eggplant, diced into ¹/₂-inch pieces	1¹/₂ to 2 eggplants	1 pound, 12 ounces	793 grams	38%
Sweet onion (such as candy or Vidalia), diced	1 small onion	3¹/₂ ounces	99 grams	4.5%
Kosher salt	3 tablespoons	1 ounce	28 grams	1%
Olive oil	¹/₄ cup	2 ounces	57 grams	2.5%
Garlic cloves, minced	15 cloves	2 ounces	57 grams	2.5%
Fresh sage, chopped	¹/₄ cup, loosely packed	—	—	—
Fresh thyme, chopped	1 tablespoon	—	—	—
Ground black pepper	2 teaspoons	—	—	—
Cherry tomatoes, halved	2 cups	1 pound, 4 ounces	567 grams	27%
Red wine vinegar	2 cups	16 ounces	454 grams	22%
Honey	scant ¹/₄ cup	2 ounces	57 grams	2.5%

1. In a colander placed over a bowl, mix together the eggplant, onion, and salt. Let drain for 1 hour.

2. Wrap the eggplant and onion in a kitchen towel and squeeze over the sink to remove excess water. In a large sauté pan over medium-high heat, warm the olive oil. Add the eggplant-onion mixture, garlic, sage, thyme, and pepper and cook, stirring frequently, for 2 to 3 minutes. Remove from the heat and stir in the tomatoes.

3. In a pot over medium-high heat, bring the vinegar and honey to a boil. Keep hot.

4. Scald 4 pint jars in a large pot of simmering water fitted with a rack—you will use this pot to process the jars. Right before filling, put the jars on the counter. Soak the lids in a pan of hot water to soften the rubber seal.

5. Divide the eggplant mixture among the jars. Transfer the brine to a heat-proof pitcher and pour over the relish, leaving a ¹/₂-inch space from the rim of the jar. Check for air pockets, adding more brine if necessary to fill in gaps. Wipe the rims with a clean towel, seal with the lids, then screw on the bands until snug but not tight.

6. Place the jars in the pot with the rack and add enough water to cover the jars by about 1 inch. Bring the water to a boil and process the jars for 15 minutes (start the timer when the water reaches a boil). Turn off the heat and leave the jars in the water for a few minutes. Remove the jars from the water and let cool completely.

At the Table: WHITEFISH ESCABECHE WITH EGGPLANT-TOMATO VINAIGRETTE (PAGE 195)

PICKLED FENNEL

This is a sharp pickle, with a distinct licorice flavor augmented by toasted fennel seeds. A few slices can gussy up robust seafood, like charred octopus. Caramelized with onions and butter, the preserve also becomes a simple side dish for roasted pork. I also use it in place of tomatoes in a summer bread salad served with grilled skirt steak (page 168).

Since the weight of the fennel is measured after the vegetable has been trimmed, cored, and sliced, start with nearly 2 pounds.

makes 4 pints

INGREDIENT	VOLUME	OUNCES	GRAMS	PERCENT
Champagne vinegar	3 cups	24 ounces	680 grams	38.25%
Water	1 1/2 cups	12 ounces	340 grams	19.25%
Sugar	3/4 cup plus 1 tablespoon	7 ounces	170 grams	9.5%
Kosher salt	4 teaspoons	1/2 ounce	15 grams	1%
Coriander seeds	2 teaspoons	—	—	—
Fennel seeds	2 teaspoons	—	—	—
Red pepper flakes	1/2 teaspoon	—	—	—
Fennel bulbs, trimmed, cored, and sliced lengthwise 1/4 inch thick	About 4 bulbs	1 pound, 4 ounces	567 grams	32%

1. In a pot, bring the vinegar, water, sugar, and salt to a boil. Keep hot. In a dry sauté pan over medium heat, toast the coriander and fennel seeds and red pepper flakes.

2. Scald 4 pint jars in a large pot of simmering water fitted with a rack—you will use this pot to process the jars. Right before filling, put the jars on the counter. Divide the spices among the jars, adding just over a teaspoon per jar, then pack the jars with fennel, using about 5 ounces per jar. Meanwhile, soak the lids in a pan of hot water to soften the rubber seal.

3. Transfer the brine to a heat-proof pitcher and pour over the fennel, leaving a 1/2-inch space from the rim of the jar. Check the jars for air pockets, adding more brine if necessary to fill in gaps. Wipe the rims with a clean towel, seal with the lids, then screw on the bands until snug but not tight.

4. Place the jars in the pot with the rack and add enough water to cover the jars by about 1 inch. Bring the water to a boil and process the jars for 15 minutes (start the timer when the water reaches a boil). Turn off the heat and leave the jars in the water for a few minutes. Remove the jars from the water and let cool completely.

At the Table: GRILLED SKIRT STEAK WITH FENNEL PANZANELLA SALAD (PAGE 168)

GIARDINIERA

Though I hate to disappoint fans of Chicago-style giardiniera—a pickled-vegetable combo packed in olive oil—this is not the same thing. Instead, it's crunchy, spicy, and sharp, a pickled vegetable medley for cured meat, pan-fried fish, or salad. But you can still serve it with grilled sausage.

While most preserves hew to one season, giardiniera is a chameleon, able to adapt to what the market bears. In early fall, I select short, round carrots, scarlet turnips, and radishes. Later in the season, I add florets of green, spiky romanesco and slices of fennel. Come spring, I turn to snap peas, green garlic, and spring onions while I wait for green beans and sweet peppers to arrive with summer. Using this recipe as a guide, I encourage you to be equally freewheeling. As long as the total weight of the vegetables (including garlic and onions—which I recommend you use in every batch) equals 57 percent of the total ingredients, you can create your own combinations depending on what you've been able to buy, grow, or forage. For the best results, look for vegetables that are either small enough to use whole or can be easily sliced into even pieces no longer than an inch.

The quantity of salt in this recipe appears excessive, but it's not a salty preserve. Salt draws out the excess water before the vegetables are packed into the jars, allowing the vegetables to absorb more brine but retain a crunchy texture. Most of the salt is rinsed away before the vegetables are packed in the jars.

makes 5 pints

INGREDIENT	VOLUME	OUNCES	GRAMS	PERCENT
Baby carrots, ideally 1 to 2 inches long, peeled, tops removed	4 cups	1 pound, 5 ounces	595 grams	23%
White or scarlet turnips, tops removed and quartered	3 cups	15¹/₂ ounces	440 grams	17%
Radishes, tops removed and halved	1 cup	5¹/₂ ounces	155 grams	6%
Kosher salt	scant ³/₄ cup	4 ounces	116 grams	4.5%
Champagne vinegar	3³/₄ cups	30 ounces	854 grams	33%
Water	¹/₂ cup	4 ounces	116 grams	4.5%
Sugar	3 tablespoons	1 ounce	28 grams	1%
Yellow onions, sliced	1 to 2	9 ounces	259 grams	10%
Garlic cloves	5	1 ounce	28 grams	1%
Red pepper flakes	2¹/₂ teaspoons	—	—	—

1. In a large colander or perforated pan, mix the carrots, turnips, and radishes with the salt. Set aside to drain for 2 hours, then rinse well.

2. In a pot, bring the vinegar, water, and sugar to a boil. Keep hot.

3. Scald 5 pint jars in a large pot of simmering water fitted with a rack—you will use this pot to process the jars. Right before filling, put the jars on the counter. Divide the onions and garlic among the jars. Add ¹/₂ teaspoon red pepper flakes to each jar, then pack in the salted vegetables. Meanwhile, soak the lids in a pan of hot water to soften the rubber seal.

4. Transfer the brine to a heat-proof pitcher and pour over the vegetables, leaving a ¹/₂-inch space from the rim of the jar. Check the jars for air pockets, adding more brine if necessary to fill in gaps. Wipe the rims with a clean towel, seal with the lids, then screw on the bands until snug but not tight.

5. Place the jars in the pot with the rack and add enough water to cover the jars by about 1 inch. Bring the water to a boil and process the jars for 15 minutes (start the timer when the water reaches a boil). Turn off the heat and leave the jars in the water for a few minutes. Remove the jars from the water and let cool completely.

At the Table: PORK RILLETES (PAGE 274); CHARCUTERIE PLATTER (PAGE 221)

PICKLED CHERRY BOMB PEPPERS

I look forward to these plump, short peppers appearing at the market at the end of July. Tamed with a dab of honey in the brine, the fiery pickles are delicious straight from the jar. I also mix the minced peppers into a spicy vinaigrette, which works well on everything from a simple heirloom tomato salad to fried cheese curds. Cherry bomb season is short—maybe just a month long—and crop yields are unpredictable. If the pepper is unavailable, the same recipe also works with fresh, shiny jalapeños, although jalapeños tend to taste more grassy and piquant. When pickling, leave the seeds and stem intact—whole peppers look striking when suspended in brine.

makes 4 pints

INGREDIENT	VOLUME	OUNCES	GRAMS	PERCENT
Champagne vinegar	2³/₄ cups	22 ounces	624 grams	34%
Water	1¹/₃ cups	11 ounces	312 grams	17%
Honey	¹/₃ cup	3 ounces	85 grams	4.6%
Kosher salt	2 teaspoons	¹/₄ ounce	8 grams	.4%
Cherry bomb peppers	about 40	1 pound, 12 ounces	794 grams	44%

1. In a pot, bring the vinegar, water, honey, and salt to a boil. Keep hot.

2. Scald 4 pint jars in a large pot of simmering water fitted with a rack—you will use this pot to process the jars. Right before filling, put the jars on the counter. Divide the peppers among the jars, using about 10 per jar. Meanwhile, soak the lids in a pan of hot water to soften the rubber seal.

3. Transfer the brine to a heat-proof pitcher and pour over the peppers, leaving a ¹/₂-inch space from the rim of the jar. Check the jars for air pockets, adding more brine if necessary to fill in gaps. Wipe the rims with a clean towel, seal with the lids, then screw on the bands until snug but not tight.

4. Place the jars in the pot with the rack and add enough water to cover the jars by about 1 inch. Bring the water to a boil and process the jars for 15 minutes (start the timer when the water reaches a boil). Turn off the heat and leave the jars in the water for a few minutes. Remove the jars from the water and let cool completely.

At the Table: CHERRY BOMB PEPPER SAUSAGE GRAVY (PAGE 186); FRIED CHEESE CURDS WITH PICKLED PEPPER VINAIGRETTE (PAGE 283)

GRILLED AND PICKLED HOT PEPPERS

Smoke and heat distinguish these pickles from other preserved peppers. I take my time getting a decent char on the peppers, and I'm not so concerned that every speck of blackened skin comes off each one. (If a few specks are left on, it gives the pickle an extra hit of smoke.) Once the peppers are peeled, I leave them intact as much as possible, since the seeds and membranes of the vegetable impart the heat to the pickle. Serrano or jalapeño chiles or even hot banana peppers will do the trick. You also can make your own mix of hot peppers. If heat isn't your thing but you like the savory flavor of a smoked pepper, try this pickle with Japanese shishito or Spanish Padrón peppers—only one in a dozen is likely to burn.

Because the ratios for this recipe are based on the weight of the grilled and skinned peppers, the instructions are divided into two parts: grilling the peppers and pickling the peppers.

makes 5 pints

GRILLING

INGREDIENT	VOLUME	OUNCES	GRAMS
Hot peppers	48	3¹/₂ pounds	1600 grams
Olive oil for roasting the peppers	—	—	—

1. To grill the peppers, prepare a fire in a grill with a mix of hardwood charcoal and wood chunks, spreading the coals evenly for direct-heat cooking. In a large bowl, toss the peppers with a splash of olive oil, coating them evenly, and arrange on the grill. Grill the peppers, turning occasionally to ensure even charring, until the skins have started to blister, 5 to 8 minutes. (Alternatively, preheat the broiler and broil the peppers until blistered.)

2. Return the peppers to the bowl and cover tightly with plastic wrap. (This will steam the peppers, allowing their skins to loosen.) Once the peppers are cool enough to handle, peel off the skins but leave the seeds intact. Weigh the peppers and set aside 2 pounds to pickle. Depending on what kind of peppers you are using, you might have leftover grilled peppers. If that is the case, refrigerate them for another use or marinate them with leftover brine.

{continued}

PICKLING

INGREDIENT	VOLUME	OUNCES	GRAMS	PERCENT
Champagne vinegar	3 cups	24 ounces	680 grams	34.6%
Water	1 cup plus 2 talespoons	9 ounces	255 grams	13%
Sugar	1/2 cup plus 2 tablespoons	4 ounces	114 grams	5.8%
Kosher salt	1 tablespoon	1/3 ounce	9 grams	.4%
Red pepper flakes	1 teaspoon	—	—	—
Coriander seeds	1 teaspoon	—	—	—
Fennel seeds	1 teaspoon	—	—	—
Mustard seeds	1 teaspoon	—	—	—
Grilled, peeled hot peppers	6 cups	2 pounds	907 grams	46.2%

1. In a medium pot, bring the vinegar, water, sugar, and salt to a boil. Keep hot. In a dry sauté pan over medium heat, toast the red pepper flakes, coriander seeds, fennel seeds, and mustard seeds until they become aromatic, about 1 minute.

2. Scald 5 pint jars in a large pot of simmering water fitted with a rack—you will use this pot to process the jars. Right before filling, put the jars on the counter. Add a little less than 1 teaspoon of the spice mix to each jar, then divide the peppers among the jar, using 7 to 10 peppers per jar. Meanwhile, soak the lids in a pan of hot water to soften the rubber seal.

3. Transfer the brine to a heat-proof pitcher and pour over the peppers, leaving a 1/2-inch space from the rim of the jar. Check the jars for air pockets, adding more brine if necessary to fill in gaps. Wipe the rims with a clean towel, seal with the lids, then screw on the bands until snug but not tight.

4. Place the jars in the pot with the rack and add enough water to cover the jars by about 1 inch. Bring the water to a boil and process the jars for 10 minutes (start the timer when the water reaches a boil). Turn off the heat and leave the jars in the water for a few minutes. Remove the jars from the water and let cool completely.

At the Table: PRESERVED GAZPACHO (PAGE 167); HOT PEPPER SAUCE (PAGE 181); BEEF CHILI (PAGE 265); FRIED CHEESE CURDS WITH PICKLED PEPPER VINAIGRETTE (PAGE 283)

GRILLED AND PICKLED SWEET PEPPERS

One word describes these pickles: generous. Each jar brims with big pieces of sweet peppers. Almost any sweet variety of pepper will do. I like Marconi, Cubanelle, and gypsy varieties, but you could use red, yellow, or orange bell peppers for a similar effect. If you select Melrose or other less meaty peppers, grill them briefly but leave the skins on. Otherwise, the peppers will be too flimsy as a pickle.

Since the pickle is based on the weight of the grilled, skinned, and seeded peppers, the instructions are divided into two parts: grilling the peppers and pickling the peppers.

makes 4 pints

GRILLING

INGREDIENT	VOLUME	OUNCES	GRAMS
Sweet peppers	10–15	5 pounds	2268 grams
Olive oil, for roasting the peppers	—	—	—

1. To grill the peppers, prepare a fire in a grill using a mix of hardwood charcoal and wood chunks, spreading the coals evenly for direct-heat cooking. In a large bowl, toss the peppers with a splash of olive oil, coating them evenly, and arrange on the grill. Grill the peppers, turning occasionally, until the skins are thoroughly blistered, about 10 minutes. (Alternatively, preheat the broiler and broil the peppers until blistered.)

2. Return the peppers to the bowl and cover tightly with plastic wrap. (This will steam the peppers, allowing their skins to loosen.) Once the peppers are cool enough to handle, peel off the skins and discard the stem and seeds. Weigh the peppers and set aside 3 pounds to pickle. Depending on what kind of peppers you are using, you might have leftover grilled peppers. If that is the case, refrigerate them for another use or marinate them with any leftover brine.

{continued}

PICKLING

INGREDIENT	VOLUME	OUNCES	GRAMS	PERCENT
Champagne vinegar	1 cup plus 2 tablespoons	9 ounces	255 grams	14%
Water	1/2 cup plus 1 tablespoon	4 1/2 ounces	128 grams	7%
Sugar	1/3 cup	2 1/4 ounces	64 grams	3.5%
Kosher salt	1 tablespoon	1/3 ounce	9 grams	.5%
Grilled sweet peppers	7 cups	3 pounds	1361 grams	75%

1. In a pot, bring the vinegar, water, sugar, and salt to a boil. Keep hot.

2. Scald 4 pint jars in a large pot of simmering water fitted with a rack—you will use this pot to process the jars. Right before filling, put the jars on the counter. Divide the peppers among the jars, using about 12 ounces per jar. Meanwhile, soak the lids in a pan of hot water to soften the rubber seal.

3. Transfer the brine to a heat-proof pitcher and pour over the peppers, leaving a 1/2-inch space from the rim of the jar. Check the jars for air pockets, adding more brine if necessary to fill in gaps. Wipe the rims with a clean towel, seal with the lids, then screw on the bands until snug but not tight.

4. Place the jars in the pot with the rack and add enough water to cover the jars by about 1 inch. Bring the water to a boil and process the jars for 15 minutes (start the timer when the water reaches a boil). Turn off the heat and leave the jars in the water for a few minutes. Remove the jars from the water and let cool completely.

At the Table: PRESERVED GAZPACHO (PAGE 167); TOMATO-PEPPER SAUCE (PAGE 47); BEEF CHILI (PAGE 265); FRIED CHEESE CURDS WITH PICKLED PEPPER VINAIGRETTE (PAGE 283)

PICKLED SNOW PEAS

I use this pickle so often that I almost take it for granted. But, in fact, flat, crisp snow peas are some of my favorite vegetables to pickle. Glazed with a splash of brine and a pat of butter, they are a perfect side for smoked or grilled trout. And they are a great stand-in for pickled green beans. But they're even better used as an accent, whether mixed into a smoked chicken salad or sprinkled onto a green salad. For a better presentation, I slice them in half at an angle.

makes 6 pints

INGREDIENT	VOLUME	OUNCES	GRAMS	PERCENT
Snow peas	8^{1}/$_{2}$ cups	2^{1}/$_{2}$ pounds	1134 grams	39%
Champagne vinegar	4^{3}/$_{4}$ cups	38 ounces	1077 grams	37.5%
Water	2^{3}/$_{4}$ cups	22 ounces	623 grams	22%
Sugar	2 tablespoons	^{2}/$_{3}$ ounce	19 grams	.75%
Kosher salt	4^{1}/$_{2}$ teaspoons	^{2}/$_{3}$ ounce	19 grams	.75%
Pickling spices (page 108)	2 tablespoons	—	—	—

1. Prepare the snow peas by snapping off the stem end and peeling away the stringy fiber. While the fiber generally comes off only one side of the pod, for older, tougher peas you may need to remove the fiber from both sides.

2. In a pot, bring the vinegar, water, sugar, and salt to a boil. Keep hot. In a dry sauté pan over medium heat, toast the pickling spices.

3. Scald 6 pint jars in a large pot of simmering water fitted with a rack—you will use this pot to process the jars. Right before filling, put the jars on the counter. Give each jar a teaspoon of the spices, and then pack with the snow peas. Meanwhile, soak the lids in a pan of hot water to soften the rubber seal.

4. Transfer the brine to a pitcher and pour over the beans, leaving a ^{1}/$_{2}$-inch space from the rim of the jar. Check the jars for air pockets, adding more brine if necessary to fill in gaps. Wipe the rims with a clean towel, seal with the lids, then screw on the bands until snug but not tight.

5. Place the jars in the pot with the rack and add enough water to ensure they are covered by about 1 inch. Bring the water to a boil and process the jars for 15 minutes (start the timer when the water reaches a boil). Turn off the heat and leave the jars in the water for a few minutes. Remove the jars from the water and let cool completely.

At the Table: SLOW-ROASTED PORK BELLY WITH GARLIC CONSERVA AND GLAZED PICKLED SUMMER BEANS (PAGE 287)

PICKLED SUMMER BEANS

From late June through July, I pickle piles of green and wax beans. During the summer, I serve them with fresh beans in a salad. By fall and winter (and spring, if any are left), I simmer them with spoonfuls of brine and butter. Glazed in their brine, the pickles complement either seared tuna with sorrel or braised brisket. I've also found that they make a great snack straight from the jar when wrapped with slices of pastrami. And to think I grew up hating green beans.

makes 7 pints

INGREDIENT	VOLUME	OUNCES	GRAMS	PERCENT
Champagne vinegar	5^1/$_2$ cups	44 ounces	1247 grams	37%
Water	2 cups	16 ounces	454 grams	13.5%
Sugar	^{1}/$_4$ cup	2 ounces	57 grams	1.7%
Kosher salt	2 tablespoons	^{3}/$_4$ ounce	20 grams	.6%
Dill seeds	2 tablespoons	—	—	—
Black peppercorns	1 tablespoon	—	—	—
Red pepper flakes	1^1/$_2$ teaspoons	—	—	—
Black mustard seeds	1^1/$_2$ teaspoons	—	—	—
Garlic cloves	7	—	—	—
Green and wax beans, trimmed	about 12 cups	3^1/$_2$ pounds	1587 grams	47.2%

1. In a medium pot, bring the vinegar, water, sugar, and salt to a boil. Keep hot. In a dry sauté pan over medium heat, toast the dill seeds, peppercorns, red pepper flakes, and mustard seeds.

2. Scald 7 pint jars in a large pot of simmering water fitted with a rack—you will use this pot to process the jars. Right before filling, put the jars on the counter. Divide the spices among the jars, giving each jar just under 2 teaspoons of the spice mix. Place 1 garlic clove in each jar. Soak the lids in a pan of hot water to soften the rubber seal.

3. In a large pot of boiling, salted water, blanch the beans for 1 minute. Drain and divide the beans among the jars.

4. Transfer the brine to a heat-proof pitcher and pour over the beans, leaving a ^{1}/$_2$-inch space from the rim of the jar. Check the jars for air pockets, adding more brine if necessary to fill in gaps. Wipe the rims with a clean towel, seal with the lids, then screw on the bands until snug but not tight.

5. Place the jars in the pot with the rack and add enough water to cover the jars by about 1 inch. Bring the water to a boil and process the jars for 10 minutes (start the timer when the water reaches a boil). Turn off the heat and leave the jars in the water for a few minutes. Remove the jars from the water and let cool completely.

At the Table: PICKLED AND FRESH SUMMER BEAN SALAD WITH PRESERVED TOMATO VINAIGRETTE (PAGE 185); FRIED CHICKEN WITH CHERRY BOMB PEPPER SAUSAGE GRAVY AND DROP BISCUITS (PAGE 186)

PICKLED AND SPICED SUMMER SQUASH

When zucchini and yellow squash are in season, it feels as if everyone with a backyard garden has too much of a good thing. I'll admit that I get tired of cooking and eating fresh squash, so I make large batches of pickles to use in colder months as a condiment with chili or stews. Zucchini and summer squash have a neutral flavor, which I spice up with smoked paprika and curry powder. If you happen to cook a lot of Southeast Asian dishes, you could just as easily make this recipe with fenugreek, cumin, and ginger, and then serve it alongside curry.

makes 5 pints

INGREDIENT	VOLUME	OUNCES	GRAMS	PERCENT
Summer squash, sliced into 1/4-inch-thick pieces	About 8 cups	3 pounds	1361 grams	56.5%
Kosher salt	2 tablespoons	1 ounce	28 grams	1.2%
Champagne vinegar	2 1/2 cups	20 ounces	567 grams	23.5%
Water	1 1/4 cups	10 ounces	283 grams	11.7%
White wine	1/2 cup	4 ounces	113 grams	4.7%
Sugar	1/4 cup	2 ounces	57 grams	2.4%
Curry powder	1 tablespoon	—	—	—
Smoked hot paprika	2 teaspoons	—	—	—

1. In a colander placed over a bowl, mix together the squash and salt. Let stand 1 hour. Place the colander in the sink and rinse the squash slices. Drain.

2. Scald 5 pint jars in a large pot of simmering water fitted with a rack—you will use this pot to process the jars. Right before filling, put the jars on the counter. Soak the lids in a pan of hot water to soften the rubber seal.

3. In a pot over medium-high heat, bring the vinegar, water, wine, sugar, curry powder, and paprika to a boil, then transfer to a heat-proof pitcher.

4. Divide the squash evenly among the jars. Pour the brine over the squash, leaving a 1/2-inch space from the rim of the jar. Check the jars for air pockets, adding more brine if necessary to fill in gaps. Wipe the rims with a clean towel, seal with the lids, then screw on the bands until snug but not tight.

5. Place the jars in the pot with the rack and add enough water to cover the jars by about 1 inch. Cover, bring the water to a boil, and process the jars for 10 minutes (start the timer when the water reaches a boil). Turn off the heat and leave the jars in the water for a few minutes. Remove the jars from the water and let cool completely.

At the Table: GRILLED AND PICKLED SUMMER SQUASH SALAD (PAGE 179); BEEF CHILI (PAGE 265)

SWEET PICKLED CHERRY TOMATOES

When in season, cherry tomatoes appear to be everywhere. This pickle offers a near-effortless way to ensure that a respectable bumper crop does not go to waste. All you need to do is fill jars with raw tomatoes and then cover them with hot brine. Compared with larger, meatier tomatoes, cherry tomatoes give off a sweet burst of flavor when you bite into them. I complement their natural sweetness with a brine that isn't as sharp as ones I use for other savory preserves. Although the tomatoes are good enough to eat straight from the jar, I often purée the entire contents of the jar, reduce the blend until slightly thick, and whisk in olive oil for a versatile vinaigrette.

Raw cherry tomatoes tend to float in the brine after they are canned. You can prevent this by pricking each tomato with a sterilized needle.

makes 5 pints

INGREDIENT	VOLUME	OUNCES	GRAMS	PERCENT
Dill seeds	5 teaspoons	—	—	—
Black peppercorns	2¹/₂ teaspoons	—	—	—
Dill sprigs	10	—	—	—
Garlic cloves	5	³/₄ ounce	20 grams	.7%
Cherry tomatoes, hulled and pricked	8 cups	3 pounds	1361 grams	49.5%
Champagne vinegar	4 cups	32 ounces	907 grams	33%
Water	1¹/₄ cups	10 ounces	284 grams	10.5%
Sugar	³/₄ cup	6 ounces	170 grams	6%
Kosher salt	1 tablespoon	¹/₃ ounce	9 grams	.3%

1. Scald 5 pint jars in a large pot of simmering water fitted with a rack—you will use this pot to process the jars. Right before filling, put the jars on the counter. In a dry sauté pan over medium heat, toast the dill seeds and peppercorns. Divide the spices among the jars, using about 1¹/₂ teaspoons per jar, then add 2 sprigs dill and 1 garlic clove to each jar. Pack the tomatoes evenly among the jars. Meanwhile, soak the lids in a pan of hot water to soften the rubber seal.

2. In a pot, bring the vinegar, water, sugar, and salt to a boil. Transfer the brine to a heat-proof pitcher and pour over the tomatoes, leaving a ¹/₂-inch space from the rim of the jar. Check the jars for air pockets, adding more brine if necessary to fill in gaps. Wipe the rims with a clean towel, seal with the lids, then screw on the bands until snug but not tight.

3. Place the jars in the pot with the rack and add enough water to cover the jars by about 1 inch. Bring the water to a boil and process the jars for 15 minutes (start the timer when the water reaches a boil). Turn off the heat and leave the jars in the water for a few minutes. Remove the jars from the water and let cool completely.

At the Table: PICKLED AND FRESH SUMMER BEAN SALAD WITH PRESERVED TOMATO VINAIGRETTE (PAGE 185)

CANNED TOMATOES

Jars of preserved tomatoes are among the most versatile and popular pantry staples to make at home. I cook 100-pound batches of tomatoes at a time, filling up several shelves with quarts of tomatoes, and yet I still burn through our inventory well before tomato season arrives again.

Since we put up so many jars, I have streamlined the process. Instead of blanching, peeling, and seeding tomatoes, I pass cooked tomatoes through a food mill, which succeeds in getting rid of much of the skin and some of the seeds. I also keep the sauce on the thin side. This not only cuts down on having a pot of tomatoes taking up space on the stove for hours, it also yields a fresher tomato flavor. If I decide to reduce the tomatoes into a sauce, I can do so later. But if I just want a spoonful of fresh-tasting tomato juice for gazpacho (page 167), all I have to do is pop open a jar.

Selecting the right tomato is crucial. I buy locally grown San Marzano tomatoes—the ultimate canning variety (just ask the Neapolitans). These meaty, firm tomatoes offer more pulp than the round, juicy heirlooms. Timing is also important. The best time to can tomatoes is peak season (typically August and September), when they are not only inexpensive but also ripe.

The decision whether to add either citric acid or lemon juice to tomatoes before canning them stokes debates among passionate canners. Although tomatoes taste acidic, their natural pH level can veer upward of 4.6, the border of safety when determining whether a product is acidic enough to water-bath process. To play it safe, food scientists recommend adding citric acid or lemon juice to tomatoes. But many old-school canners who have made tomato sauce for years without adding any acid feel this recommendation is overkill.

While I tend toward the cautious side, I prefer not to add ingredients that do nothing to enhance the natural flavor of the product, so I don't acidify my tomatoes. Instead, I test a jar from each batch with a pH meter. (For instructions on how to use a pH meter, see page 6.) In general, I have found that late-summer tomatoes yield an average pH of 3.5. While it is a good exercise to check the pH of canned items, it is absolutely necessary with this recipe.

If you don't have a pH meter to test your tomatoes, play by the book and add 1 tablespoon lemon juice or ¼ teaspoon of citric acid to each pint, double for each quart. Or you can pressure-can the tomatoes. Pressure canning, as discussed on page 122, brings the internal temperature of the jar high enough to kill spoilers even if acidity levels aren't below 4.6 pH. Another alternative is to divide the sauce among resealable plastic bags and freeze them. If you make a much larger batch than the one I've provided here, factor in an extended simmering time for the tomatoes.

makes 4 to 5 pints

INGREDIENT	VOLUME	OUNCES	GRAMS	PERCENT
Tomatoes, preferably San Marzano or Roma	about 12 cups	6 pounds	2700 grams	99.5%
Kosher salt	2 teaspoons	¼ ounce	10 grams	.5%

1. Core and quarter the tomatoes. Put the tomatoes and their juices into a large pot. Bring to a boil, decrease to a gentle simmer, cover, and cook, stirring every 5 minutes to prevent the bottom from scorching, for about

20 minutes. Uncover the tomatoes and cook until the tomatoes have released all of their juices and become very soft but before the juices have thickened substantially, 15 to 20 minutes more. Pass through a food mill fitted with a coarse disk and season with salt to your liking (about 2 teaspoons).

2. Scald 5 pint jars in a large pot of simmering water fitted with a rack—you will use this pot to process the jars. Right before filling, put the jars on the counter. Meanwhile, soak the lids in a pan of hot water to soften the rubber seal.

3. Using a ladle, divide the tomato sauce among the jars, leaving a $^1/_2$-inch space from the rim of the jar. Check the jars for air pockets, adding more tomatoes if necessary to fill in any gaps. Wipe the rims with a clean towel, seal with the lids, then screw on the bands until snug but not tight.

4. Place the jars in the pot with the rack and add enough water to cover the jars by about 1 inch. Bring the water to a boil and process the jars for 15 minutes (start the timer when the water reaches a boil). Turn off the heat and leave the jars in the water for a few minutes. Remove the jars from the water and let cool completely.

At the Table: ROASTED LAMB MEATBALLS WITH TOMATO-BEAN RAGOUT AND GREEN GARLIC (PAGE 142); PRESERVED GAZPACHO (PAGE 167); BEEF CHILI (PAGE 265); POTATO GNOCCHI WITH SAN MARZANO TOMATO SAUCE AND PECORINO (PAGE 286)

TOMATO-PEPPER SAUCE

One February afternoon I made this sauce straight from the canned tomatoes and peppers in our pantry. The result was fresh and lively, and I saw its potential immediately. With lime and chile, it made a fine salsa. But it worked equally well with parsley, basil, and olive oil for a simple Mediterranean-style pan-seared fish dish. Not bad for a few jars saved from last summer.

makes about $4^1/_2$ cups

2 pints Canned Tomatoes (page 46)
1 pint Grilled and Pickled Sweet Peppers
(page 39), drained and chopped
$^1/_2$ sweet onion, minced

2 tablespoons chopped cilantro
$1^1/_2$ tablespoons extra-virgin olive oil
Kosher salt and freshly ground
black pepper

1. In a medium pot over low heat, cook the tomatoes down until thickened to a salsa consistency. Transfer to a bowl and stir in the peppers and onion. Let cool to room temperature, then mix in the cilantro and olive oil. Season with salt and pepper.

TOMATO JAM

When heaps of tomatoes start to arrive through the back door, we have a little room for tomato experimentation. This preserve is a nice alternative to canned tomatoes. Although noticeably sweet, it is balanced by a generous helping of black pepper. When simmered with onions and apple cider vinegar, it becomes a convincing glaze for barbecued goat (page 198) or meatloaf. Straight from the jar, I use it to garnish goat cheese–topped crostini. And with a few additions— roasted peppers and almonds, say—the jam can also be turned into a quick sauce akin to Spanish romesco.

Because the tomato jam yield will vary depending on the tomatoes used and how long they cook, scald a few smaller jars with the pints in case you have a bit of the valuable stuff left over.

makes 3 to 4 pints

INGREDIENT	VOLUME	OUNCES	GRAMS	PERCENT
Tomatoes, preferably Romas or San Marzanos	about 10 cups	5 pounds	2268 grams	75.5%
Extra-virgin olive oil	1/4 cup	2 ounces	57 grams	2%
Sweet onion (such as candy or Vidalia), thinly sliced	1	7 ounces	198 grams	6.6%
Kosher salt	1 tablespoon	1/3 ounce	9 grams	.3%
Freshly ground black pepper	1 teaspoon	—	—	—
Sugar	1 1/4 cups	8 ounces	227 grams	7.6%
White wine	1 cup plus 2 tablespoons	8 1/2 ounces	241 grams	8%

1. Core the tomatoes and score the ends with an X. In a large pot of boiling, salted water, blanch for 1 minute. Using a slotted spoon, transfer the tomatoes to a baking sheet. Once they are cool enough to handle, peel away and discard the skins and quarter the tomatoes. Remove the tomato seeds over a bowl fitted with a fine-mesh strainer to reserve as much juice as possible. Discard the seeds and dice the tomato flesh into small squares.

2. In a large pot over medium heat, warm the olive oil. Stir in the onion and season with the salt and pepper. Cook until the onions begin to brown, then stir in the sugar. Once the sugar has dissolved, pour in the wine and cook over medium heat until the pot is nearly dry, about 15 minutes. Pour in the tomatoes and reserved juices and simmer until the tomatoes have softened and the juice reaches about 212°F, or until the jam is thick enough to lightly coat the back of a spoon, about 45 minutes.

3. Scald 3 pint jars and 2 half-pint jars in a large pot of simmering water fitted with a rack—you will use this pot to process the jars. Right before filling, put the jars on the counter. Meanwhile, soak the lids in a pan of hot water to soften the rubber seal.

4. Ladle the jam into the jars, leaving a $^1/_2$-inch space from the rim of the jar. Wipe the rims with a clean towel, seal with the lids, then screw on the bands until snug but not tight.

5. Place the jars in the pot with the rack and add enough water to cover the jars by about 1 inch. Bring the water to a boil and process the jars for 10 minutes (start the timer when the water reaches a boil). Turn off the heat and leave the jars in the water for a few minutes. Remove the jars from the water and let cool completely.

At the Table: TOMATO JAM–GLAZED BARBECUED GOAT (PAGE 198), TOMATO JAM–ROASTED POTATOES (PAGE 237).

PICKLED WATERMELON RIND

My family has always embraced Southern cooking, from my mom's skillet-fried chicken to my brother's Carolina barbecue. This pickle is a tribute to that rich culinary culture.

Made from an ingredient that typically goes straight into the compost bin, watermelon rind makes for a humble pickle. Actually, it's a pickle only in the sense that a splash of vinegar curbs some of the preserve's sticky sweetness. The not-insignificant amount of sugar in this recipe is added in three stages, which allows the sugar and spices to gradually permeate the rind. The layering process also changes the texture of the rind, turning it translucent, similar to what happens when you candy citrus peel. In the end, the layers contribute to a pickle destined for cured meat. Adding these layers takes patience—plan on making this pickle over the course of several days—but the result is a perfect condiment for salty cured meat. I also like to serve it alongside grilled bread, sliced prosciutto, and arugula dressed with lemon juice and olive oil.

makes 3 pints

INGREDIENT	VOLUME	OUNCES	GRAMS	PERCENT
Peeled watermelon rind, finely diced	6 cups (from about 1 medium or two small melons)	2 pounds	907 grams	25.5%
Water	6 cups	48 ounces	1360 grams	39%
Kosher salt	$^1/_4$ cup plus 2 tablespoons	3$^1/_4$ ounces	92 grams	2.5%
Sugar	3 cups	1 pound, 7 ounces	652 grams	18.5%
Champagne vinegar	1$^1/_2$ cups	12 ounces	340 grams	9.5%
Lemon, sliced thinly	1$^1/_2$ lemons	6 ounces	170 grams	5%
Cinnamon sticks	3	—	—	—
Allspice berries	1$^1/_2$ teaspoons	—	—	—
Cloves	1$^1/_2$ teaspoons	—	—	—

{continued}

1. Place the rind in a large bowl. In a separate bowl, mix together the water and salt. Pour the salted water over the watermelon rind and let stand for 4 hours, then drain and rinse. Transfer the rind to a pot and cover with about 1 inch of fresh water. Bring to a boil, decrease to a simmer, and cook until tender, about 20 minutes. The rinds will start to look translucent, like slices of onions. Drain and chill.

2. In a pot over medium-high heat, simmer together 1 cup of the sugar, the vinegar, and the lemon slices. In a dry sauté pan over medium heat, toast the cinnamon, allspice berries, and cloves until fragrant. Mix the spices into the vinegar and pour over the rind. Cover and refrigerate for at least 24 hours or up to 2 days.

3. Strain the brine into a pot, reserving the rind and spices. Place the pot over medium-high heat, mix in 1 cup of the sugar, and bring to boil. Pour over the rind, cover, and refrigerate for another 24 hours or up to 2 days.

4. Strain the brine into a pot, reserving the rind and spices. Place the pot over medium-high heat, mix in the remaining 1 cup sugar, and bring to boil. Meanwhile, scald 3 pint jars in a large pot of simmering water fitted with a rack—you will use this pot to process the jars. Right before filling, put the jars on the counter. Divide the rind among the jars. Place 1 cinnamon stick in each jar. Soak the lids in a pan of hot water to soften the rubber seal.

5. Transfer the brine to a heat-proof pitcher and pour over the rind, leaving a $^1/_2$-inch space from the rim of the jar. Check the jars for air pockets, adding more liquid if necessary to fill in gaps. Wipe the rims with a clean towel, seal with the lids, then screw on the bands until snug but not tight.

6. Place the jars in the pot with the rack and add enough water to cover the jars by about 1 inch. Bring the water to a boil and process the jars for 15 minutes (start the timer when the water reaches a boil). Turn off the heat and leave the jars in the water for a few minutes. Remove the jars from the water and let cool completely.

At the Table: CHARCUTERIE PLATTER (PAGE 221)

PICKLED CELERY ROOT

With gnarled skin and shrunken stalks, celery root isn't much of a looker. But peel away the craggy surface and the vegetable quickly gains favor. Similar to, but sharper than, celery stalks, this vegetable with a dense, starchy texture lends itself well to being puréed or roasted. When pickled, celery root is a natural addition to remoulade (page 180), a creamy condiment versatile enough to pinch hit at a barbecue in the summer or a roast chicken dinner in the winter.

The quantity of celery root below is based on celery roots that have been peeled and shredded, and yield can vary depending on how craggy the skin is. Start with around 3 pounds of celery root.

makes 4 pints

INGREDIENT	VOLUME	OUNCES	GRAMS	PERCENT
Celery root, peeled and grated	16 cups	2 pounds	907 grams	40.35%
Champagne vinegar	2³/₄ cups	22 ounces	624 grams	27.75%
Water	2³/₄ cups	22 ounces	624 grams	27.75%
Honey	3 tablespoons	2 ounces	57 grams	2.54%
Lemon, juice and zest	1	1 ounce	28 grams	1.25%
Kosher salt	1 tablespoon	¹/₄ ounce	8 grams	.36%
Black peppercorns	2 teaspoons	—	—	—
Thyme sprigs	12	—	—	—
Bay leaves	4	—	—	—

1. Combine the celery root, vinegar, water, honey, lemon juice and zest, and salt in a pot. Cover and bring to a boil. Strain the brine into a heat-proof pitcher and keep hot.

2. Scald 4 pint jars in a large pot of simmering water fitted with a rack—you will use this pot to process the jars. Right before filling, put the jars on the counter. Put ¹/₂ teaspoon peppercorns, 3 sprigs thyme, and 1 bay leaf in each jar. Meanwhile, soak the lids in a pan of hot water to soften the rubber seal.

3. Pack the celery root into the jars. Pour the brine over the celery root, leaving a ¹/₂-inch space from the rim of the jar. Check the jars for air pockets, adding more brine if necessary to fill in gaps. Wipe the rims with a clean towel, seal with the lids, then screw on the bands until snug but not tight.

4. Place the jars in the pot with the rack and add enough water to cover the jars by about 1 inch. Bring the water to a boil and process the jars for 15 minutes (start the timer when the water reaches a boil). Turn off the heat and leave the jars in the water for a few minutes. Remove the jars from the water and let cool completely.

At the Table: PICKLED CELERY ROOT REMOULADE (PAGE 180)

RED WINE–PICKLED BEETS

Even when the ground is frozen solid, I can depend on a good crop of beets, one of the few fresh vegetables that I can buy year round. Yet a steady supply doesn't stop me from putting up a few jars, because beets have a natural affinity for vinegar.

There are two steps in this recipe: roasting and pickling. The pickling recipe is based on the weight of beets once they have been roasted, peeled, and sliced. If you have more roasted beets than you need, serve them like we do at Vie, with a few pieces of the finished pickled beets, as in the Roasted and Pickled Beet Salad (page 236). Or marinate any remaining beets in leftover brine and refrigerate for a quick pickle.

makes 4 pints

ROASTING

INGREDIENT	VOLUME	OUNCES	GRAMS
Red beets	7	3 pounds	1362 grams
Olive oil, for roasting the beets	—	—	—
Kosher salt, for seasoning	—	—	—

1. Preheat the oven to 400°F. Trim away the beet greens. (If they are in good condition, you can use them with the kale dish, page 200.) Nestle the beets in a baking pan and coat with a splash of olive oil and a few generous pinches of salt. Cover with aluminum foil and roast for 1 hour, or until the beets are tender when pierced with a paring knife or a wooden skewer, about an hour. Once the beets are cool enough to handle, rub the skins off with your fingers or a kitchen towel that you don't mind staining with beet juice.

2. Slice the beets into $1/4$-inch-thick wedges. Weigh the slices, setting aside $2^1/_2$ pounds to pickle.

PICKLING

INGREDIENT	VOLUME	OUNCES	GRAMS	PERCENT
Red wine vinegar (at least 5% acidity)	2 cups	16 ounces	454 grams	22%
Red wine	1 cup	8 ounces	227 grams	11%
Water	1/2 cup	4 ounces	114 grams	5.5%
Honey	1/4 cup	3 ounces	85 grams	4.05%
Brown sugar	1/3 cup, packed	2 ounces	57 grams	3%
Kosher salt	1 tablespoon	1/3 ounce	9 grams	.45%
Black peppercorns	2 teaspoons	—	—	—
Thyme sprigs	8	—	—	—
Rosemary sprigs	4	—	—	—
Red beets, roasted, peeled, and sliced	6 3/4 cups	2 1/2 pounds	1132 grams	54%

1. In a pot, bring the vinegar, wine, water, honey, sugar, and salt to a boil. Keep hot.

2. Scald 4 pint jars in a large pot of simmering water fitted with a rack—you will use this pot to process the jars. Right before filling, put the jars on the counter. Add 1/2 teaspoon peppercorns, 2 thyme sprigs, and 1 rosemary sprig into each jar, and then pack in the beets. Meanwhile, soak the lids in a pan of hot water to soften the rubber seal.

3. Transfer the brine to a heat-proof pitcher and pour over the beets, leaving a 1/2-inch space from the rim of the jar. Check the jars for air pockets, adding more brine if necessary to fill in gaps. Wipe the rims with a clean towel, seal with the lids, then screw on the bands until snug but not tight.

4. Place the jars in the pot with the rack and add enough water to cover the jars by about 1 inch. Bring the water to a boil and process the jars for 10 minutes (start the timer when the water reaches a boil). Turn off the heat and leave the jars in the water for a few minutes. Remove the jars from the water and let cool completely.

At the Table: ROASTED AND PICKLED BEET SALAD WITH PICKED HERBS (PAGE 236)

JAMS, MARMALADES, CONSERVES, AND BUTTERS

Our first forays into jam making at Vie started innocently enough: a few jars of strawberry jam, an apricot jelly. But soon we were infusing vanilla beans into melon, mixing sour cherries with almonds, and macerating kumquats in sugar and wine. Then the list kept growing.

Along the way, we started challenging the conventional rules of jam making. I dialed the sugar way back so that the true taste of the fruit wasn't eclipsed by added sweetness. The results were preserves that could be slathered on a piece of Irish soda bread but wouldn't be out of place next to a piece of aged raw-milk Cheddar.

Sugar is not necessarily a bad thing in jam. It soaks up water molecules, which eventually dehydrates microorganisms in the fruit. Using sugar to stave off spoilage goes back centuries. But the sweet, breakfast-ready preserves we know today did not become widespread in Europe until the eighteenth and nineteenth centuries, when booming sugar plantations in the West Indies drove sugar prices down. Then, sugar was crucial for shelf-stability: an open jar of a high-sugar jam could be stored at room temperature without spoiling for months. But we have refrigerators now, and jams made with far less sugar will hold up fine for a few months as long as they are kept chilled.

Sugar comes in handy in another important part of jam making. Jam makers like to talk about pectin, the naturally occurring thickeners in plant cells. With the addition of an acid, pectin molecules bond, and jam and jellies thicken. But pectin won't bond as well if there is too much water in a mixture (it will bond with water molecules instead). Since sugar wicks away water, it also encourages pectin to form a web of bonded molecules.

In addition to being lower in sugar, my fruit preserves differ in other ways from the kinds that win blue ribbons at state fairs. Made with some of the fruit pulp, my apricot jelly isn't clear, and my jams are looser than conventional jams. But I'll compromise conventional textures to preserve the integrity and flavor of the fruit every time.

Often, my jams start with an overnight maceration. I bring fruit and sugar to a brief boil, then cool the mixture down and refrigerate it at least overnight but occasionally for as many as five days. Conveniently, maceration acts as a preliminary form of preservation. If I buy several baskets of perfectly ripe berries but find myself short on time, I run the risk of letting them get moldy if I store them in my walk-in cooler for a week. So five minutes of work buys me a five-day window to complete the job. Apart from time, maceration allows the sugar to penetrate the fruit and draw out juices. After macerating overnight, the fruit expels a lot of its water. In jams where it is necessary to strain the liquid and boil it before returning the fruit to the pot, maceration is a crucial step.

When making jam, I monitor temperatures with a calibrated digital thermometer. The temperature tells me that the jam has reached a point at which the juices have started to gel. It's easy for me to reach higher temperatures on my professional stove, but home jam makers occasionally have the problem of encouraging their jams to get up to high temperatures without extended boiling periods. If you're worried your jam isn't registering the temperature indicated in the recipe, it's okay. Since all of the jams in this book are processed in a water bath for at least 10 minutes, the temperature reading isn't a food-safety precaution (the boiling alone will sterilize the jar and its contents). But if you want to get the right thickness, you do need to cook it to the temperatures indicated in the recipes. If you're concerned, you can turn to the old chilled-plate trick to check the jam's consistency: put a couple of plates in the freezer before making the jam. When the bubbles in the jam start to turn glossy and large, dab a speck on the chilled plate and push it with your finger. If it feels tacky and doesn't drip all over the plate, the jam is probably done.

A NOTE ON PRESERVING PANS

Since the key to a good jam or conserve is a quick cooking time, the best kind of pots to use for jam making are wide, with sloping sides if possible, and finished with a non-reactive material like stainless steel. In contrast, a narrow stock pot with less surface area exposed to the burners offers less heat conduction and slower evaporation. Good for stocks, not for jams.

Some jam makers swear by wide-bottomed copper preserving pans. Copper conducts heat amazingly well, which helps a jam reach a high temperature without having to simmer the fruit so long that it tastes overcooked. I don't use copper preserving pans in the restaurant kitchen. Not only are they very expensive but they also come with issues regarding copper toxicity. Unlined copper pans react with the acidity in fruit. Although sugar protects the fruit from the reaction, this is a big problem if you are making a sugar-free jam or if you plan on macerating fruit without sugar. If you use a copper preserving pan, avoid copper toxicity by mixing the fruit with sugar before adding it to the pan.

BASE RECIPE: PECTIN

Four components ensure that a jam will set up: fruit, pectin, sugar, and acid. Pectin, a substance that thickens jams, naturally occurs in citrus fruits and apples, particularly in their skins and cores. Berries, such as gooseberries and cranberries, also have high quantities of naturally occurring pectin. But strawberries and stone fruit like peaches do not. This can mean the jam needs extra cooking time, which is often the case with strawberry jam, or that it requires the addition of pectin.

Commercial pectin is sold as a powder or liquid, but it's not hard to make, and more home canners are trying their hand at making their own "pectin stocks." This recipe is technically a mild apple jelly. In fact, if you happen to have a bunch of crab apples, there isn't much more you can do with them than make this jelly.

Once made, it keeps in the refrigerator for a few weeks, though I prefer to water-bath process pectin in half-pint jars so it is on the shelf whenever I need it. Or you could freeze the pectin in small portions and thaw it before using.

makes 6 to 8 half-pints

INGREDIENT	VOLUME	OUNCES	GRAMS	PERCENT
Green apples, quartered (seeds, cores, and skins left on)	16 cups	4½ pounds	2045 grams	40.7%
Sugar	5¼ cups	2½ pounds	1135 grams	22.6%
Water	8 cups	64 ounces	1816 grams	36.1%
Lemon, juiced	1	1 ounce	28 grams	.6%

1. In a large pot over high heat, bring the apples, sugar, water, and lemon juice to a boil. Decrease to a simmer and cook, stirring occasionally, for 1 hour, or until the apples are completely soft.

2. Using a fine-mesh strainer, strain the mixture into a clean pot, pressing on the solids gently with a wooden spoon. (You can allow the mixture to strain overnight in the refrigerator if you desire.) Discard the solids and bring the liquid to 210°F (just under a boil), about 20 minutes. At this point you can cool the pectin and refrigerate it for up to 2 weeks or freeze it for up to a year. Or, while the pectin is still hot, you can process it into jars using a water bath.

3. Scald 8 half-pint jars in a large pot of simmering water fitted with a rack—you will use this pot to process the jars. Before filling, put the jars on the counter. Meanwhile, soak the lids in a pan of hot water to soften the rubber seal.

4. Divide the pectin among the jars, leaving a ½-inch space from the rim of the jar. Seal with the lids and screw on the bands until snug but not tight.

5. Place the jars in the pot fitted with the rack and add enough water to cover by about 1 inch. Bring the water to a boil and process the jars for 10 minutes. Turn off the heat and leave the jars in the water for a few minutes. Remove the jars from the water and let cool completely.

JAMS, MARMALADES, CONSERVES, AND BUTTERS

BEER JAM

This isn't really jam in the classic sense. Formed by simmering a few bottles of stout with sugar, spices, and apple pectin, it's more like a delicious, dark syrup. It is also the rare year-round preserve at Vie. Most of it goes into our popular beer jam Manhattans (page 209), but some finds its way into the kitchen, where I've used it to glaze beef cheeks (page 275) or pair with a wedge of Irish-style Cheddar.

For the ultimate beer jam, you can splurge on four bottles of Goose Island's Bourbon County Stout, a special-occasion beer aged for 100 days in barrels that previously held bourbon. After aging, the inky beer gives off notes of vanilla, cara-mel, and smoke, which echo the spices in the jam. But that beer is special—and expensive. Unaged dark beers, like milk stout, also make fine beer jam. Nathan Sears, my chef de cuisine at Vie, has also made this recipe with balsamic vinegar instead of beer, which makes a nice accent for blanched green beans.

makes 6 half-pints, plus one 4-ounce jar

INGREDIENT	VOLUME	OUNCES	GRAMS	PERCENT
Stout beer	4 (12-ounce) bottles	48 ounces	1361 grams	55%
Sugar	4²/₃ cups	2 pounds	907 grams	35%
Lemon, juiced	1	1 ounce	28 grams	1%
Vanilla beans, split	2	—	—	—
Allspice berries	10	—	—	—
Cloves, whole	3	—	—	—
Star anise	2	—	—	—
Orange zest	1 large strip	—	—	—
Pectin (page 58)	1 cup	8 ounces	227 grams	9%

1. In a large, heavy-bottomed pot over high heat, bring the beer, sugar, lemon juice, vanilla beans, allspice berries, cloves, star anise, and orange zest to a boil. Remove from the heat, transfer to a storage container, and refriger-ate overnight or up to 5 days.

2. Strain the liquid and save the vanilla beans for another use. Pour into a large, wide pot and bring to a boil over high heat—be careful that the beer doesn't boil over. Cook, stirring occasionally, until the mixture reaches about 215°F and has the texture of light syrup, 25 to 35 minutes.

3. Scald 6 half-pint jars and one 4-ounce jar in a large pot of simmering water fitted with a rack—you will use this pot to process the jars. Right before filling, put the jars on the counter. Meanwhile, soak the lids in a pan of hot water to soften the rubber seal.

4. Transfer the jam to a heat-proof pitcher and pour into the jars, leaving a $^1/_2$-inch space from the rim of the jar. (Depending on how much you reduced the jam, you may not need the small jar.) Wipe the rims with a clean towel, seal with the lids, then screw on the bands until snug but not tight.

5. Place the jars in the pot with the rack and add enough water to cover the jars by about 1 inch. Bring the water to a boil and process the jars for 10 minutes (start the timer when the water reaches a boil). Turn off the heat and leave the jars in the water for a few minutes. Remove the jars from the water and let cool completely.

At the Table: BEER JAM MANHATTAN (PAGE 209); BEER JAM–GLAZED BEEF CHEEKS WITH WHOLE-WHEAT SPAETZLE AND ROASTED BEETS (PAGE 275)

IRISH SODA BREAD

Chicago celebrates St. Patrick's Day by opening the bars early and dyeing the river green. I celebrate it by making corned beef and baking this simple soda bread, using dried fruits from local growers. Currants are classic, but diced dried apricots or cherries are easy stand-ins. This bread is too good to be limited to once a year. Served toasted as part of a cheese course, it is an excellent carrier for beer jam and aged Cheddar (be it from Wisconsin or County Cork). For breakfast, try it with any favorite fruit preserve.

makes 1 large round loaf

3 cups all-purpose flour
$^1/_2$ cup sugar
1 tablespoon baking powder
1 teaspoon baking soda

$^1/_2$ teaspoon kosher salt
4 tablespoons cold unsalted butter, cubed
1 cup buttermilk, plus 1 or 2 tablespoons more for glazing the top

1 large egg
1 cup dried currants, diced dried apricots, or dried cherries

1. Preheat the oven to 375°F. Butter a baking sheet or line it with parchment paper.

2. In a large bowl, whisk together the flour, sugar, baking powder, baking soda, and salt. Using your fingers, rub the butter into the flour until it forms a coarse, crumbly mixture. (Alternatively, pulse all of the ingredients together briefly in a food processor.) In a liquid measuring cup, whisk the buttermilk and egg together. Gradually stir the buttermilk into the flour and mix or pulse briefly, just until a tacky dough forms. Gently fold in the currants.

3. Turn the dough onto a lightly floured counter and pat it into a round. Transfer to the prepared baking sheet and brush the top with buttermilk. With a sharp knife, cut an X on the top. Bake until the top is golden brown and the bread is cooked through, 40 to 45 minutes.

RHUBARB-BEER JAM

This jam takes advantage of two things that the Midwest has in abundance: beer and rhubarb. Pair a locally made wheat beer with rhubarb, which grows like a weed in some parts, and we have one heck of a regional jam. The tang of both ingredients is mellowed with a long maceration process. I refrigerate the beer and rhubarb with the sugar and lemon at least overnight to allow the sugar to gently soften the rhubarb and extract its juices. Like the Beer Jam (page 60), this tart preserve gets put to work at the bar. It's especially endearing in the Vie version of a Normandy (page 212), a cocktail featuring Calvados.

makes 7 half-pints

INGREDIENT	VOLUME	OUNCES	GRAMS	PERCENT
Rhubarb, diced	about 9 cups	3 pounds	1361 grams	59%
Wheat beer	3 cups	24 ounces	680 grams	29%
Sugar	1 1/2 cups	9 ounces	255 grams	11%
Lemon juice	1 lemon	1 ounce	28 grams	1%
Lemon zest	2 tablespoons	—	—	—

1. In a wide, heavy-bottomed pot, bring the rhubarb, beer, sugar, and lemon juice and zest to a simmer over medium-high heat. Cool, transfer to a storage container, and refrigerate overnight or up to 5 days.

2. Strain the liquid into a wide, heavy-bottomed pot and reserve the rhubarb. Bring to a boil and cook briskly, stirring occasionally, until it reaches 215°F, about 12 minutes. Stir in the rhubarb and return to a simmer. Cook, stirring occasionally to prevent scorching, until the jam nears 215°F, about 10 minutes. The jam should lightly coat the back of a spoon.

3. Scald 7 half-pint jars in a large pot of simmering water fitted with a rack—you will use this pot to process the jars. Right before filling, put the jars on the counter. Meanwhile, soak the lids in a pan of hot water to soften the rubber seal.

4. Transfer the jam to a heat-proof pitcher and pour into the jars, leaving about a 1/2-inch space from the rim of the jar. Wipe the rims with a clean towel, seal with the lids, then screw on the bands until snug but not tight.

5. Place the jars in the pot with the rack and add enough water to cover the jars by about 1 inch. Bring the water to a boil and process the jars for 10 minutes (start the timer when the water reaches a boil). Turn off the heat and leave the jars in the water for a few minutes. Remove the jars from the water and let cool completely.

At the Table: RHUBARB NORMANDY (PAGE 212)

DEHYDRATED STRAWBERRY JAM

With strawberry jam, the name of the game is intensity. I want a jam that captures the flavor of just-picked berries, the kind that are red all the way through, not just on the surface, so I dehydrate the strawberries before making jam to concentrate the flavor. A fruit dehydrator is the best way to dehydrate the strawberries for this recipe, but you also can use an oven. I find 135°F is ideal for strawberries, but not everyone's oven can go as low. That's okay: just preheat your oven to its lowest setting. If that happens to be 170°F, the berries may look soggy rather than dehydrated, but the resulting jam will still taste delicious. (The process will also be much faster, about 4 hours compared with 8 or 9.)

Because strawberries are naturally low in pectin, this recipe requires a cup of pectin (page 58). If you don't have homemade pectin handy, add about 5 teaspoons of powdered pectin instead.

makes 5 half-pints

INGREDIENT	VOLUME	OUNCES	GRAMS	PERCENT
Strawberries	14 cups	4 pounds	1815 grams	84%
Sugar	$^2/_3$ cup	4$^1/_2$ ounces	128 grams	6%
Pectin (page 58)	1 cup	8 ounces	226 grams	10%

1. Set up a dehydrator or preheat the oven to 135°F. Line 2 baking sheets with nonstick silicone baking sheets or parchment paper.

2. Hull the strawberries. Quarter or halve the large ones but leave the small ones whole. Lay them on the tray of a dehydrator or on lined baking sheets, cut side up if applicable, and place in the dehydrator or oven. Dehydrate the strawberries until they are nearly half of their original size and the juices have stopped running, about 8 hours. (If using a low oven instead, this might take only 4 hours.) Transfer the strawberries to a bowl and mix in the sugar. Cover, refrigerate, and allow the fruit to macerate at least overnight or up to 4 days.

3. Pour the strawberries into a heavy-bottomed pot and stir in the pectin. Bring the jam to a boil, then decrease the heat and cook until the juices reduce by half, 5 to 8 minutes.

4. Scald 5 half-pint jars in a large pot of simmering water fitted with a rack—you will use this pot to process the jars. Right before filling, put the jars on the counter. Soak the lids in a pan of hot water to soften the rubber seal.

5. Transfer the strawberry jam to a heat-proof pitcher and pour into the jars, leaving a $^1/_2$-inch space from the rim. Wipe the rims with a clean towel, seal with the lids, then screw on the bands until snug but not tight.

6. Place the jars in the pot with the rack and add enough water to cover the jars by about 1 inch. Bring the water to a boil and process the jars for 10 minutes (start the timer when the water reaches a boil). Turn off the heat and leave the jars in the water for a few minutes. Remove the jars from the water and let cool completely.

At the Table: POUND CAKE WITH DEHYDRATED STRAWBERRY JAM AND SWEETENED CRÈME FRAÎCHE (PAGE 137)

STRAWBERRY AND PINOT NOIR JAM

It's not every day I allocate a nice bottle of wine to a simmering pot for the purpose of making jam, but local strawberries deserve the four-star treatment. Inspired by Christine Ferber, the French jam maker whom I met at the French Pastry School in Chicago, this jam was one of the first I started making at Vie. A natural pair with foie gras or chicken liver mousse, it's also decadent with Camembert and other creamy cheeses.

I call for Pinot Noir because the wine often reflects characteristics of strawberries, but you can also choose a light-bodied wine with similar properties, like Italian Cesanese or Cirò.

makes about 6 half-pints

INGREDIENT	VOLUME	OUNCES	GRAMS	PERCENT
Strawberries	14 cups	4 pounds	1815 grams	60%
Sugar	2¹/₄ cups plus 1 tablespoon	1 pound	454 grams	15%
Light red wine, such as Pinot Noir	1 (750-ml) bottle	25 ounces	710 grams	24%
Lemon, juiced	1	1 ounce	28 grams	1%

1. Hull the strawberries. Quarter or halve the large ones but leave the small ones whole. In a large, heavy-bottomed pot over high heat, bring the strawberries, sugar, wine, and lemon juice to a boil. Give the mixture a good stir and cook to dissolve the sugar and release some of the strawberry juices, about 10 minutes. Cool, transfer to a storage container, and refrigerate overnight or up to 5 days.

2. Strain the liquid into a large pot, reserving the strawberries. Cook the liquid over medium-high heat until the mixture has reduced by half and reaches 215°F, about 25 minutes. Return the strawberries to the liquid and continue to cook, skimming foam off the surface with a ladle, until the mixture reaches 212°F, about 15 minutes.

3. Scald 6 half-pint jars in a large pot of simmering water fitted with a rack—you will use this pot to process the jars. Right before filling, put the jars on the counter. Meanwhile, soak the lids in a pan of hot water to soften the rubber seal.

4. Transfer the strawberry jam to a heat-proof pitcher and pour into the jars, leaving a ¹/₂-inch space from the rim of the jar. Wipe the rims with a clean towel, seal with the lids, then screw on the bands until snug but not tight.

5. Place the jars in the pot with the rack and add enough water to cover the jars by about 1 inch. Bring the water to a boil and process the jars for 10 minutes (start the timer when the water reaches a boil). Turn off the heat and leave the jars in the water for a few minutes. Remove the jars from the water and let cool completely.

At the Table: VANILLA PANNA COTTA (PAGE 75); BITTERSWEET CHOCOLATE MARQUISE WITH SUMMER BERRY JAM (PAGE 288)

APRICOT JELLY

Many jelly makers boast about how their jellies hold their shape in quivering, clear spoonfuls. This is not one of those jellies. First of all, it's not that thick. Second, it's not impeccably clear. So, realistically, it's more of a jelly-jam hybrid, but it is still one of my most-used fruit preserves. I brush it over fresh fruit tarts for a shiny finish or drizzle it on pound cake for moisture and flavor. I also use it on the savory side of the kitchen, basting a few tablespoons over pan-seared scallops and or roasted chicken for a sweet, tangy glaze. This recipe calls for pitted apricots. Start with about 4¼ pounds whole fruit.

makes 3 to 4 half-pints

INGREDIENT	VOLUME	OUNCES	GRAMS	PERCENT
Apricots, pitted	6 cups	4 pounds	1814 grams	69%
Honey	½ cup plus 1 tablespoon	6⅓ ounces	180 grams	7%
Pectin (page 58)	2 cups	1 pound, 6 ounces	624 grams	24%

1. In a heavy-bottomed pot over medium-high heat, bring the apricots and honey to a boil. Simmer until the honey has dissolved, about 6 minutes. Cool, transfer to a storage container, and refrigerate overnight or up to 5 days.

2. Pour the apricots back into a heavy-bottomed pot, stir in the pectin, and bring to a boil. Simmer over medium-high heat for 5 to 6 minutes, then strain through a fine-mesh strainer lined with cheesecloth into a clean pot, using a ladle to push as much of the jelly through as you can. Alternatively, omit the cheesecloth and strain directly through a fine-mesh strainer. (You will have more pulp in the end, but it won't affect the flavor.)

3. Discard the solids and return the jelly to the stove. Cook over medium-high heat until the jelly reaches 215°F, about 15 minutes. While the jelly is cooking, use a ladle to skim off any foam that rises to the surface.

4. Scald 4 half-pint jars in a large pot of simmering water fitted with a rack—you will use this pot to process the jars. Depending on how you strained the jelly, you might have enough for a fourth jar, or you can use a small, 4-ounce jar to capture the rest. Right before filling, put the jars on the counter. Meanwhile, soak the lids in a pan of hot water to soften the rubber seal.

5. Transfer the apricot jelly to a heat-proof pitcher and pour into the jars, leaving about a ½-inch space from the rim of the jar. Wipe the rims with a clean towel, seal with the lids, then screw on the bands until snug but not tight.

6. Place the jars in the pot with the rack and add enough water to cover the jars by about 1 inch. Bring the water to a boil and process the jars for 10 minutes (start the timer when the water reaches a boil). Turn off the heat and leave the jars in the water for a few minutes. Remove the jars from the water and let cool completely.

At the Table: THUMBPRINT COOKIES (PAGE 224); CHEESE TART WITH APRICOT PRESERVES (PAGE 277)

BLACKBERRY JAM

This jam is purposefully simple: it's all about emphasizing the pure sweet-tart flavor of fresh blackberries. Because it is relatively low in sugar, this preserve's texture is naturally softer than classic berry jams. It is also easy to overcook. I use a lid to get the juices to temperature quickly without losing a lot of moisture, then I remove the lid and monitor the temperature and consistency of the jam. When in doubt, test a small dab on a chilled plate. If it sets up softly on the plate (see page 57), the jam is ready to be packed into jars. As long as the weight of the fruit stays the same, you could use any combination of blackberries, mulberries, and raspberries in this recipe.

makes 2 to 3 half-pints

INGREDIENT	VOLUME	OUNCES	GRAMS	PERCENT
Blackberries, hulled if necessary	6 cups	2 pounds	907 grams	89%
Sugar	1/2 cup	3 1/4 ounces	91 grams	10%
Lemon juice	1 tablespoon	1/2 ounce	14 grams	1%

1. In a wide, heavy-bottomed pot, combine the blackberries, sugar, and lemon juice. Cover and bring to a simmer over medium-high heat, checking the pot frequently until the juices start to release, about 5 minutes. Cool, transfer to a storage container, and refrigerate overnight or up to 5 days.

2. Pour the blackberries into a wide, heavy-bottomed pot, cover, and bring to a boil. Once the juices are boiling, uncover the jam and continue to cook briskly until the mixture hits 212°F and sets up softly when tested on a chilled plate (see page 57), about 15 minutes. While the jam is cooking, use a ladle to skim off any foam that rises to the surface.

3. Scald 3 half-pint jars in a large pot of simmering water fitted with a rack—you will use this pot to process the jars. Right before filling, put the jars on the counter. Meanwhile, soak the lids in a pan of hot water to soften the rubber seal.

4. Transfer the blackberry jam to a heat-proof pitcher and pour into the jars, leaving about a 1/2-inch space from the rim of the jar. Wipe the rims with a clean towel, seal with the lids, then screw on the bands until snug but not tight.

5. Place the jars in the pot with the rack and add enough water to cover the jars by about 1 inch. Bring the water to a boil and process the jars for 10 minutes (start the timer when the water reaches a boil). Turn off the heat and leave the jars in the water for a few minutes. Remove the jars from the water and let cool completely.

At the Table: BITTERSWEET CHOCOLATE MARQUISE WITH SUMMER BERRY JAM (PAGE 288)

A NOTE ON
BRANDIED FRUIT

Plunging fruit into brandy is an easy way to preserve it. Alcohol inhibits spoilers from growing while adding a sweet punch of flavor. On their own, brandied fruits own make for an easy, decadent topping on ice cream or cake. But I also apply them in savory sauces, compotes, and cocktails.

These three recipes follow the same approach: fresh fruit, pitted or sliced, is packed into a jar; hot brandy is poured over the fruit; the jar is sealed and processed. But the end results are all quite different depending on the fruit itself. An opened jar keeps in the refrigerator for several months, provided the fruit stays submerged in the brandy.

BRANDIED CHERRIES

We use these cherries year-round, so we make big batches. Nine pints in this recipe might seem excessive (and time-consuming for whoever was assigned the task of pitting), but if I still have a few jars remaining by December, I know it was time well spent.

A few plump cherries atop a bowl of ice cream is one way to serve these cherries, but it's hardly the only one. In Cherry Clafoutis with Milk Jam (page 189), they easily take the place of fresh cherries. I also put the cherries and brandy to work in a simple sauce for duck, squab, or other game birds. Just strain the cherries, reduce the brandy, and mix in a splash of roasted chicken jus. Simmer until the sauce lightly coats the back of a spoon, then swirl in a knob of butter, a pinch of minced shallots, and a few brandied cherry halves, and you have a fine sauce for roasted meat. If cocktails are more your speed, use this recipe to garnish a Beer Jam Manhattan (page 209). While the recipe below uses sweet cherries, sour cherries work equally well brandied.

Since the weight of the cherries is based on pitted cherries, you will need to start with just under 6½ pounds.

makes 9 pints

INGREDIENT	VOLUME	OUNCES	GRAMS	PERCENT
Brandy	3¾ cups	30 ounces	850 grams	18%
Water	2¾ cups plus 2 tablespoons	23 ounces	652 grams	14%
Sugar	2¼ cups plus 1 tablespoon	1 pound	454 grams	10%
Cherries, pitted and stemmed	16 cups	6 pounds	2720 grams	58%

1. In a large pot over high heat, bring the brandy, water, and sugar to a boil. Decrease to a simmer and cook until the sugar dissolves.

2. Scald 9 pint jars in a large pot of simmering water fitted with a rack—you will use this pot to process the jars. Right before filling, put the jars on the counter. Meanwhile, soak the lids in a pan of hot water to soften the rubber seal.

3. Pack the cherries into the jars. Transfer the brandy syrup into a heat-proof pitcher and pour over the cherries, leaving a $^1/_2$-inch space from the rim of the jar. Remove air bubbles (this is especially important with pitted cherries, since the center of the fruit can trap air), adding more syrup if needed to cover the cherries. Wipe the rims with a clean towel, seal with the lids, then screw on the bands until snug but not tight.

4. Place the jars in the pot with the rack and add enough water to cover the jars by about 1 inch. Bring the water to a boil and process the jars for 15 minutes (start the timer when the water reaches a boil). Turn off the heat and leave the jars in the water for a few minutes. Remove the jars from the water and let cool completely.

At the Table: CHERRY CLAFOUTIS WITH MILK JAM (PAGE 189); BEER JAM MANHATTAN (PAGE 209); SWEET MILK PUNCH (PAGE 213)

BRANDIED BLACK MISSION FIGS

Even though fresh figs have two seasons—one in early summer, one in the fall—harvests are short and can be uneven. By preserving figs in brandy, I ensure that they stick around longer to grace cheese and charcuterie plates. Brandied figs in a light syrup also pair well with venison. To make a sauce, set a few halves aside for a garnish. Reduce some of the brandy by half, whisk in a knob of butter, then stir the figs back in before spooning the sauce on the plate.

makes 4 pints

INGREDIENT	VOLUME	OUNCES	GRAMS	PERCENT
Brandy	1 $^2/_3$ cups	13 $^1/_2$ ounces	390 grams	18.5%
Sugar	1 $^1/_3$ cup, plus 2 tablespoons	10 ounces	290 grams	13.5%
Water	$^3/_4$ cup plus 1 tablespoon	6 $^1/_2$ ounces	189 grams	9%
Black mission figs (washed, stemmed, and halved or quartered)	8 cups	2 pounds, 11 ounces	1247 grams	59%

1. In a large pot over high heat, bring the brandy, sugar, and water to a boil. Decrease to a simmer and cook until the sugar dissolves.

{continued}

2. Scald 4 pint jars in a large pot of simmering water fitted with a rack—you will use this pot to process the jars. Right before filling, put the jars on the counter. Meanwhile, soak the lids in a pan of hot water to soften the rubber seal.

3. Divide the figs among the jars. Transfer the brandy syrup into a heat-proof pitcher and pour over the figs, leaving a $^1/_2$-inch space from the rim of the jar. Remove air bubbles, adding more syrup if needed to cover the figs. Wipe the rims with a clean towel, seal with the lids, then screw on the bands until snug but not tight.

4. Place the jars in the pot with the rack and add enough water to cover the jars by about 1 inch. Bring the water to a boil and process the jars for 15 minutes (start the timer when the water reaches a boil). Turn off the heat and leave the jars in the water for a few minutes. Remove the jars from the water and let cool completely.

At the Table: SALTED CARAMEL ICE CREAM WITH BRANDIED FIGS (PAGE 260)

BRANDIED PEACHES

Added to ice cream, yogurt, pudding, or cake, these peaches can turn a simple sweet into something more indulgent. I also like them in place of brandied cherries in clafoutis (page 189). Or try them in sangria. On a hot evening, pour an entire jar into a pitcher and stir in lemon slices, mint leaves, and white wine. Let it marinate for a couple of hours in the refrigerator before you pour it for thirsty friends.

I leave the skins intact because they help the peach slices hold their shape. If you hate peach skin, blanch the peaches in a large pot of boiling water for about 1 minute, shock them in an ice bath, and peel off the skins. But be prepared for a softer preserve.

The weight provided in the recipe is based on pitted peaches, so start with about 4 pounds total, or 2 large peaches per jar.

makes 6 pints

INGREDIENT	VOLUME	OUNCES	GRAMS	PERCENT
Brandy	$3^1/_2$ cups	28 ounces	769 grams	24%
Sugar	2 cups	15 ounces	435 grams	14%
Water	$1^1/_4$ cups	10 ounces	290 grams	9%
Peaches (washed, pitted, and cut into 8 pieces each)	About 12 peaches	$3^1/_2$ pounds	1624 grams	53%

1. In a large pot over high heat, bring the brandy, sugar, and water to a boil. Decrease to a simmer and cook until the sugar dissolves.

2. Scald 6 pint jars in a large pot of simmering water fitted with a rack—you will use this pot to process the jars. Right before filling, put the jars on the counter. Meanwhile, soak the lids in a pan of hot water to soften the rubber seal.

3. Divide the peaches among the jars. Transfer the brandy syrup into a heat-proof pitcher and pour over the peaches, leaving a $^1/_2$-inch space from the rim of the jar. Remove air bubbles, adding more syrup if needed to cover the peaches. Wipe the rims with a clean towel, seal with the lids, then screw on the bands until snug but not tight.

4. Place the jars in the pot with the rack and add enough water to cover the jars by about 1 inch. Bring the water to a boil and process the jars for 15 minutes (start the timer when the water reaches a boil). Turn off the heat and leave the jars in the water for a few minutes. Remove the jars from the water and let cool completely.

At the Table: BUTTERMILK ICE CREAM WITH BRANDIED PEACHES (PAGE 161)

GOOSEBERRY JAM

A shiny purple-green marble of a fruit, gooseberries look harmless enough, but one bite delivers a significant shot of tart juice. While vanilla bean tames some of the high-pectin fruit's acidity, I leave most of that tart bite intact. This makes the jam a good counterpoint to young goat and sheep's milk cheeses. A spoonful of gooseberry jam can enliven a fruit salad. Mixed with minced shallot, it also can act as a condiment for coppa and other cured meats. As with the blackberry jam, I use a lid to cook the jam quickly without losing a significant amount of juice in the process.

makes 4 half-pints

INGREDIENT	VOLUME	OUNCES	GRAMS	PERCENT
Gooseberries	6 cups	2 pounds	907 grams	75.5%
Sugar	1$^2/_3$ cups	10 ounces	282 grams	23%
Lemon juice	1$^1/_2$ tablespoons	$^1/_2$ ounce	14 grams	1.5%
Vanilla bean	1	—	—	—

1. Hull the gooseberries and trim the spiky ends with scissors or a paring knife. In a heavy-bottomed pot, combine the gooseberries, sugar, and lemon juice. Cover with a lid and bring to a simmer over medium-high heat. Once the pot is simmering, remove the lid. Split the vanilla bean in half and scrape out the seeds with the tip of a spoon. Add the seeds to the pot (reserve the pod for another use), and continue to cook until the jam reaches 212°F, about 15 minutes (the gooseberries will release their juices quickly).

{continued}

2. Scald 4 half-pint jars in a large pot of simmering water fitted with a rack—you will use this pot to process the jars. Right before filling, put the jars on the counter. Meanwhile, soak the lids in a pan of hot water to soften the rubber seal.

3. Transfer the gooseberry jam to a heat-proof pitcher and pour into the jars, leaving a $^1/_2$-inch space from the rim of the jar. Wipe the rims with a clean towel, seal with the lids, then screw on the bands until snug but not tight.

4. Place the jars in the pot with the rack and add enough water to cover the jars by about 1 inch. Bring the water to a boil and process the jars for 10 minutes (start the timer when the water reaches a boil). Turn off the heat and leave the jars in the water for a few minutes. Remove the jars from the water and let cool completely.

At the Table: GOOSEBERRY SMASH (PAGE 212)

PEACH SAFFRON JAM

It's a color-coordinated pair: orange peaches only get brighter with the addition of saffron. But there is more to this match than appearances. The saffron turns simple sweet peaches into something quite different—earthy, musky, savory. In other words, this may not be the best choice for a thumbprint cookie destined for a bake sale.

But while this recipe is less versatile than apricot jam, for instance, it shines in certain dishes. Taking cues from the saffron-and-seafood pairing in paella, I've used it to accent shrimp and scallops, and I also like it with lamb and Merguez sausages. A tablespoon blended into a tomato vinaigrette makes a sweet-sour salad dressing. And it's not off-limits at dessert. Try it with something neutral, like Vanilla Panna Cotta (page 75). Or layer it into a trifle with pastry cream and ladyfingers soaked in the juices from brandied peaches.

Since the weight of the peaches is based on pitted peaches, start with just under 5 pounds of whole fruit.

makes 4 half-pints

INGREDIENT	VOLUME	OUNCES	GRAMS	PERCENT
Peaches, pitted	12 cups	4½ pounds	2040 grams	86%
Sugar	1½ cups, plus 1 tablespoon	11 ounces	312 grams	13%
Lemon, juiced	1	1 ounce	28 grams	1%
Saffron	1 tablespoon	—	—	—

1. In a large, heavy-bottomed pot over high heat, bring the peaches, sugar, lemon juice, and saffron to a boil. Give the peaches a good stir and cook until they release their juices, about 12 minutes. Cool, transfer to a storage container, and refrigerate overnight or up to 5 days.

2. Pass the peaches and the juices through a food mill fitted with the coarse plate into a large, heavy-bottomed pot. Bring to a boil and continue to cook, stirring occasionally, until the jam reaches 215°F, about 15 minutes.

3. Scald 4 half-pint jars in a large pot of simmering water fitted with a rack—you will use this pot to process the jars. Right before filling, put the jars on the counter. Meanwhile, soak the lids in a pan of hot water to soften the rubber seal.

4. Transfer the peach jam to a heat-proof pitcher and pour into the jars, leaving about a ½-inch space from the rim of the jar. Wipe the rims with a clean towel, seal with the lids, then screw on the bands until snug but not tight.

5. Place the jars in the pot with the rack and add enough water to cover the jars by about 1 inch. Bring the water to a boil and process the jars for 10 minutes (start the timer when the water reaches a boil). Turn off the heat and leave the jars in the water for a few minutes. Remove the jars from the water and let cool completely.

At the Table: VANILLA PANNA COTTA (PAGE 75)

YELLOW PLUM AND RIESLING JAM

When adding wine to a red or purple plum preserve, I turn to red wine because darker plums, with their tannic skins, can take it. More delicate in flavor, yellow plums are overwhelmed by red wines but do well with aromatic Riesling, which matches the fruit's acidity, complements its sweetness, and emphasizes the floral stone-fruit flavors. Plum preserves naturally pair with cheese, but I also serve spoonfuls with Pork Milanese (page 258).

Since the weight of the plums is based on pitted plums, you will need to start with a plum or two over 4 pounds.

makes 4 half-pints

INGREDIENT	VOLUME	OUNCES	GRAMS	PERCENT
Yellow plums, pitted and chopped	7 cups	3 pounds, 12 ounces	1700 grams	69%
Riesling	2^{1}/$_{8}$ cups	17 ounces	482 grams	20%
Sugar	1^{1}/$_{8}$ cups	9 ounces	255 grams	11%
Lemon thyme, stems removed, chopped	8 sprigs	—	—	—

1. In a large, heavy-bottomed pot over high heat, bring the plums, wine, sugar, and lemon thyme to a boil. Give the mixture a good stir and cook until it reaches a boil, about 11 minutes. Cool, transfer to a storage container, and refrigerate overnight or up to 5 days.

2. Strain the liquid into a large pot, reserving the plums. Cook the liquid over high heat until the mixture has reduced by one-third and reaches 215°F, about 20 minutes. Return the plums to the liquid and continue to cook, skimming foam off the surface with a ladle, until the jam reaches 215°F, about 8 minutes.

3. Scald 4 half-pint jars in a large pot of simmering water fitted with a rack—you will use this pot to process the jars. Right before filling, put the jars on the counter. Meanwhile, soak the lids in a pan of hot water to soften the rubber seal.

4. Transfer the jam to a heat-proof pitcher and pour into the jars, leaving a ^{1}/$_{2}$-inch space from the rim of the jar. Wipe the rims with a clean towel, seal with the lids, then screw on the bands until snug but not tight.

5. Place the jars in the pot with the rack and add enough water to cover the jars by about 1 inch. Bring the water to a boil and process the jars for 10 minutes (start the timer when the water reaches a boil). Turn off the heat and leave the jars in the water for a few minutes. Remove the jars from the water and let cool completely.

At the Table: PORK MILANESE WITH YELLOW PLUM AND RIESLING JAM AND ARUGULA (PAGE 258)

VANILLA PANNA COTTA

When you have a selection of preserves within reach, a simple way to showcase them is with panna cotta. A classic Italian dessert of cream and sugar bound with gelatin, it offers a neutral canvas to serve some of the more unusual jams, such as Peach Saffron (page 73), Vanilla Melon (page 77), and Strawberry and Pinot Noir (page 63).

You can use the panna cotta with the preserves in one of two ways. For a more stylized presentation, layer the jam and the panna cotta: heat the jam, pour a thin layer into chilled panna cotta molds (nonstick flexible silicone muffin pans work well), and refrigerate until cooled. Then pour the warm panna cotta on top and refrigerate again until set, about two hours. To serve, invert the panna cotta on a plate to show off the layers. Or you can make a straightforward panna cotta in a ramekin and serve a spoonful of jam on top. I prefer using gelatin sheets, which offer a higher-quality gelatin than powdered. (One box, purchased at a specialty foods store or online, will keep you in business for a while.) Otherwise, use 2 teaspoons of powdered gelatin dissolved in 2 tablespoons ice water.

makes 6

2^1/$_2$ cups heavy cream
^{1}/$_2$ cup sugar
2^1/$_2$ tablespoons unsalted butter

^{1}/$_2$ vanilla bean, split lengthwise
2^1/$_2$ gelatin sheets

1. In a medium pot over medium-high heat, bring the cream, sugar, butter, and vanilla bean to a boil. Remove from the heat and let the vanilla infuse into the cream for 15 minutes. Remove the vanilla bean. Using a spoon, scrape the vanilla seeds into the cream, discarding the pod.

2. Soak the gelatin sheets in ice water for at least 2 minutes or until softened. Squeeze out any excess water from the gelatin and whisk it into the cream. Strain the panna cotta through a fine-mesh strainer into a heat-proof pitcher (this removes any extra bits of gelatin). Pour into 6 ramekins or 6 silicon muffin cups and refrigerate until set, about 2 hours. To unmold, run a palette knife or paring knife along the edges and invert it onto a plate.

RAINIER CHERRY JAM

While fresh cherries are a quintessentially summer fruit, I find that preserved cherries taste their best in the fall.

Because cherries are naturally low in pectin, this recipe requires a cup of homemade pectin (page 58). If you don't have apple pectin handy, add ¼ cup of powdered pectin instead. Start with about 2½ pounds before pitting the cherries. To pit cherries, I recommend using a cherry pitter, a handheld contraption that pushes the pit through the flesh. You also can gently smash the cherry with the flat side of a chef's knife to loosen the pit. For a variation with sour cherries, leave out the pectin and add 1⅓ cups toasted Marcona almonds and 2½ ounces of Amaretto. The cherries take on an almond flavor. In turn, the almonds soak up the color and tang of the cherries.

makes 4 half-pints

INGREDIENT	VOLUME	OUNCES	GRAMS	PERCENT
Rainier cherries, stemmed and pitted	6½ cups	2 pounds, 4 ounces	1020 grams	67%
Sugar	1¼ cups	9 ounces	255 grams	17%
Lemon, juiced	1	1 ounce	28 grams	1%
Pectin (page 58)	1 cup	8 ounces	226 grams	15%

1. In a large, heavy-bottomed pot over high heat, bring the cherries, sugar, and lemon juice to a boil. Give the mixture a good stir and cook until the cherries begin releasing their juices, about 5 minutes. Cool, transfer to a storage container, and refrigerate overnight or up to 5 days.

2. Strain the juice into a large pot, reserving the cherries. You should have about 2 cups of juice. Stir the pectin into the juice and cook over high heat until the juice has reduced by about ½ cup and reaches 215°F, about 10 minutes. Return the cherries to the juice and continue to cook, skimming foam off the surface with a ladle, until the mixture returns to 215°F, about 7 minutes.

3. Scald 4 half-pint jars in a large pot of simmering water fitted with a rack—you will use this pot to process the jars. Right before filling, put the jars on the counter. Meanwhile, soak the lids in a pan of hot water to soften the rubber seal.

4. Transfer the cherry jam to a heat-proof pitcher and pour into the jars, leaving a ½-inch space from the rim of the jar. Wipe the rims with a clean towel, seal with the lids, then screw on the bands until snug but not tight.

5. Place the jars in the pot with the rack and add enough water to cover the jars by about 1 inch. Bring the water to a boil and process the jars for 10 minutes (start the timer when the water reaches a boil). Turn off the heat and leave the jars in the water for a few minutes. Remove the jars from the water and let cool completely.

At the Table: THUMBPRINT COOKIES (PAGE 224); BITTERSWEET CHOCOLATE MARQUISE WITH SUMMER BERRY JAM (PAGE 288); WHOLE-WHEAT SHORTBREAD WITH RAINIER CHERRY JAM AND YOGURT (PAGE 153)

VANILLA MELON JAM

In contrast to bright, citruslike honeydew, an orange-fleshed muskmelon or cantaloupe is creamy—almost buttery. For this reason, the late-summer fruit harmonizes well with vanilla. This melon jam is memorable spooned over a bowl of fresh ricotta, one of my favorite breakfast dishes. But, like the classic melon-ham pairings, it also offers a deft accent to prosciutto. For a condiment on a cured-meat platter, I mix it with lemon juice, minced shallot, and olive oil (page 221).

makes 6 half-pints

INGREDIENT	VOLUME	OUNCES	GRAMS	PERCENT
Melon, preferably musk-melon or cantaloupe, peeled and diced	16 cups (about 2 medium melons)	5¹/₂ pounds	2495 grams	90.7%
Honey	²/₃ cup	8 ounces	227 grams	8.3%
Vanilla bean	1	—	—	—
Lemon, juiced	1	1 ounce	28 grams	1%

1. In a large heavy-bottomed pot over medium-high heat, bring the melon and honey to a simmer. Split the vanilla bean in half and scrape out the seeds with the tip of a spoon. Mix in the seeds and bean and simmer for a minute more. Cool, transfer to a storage container, and refrigerate overnight or up to 3 days.

2. In a large, heavy-bottomed pot over medium-high heat, bring the melon to a boil and cook, stirring occasionally, until the jam has thickened into a jamlike consistency, about 30 to 40 minutes.

3. Scald 6 half-pint jars in a large pot of simmering water fitted with a rack—you will use this pot to process the jars. Right before filling, put the jars on the counter. Meanwhile, soak the lids in a pan of hot water to soften the rubber seal.

4. Remove the vanilla bean and reserve for another use. Transfer the melon jam to a heat-proof pitcher and pour into the jars, leaving about a ¹/₂-inch space from the rim of the jar. Wipe the rims with a clean towel, seal with the lids, then screw on the bands until snug but not tight.

5. Place the jars in the pot with the rack and add enough water to cover the jars by about 1 inch. Bring the water to a boil and process the jars for 10 minutes (start the timer when the water reaches a boil). Turn off the heat and leave the jars in the water for a few minutes. Remove the jars from the water and let cool completely.

At the Table: CHARCUTERIE PLATTER (PAGE 221)

CARAMEL APPLE JAM

Put aside images of oversized caramel apples propped on sticks; this jam shares few similarities. Instead, it's a near-perfect cheese condiment, where caramel is balanced by the savory leanings of thyme and pepper. Sugar takes time to caramelize, but once it starts turning brown, it cooks quickly. This is the point when people freak out a little, pulling the sugar off the heat too early. But if you play it safe, you'll never achieve the complex flavors that a proper caramel delivers. When the caramel starts to brown, pick up the pan from the heat and tilt it to gauge how dark the caramel has turned. Once the caramel is amber and nearly smoking, pour in the cider. This causes a rather dramatic reaction—the pot will sputter and the sugars seize up and harden—but it also stops the sugar from cooking further.

The quantity of apples below is based on fruit that has been cored and shredded. I leave the skins on for texture and color, but you can peel the apple if you prefer a softer preserve. Either way, start with about 4¹/₂ pounds of apples.

makes 7 half-pints

INGREDIENT	VOLUME	OUNCES	GRAMS	PERCENT
Sugar	1¹/₄ cups	9 ounces	255 grams	10%
Thyme	2 tablespoons	—	—	—
Freshly ground black pepper	1 teaspoon	—	—	—
Apple cider	2 cups	16 ounces	454 grams	18%
Apples, cored and shredded	12 cups	4 pounds	1815 grams	72%

1. In a heavy-bottomed pot over medium-high heat, melt the sugar with a splash of water, just enough for the sugar to look like wet sand. Continue to cook until the sugar begins to brown. Swirl the pan and continue to cook the sugar until it has reached a deep golden brown color, 5 to 7 minutes. Decrease the heat and cautiously add the thyme and pepper—it will splatter and fry. Remove the pot from the heat and pour in the cider. Be careful: the cider will sputter on contact and the caramel will seize up and harden.

2. Return the pot to the stove. Over medium heat, simmer until the caramel dissolves into the cider. Reduce the cider by half, about 3 minutes. Stir in the apples, cover, and cook for 5 minutes. Uncover and continue to cook, stirring occasionally, until the mixture has thickened to a jamlike consistency, 5 to 10 minutes.

3. Scald 7 half-pint jars in a large pot of simmering water fitted with a rack—you will use this pot to process the jars. Right before filling, put the jars on the counter. Meanwhile, soak the lids in a pan of hot water to soften the rubber seal.

4. Spoon the jam among the jars, leaving about a ¹/₂-inch space from the rim of the jar. Wipe the rims with a clean towel, seal with the lids, then screw on the bands until snug but not tight.

5. Place the jars in the pot with the rack and add enough water to cover by about 1 inch. Bring the water to a boil and process the jars for 10 minutes (start the timer when the water reaches a boil). Turn off the heat and leave the jars in the water for a few minutes. Remove the jars from the water and let cool completely.

At the Table: CHEESE AND CRACKERS WITH CARAMEL APPLE JAM (PAGE 163)

SMOKED APPLE BUTTER

The smell of wood fires and the taste of crisp local apples are so intrinsically linked to fall that combining the two elements in a preserve makes perfect sense. The result is apple flavor embellished with smoke and caramel—a fine addition to seared scallops, a bourbon cocktail (Kentucky Burnt Apples, page 213), or just about anything that benefits from smoke and sweetness.

This apple butter requires adequate time for smoking, cooking, and processing. I save the cores and cook them with lemon rind and juice to make a light pectin-fortified broth. The broth is folded into the apples after they are smoked.

While a stovetop smoker works well for small smoking projects, this recipe requires a more dedicated setup. I smoke the apples for 2 hours in a Weber Smokey Mountain. Below I've outlined the steps for setting up the Smokey Mountain, though the instructions can be modified to suit other outdoor smokers as long as the time and temperature stay the same. For more on slow-smoked foods, see The Draw of Smoke (page 197). For this recipe, you will need hardwood lump charcoal and untreated wood chunks, such as hickory or cherry.

makes about 7 pints

INGREDIENT	VOLUME	OUNCES	GRAMS	PERCENT
Golden apples	—	10 pounds	4536 grams	86%
Lemon, juice and strips of zest	1	2 ounces	57 grams	1%
Sugar	3¹/₂ cups	1¹/₂ pounds	680 grams	13%

1. Core and halve the apples. Put the cores in a pot with the juice and zest from the lemon. Cover the cores with 4 cups water and bring to a boil. Decrease to a simmer and cook for 1 hour, then strain and discard the solids.

2. Meanwhile, prepare the smoker. Remove the lid and the large center cylinder. Open the vent in the charcoal basin, ensuring that the holes aren't blocked by bits of charcoal or ash. Place the center ring down and the charcoal chamber on top of it. Fill the chamber halfway up with hardwood lump charcoal.

{continued}

3. Put about 3 sheets of crumpled newspaper at the base of a heavy-duty chimney starter. Place the chimney on a grate or a heat-proof surface that allows air to flow into its base and light the paper on about 3 sides. After 5 to 10 minutes, the charcoal should start to catch fire, begin to glow red, and turn ashen around the edges.

4. Dump the contents of the chimney onto the unlit charcoal, using metal tongs to pick up any pieces that stray to the sides. Once the smoke subsides, place three 3- to 5-inch chunks of wood on the charcoal.

5. Reassemble the smoker: Return the center cylinder (which should be fitted with a water bowl and two grates) on top of the charcoal basin. With a heat-proof pitcher gently pour water through the grates into the bowl, trying not to splash the coals underneath, until it is nearly full. Once the smoke has subsided, about 5 minutes later, put the apples, skin side down, on the top grate and cover with the lid, ensuring that the vent is open.

6. Smoke the apples for 2 hours between 225°F and 250°F, checking only periodically to ensure the coals are still burning (the less you open the lid, the more smoke stays with the fruit). After 2 hours, the apples should be golden brown and tender.

7. In a large pot, stir together the smoked apples, the strained apple broth, and the sugar. Cover and bring to a boil. Decrease to a simmer and cook gently for $^1/_2$ hour. In batches, purée the apples until smooth. Return to the pot and cook to 200°F, about 20 minutes.

8. Scald 7 half-pint jars in a large pot of simmering water fitted with a rack—you will use this pot to process the jars. (Depending on the apples, you might have enough for an additional small, 4-ounce jar.) Right before filling, put the jars on the counter. Meanwhile, soak the lids in a pan of hot water to soften the rubber seal.

9. Ladle the apple butter into the jars, leaving about a $^{1}/_{2}$-inch space from the rim of the jar. Wipe the rims with a clean towel, seal with the lids, then screw on the bands until snug but not tight.

10. Place the jars in the pot with the rack and add enough water to cover the jars by about 1 inch. Bring the water to a boil and process the jars for 10 minutes (start the timer when the water reaches a boil). Turn off the heat and leave the jars in the water for a few minutes. Remove the jars from the water and let cool completely.

At the Table: KENTUCKY BURNT APPLES (PAGE 213)

PUMPKIN BUTTER

I look forward to pumpkin butter as soon as fall arrives. For the most concentrated flavor, I roast the pumpkin in two stages. First, I roast the pumpkin to cook it, then I mix the pulp with spices and butter and roast it again until it achieves a velvety, dense texture. While I can eat it slathered on toast, I also like to leverage it in Pumpkin Butter Bars (page 233) and Pumpkin Butter Ice Cream (page 253).

All-purpose, naturally creamy butternut squash works well in this recipe, but I like to mix it up with darker varieties, such as red kuri, kabocha, or acorn. Small sugar pumpkins and deep-orange Cinderella pumpkins are also good.

Pumpkin butter is low in acidity, so it is not safe for water-bath processing. That's fine with me, because I never store it for very long. Either divide the butter into pint containers to freeze or store it in the refrigerator for a few weeks.

makes about 6 cups

ROASTING

INGREDIENT	VOLUME	OUNCES	GRAMS
Pumpkin or winter squash, halved and seeded	2 to 3 pumpkins	5 pounds	2260 grams
Vegetable oil for coating	—	—	—

1. Preheat the oven to 400°F. Brush the cut sides of the pumpkins with oil. Place the halves, cut side down, in a baking pan and roast for 45 minutes, or until the pumpkin is tender when pierced with a knife. (This varies widely depending on the squash variety. A delicata may cook in 35 minutes while a butternut or kabocha can take 1 hour.) Using a spoon, scrape the flesh into a bowl and discard the skins.

{continued}

INGREDIENT	VOLUME	OUNCES	GRAMS	PERCENT
Roasted pumpkin or winter squash pulp	6 cups	3 pounds	1360 grams	75%
Brown sugar	2 cups	12 ounces	340 grams	18.8%
Unsalted butter, cubed	1 stick	4 ounces	113 grams	6%
Kosher salt	1 teaspoon	$^1/_8$ ounces	3 grams	.2%
Cinnamon, ground	1 teaspoon	—	—	—
Nutmeg, ground	$^1/_2$ teaspoon	—	—	—
Ginger, ground	$^1/_2$ teaspoon	—	—	—
Cloves, ground	$^1/_4$ teaspoon	—	—	—

1. Preheat the oven to 350°F. In a bowl, mix together the roasted pumpkin, sugar, butter, salt, cinnamon, nutmeg, ginger, and cloves. Spread onto a 9 by 13-inch baking pan and bake, stirring every 15 minutes with a spatula, until the pumpkin has become thick and slightly caramelized, about 1½ hours. Give it a good stir at the end; it should be smooth and spreadable. If the pumpkin is too fibrous for your liking, blend it in a food processor to even out the texture. Cool and refrigerate or freeze in a couple of plastic deli containers until ready to use.

At the Table: PUMPKIN BUTTER BARS (PAGE 233); PUMPKIN BUTTER ICE CREAM (PAGE 253)

KUMQUAT MARMALADE

Small, oblong kumquats are unique among citrus. Not only are they good enough to eat whole, but they also retain enough acidity to be versatile in both savory and sweet preparations. Compared with other citrus fruits, kumquats arrive later in the season.

This marmalade mirrors the fruit's flexibility. Not only does it pair well with pound cake (page 137), but it also works as a glaze for shrimp or chicken. For a variation, make this with Meyer lemons, which are similarly sweet. Slice the fruit into six wedges, then slice each wedge crosswise into thin pieces. The recipe will yield about a pint more than the kumquat marmalade and is just as delicious.

makes 5 half-pints

INGREDIENT	VOLUME	OUNCES	GRAMS	PERCENT
Kumquats	125 kumquats	2¹/₂ pounds	1134 grams	44%
Sugar	3 cups	1 pound, 4 ounces	567 grams	22%
White wine	2¹/₂ cups	20 ounces	567 grams	22%
Orange juice	a scant 1 cup	7¹/₂ ounces	213 grams	9%
Lemon juice	a scant ¹/₃ cup	2¹/₂ ounces	71 grams	3%

1. Halve the kumquats lengthwise and remove most of the seeds (some are okay). In a large, heavy-bottomed pot, bring the kumquats, sugar, wine, and juices to a boil. Remove from the heat, transfer to a storage container, and refrigerate overnight or up to 5 days.

2. Strain the liquid into a large, wide pot and cook over high heat until it reaches 218°F, about 25 minutes. Stir in the kumquats and continue to cook until the marmalade returns to 216°F, about 12 minutes. Continue to cook until the marmalade has thickened into a light syrup. To test its consistency, dab a small spoonful on a chilled plate. If the syrup is runny, keep cooking the marmalade. If the syrup feels tacky and wrinkles slightly when you push it with your finger, the marmalade is done.

3. Scald 5 half-pint jars in a large pot of simmering water fitted with a rack—you will use this pot to process the jars. Right before filling, put the jars on the counter. Meanwhile, soak the lids in a pan of hot water to soften the rubber seal.

4. Spoon the jam into the jars, leaving a ¹/₂-inch space from the rim of the jar. Wipe the rims with a clean towel, seal with the lids, then screw on the bands until snug but not tight. Place the jars in the pot with the rack and add enough water to cover the jars by about 1 inch. Bring the water to a boil and process the jars for 10 minutes (start the timer when the water reaches a boil). Turn off the heat and leave the jars in the water for a few minutes. Remove the jars from the water and let cool completely.

At the Table: RHUBARB SUMMER PUDDING WITH KUMQUAT MARMALADE (PAGE 145)

MAPLE–BLACK WALNUT BUTTER

The distinctive scent of black walnuts takes me back to family vacations in Florida. My mom, never short on cooking projects—even on vacation—would bake loaves of bread studded with walnuts she brought from Missouri. Compared to conventional walnuts, black walnuts have an earthier, almost musky flavor. Blended with maple into a paste, they turn into a preserve that is a whole lot more versatile than you might think. I mix the paste with buttermilk for a sweet, tangy dressing to add to roasted sunchokes (page 157). Similarly, I mix a few spoonfuls into crème fraîche to garnish a bowl of sunchoke soup. I've even found that the crème fraîche sauce works for glazing roasted beets or parsnips. When black walnuts are scarce, I've found that hickory nuts make a fine butter, too.

Be patient as you purée the walnut mixture—it will take some time in the food processor before it reaches the optimal consistency. Since the butter is a low-acid food, it is not safe for water-bath processing, but it keeps well stored in the refrigerator like freshly ground peanut butter. You also can freeze it.

makes 4 cups

INGREDIENT	VOLUME	OUNCES	GRAMS	PERCENT
Maple syrup	1¾ cups	1 pound, 4 ounces	567 grams	55.5%
Black walnuts	about 4 cups	1 pound	454 grams	44.5%
Kosher salt	1 teaspoon	—	—	—

1. Pour the maple syrup into a wide, heavy-bottomed pot and cook over high heat until a candy thermometer reaches between 230°F and 240°F. This is the soft ball stage—when a drop of hot syrup immersed in ice water will form a soft ball. Stir in the walnuts and salt and cook, stirring constantly, until the walnuts are coated with the syrup and look frosted, about 5 minutes. The maple syrup may appear crystallized at this point. Continue to cook until the crystals melt and the nuts begin to smell toasted, about 5 more minutes. Once the nuts are evenly toasted and the syrup has lost any crystallization, cool slightly and transfer to a food processor.

2. Blend the preserve in a food processor until it forms a smooth paste. Be patient—this will take a while. Cool and store in the refrigerator for up to a month.

At the Table: ROASTED SUNCHOKES WITH MAPLE–BLACK WALNUT BUTTER AND PARSLEY (PAGE 157)

BITTERSWEET PRESERVES:
AIGRE-DOUX AND
MOSTARDA

Complex and nuanced, aigre-doux and mostarda are preserves for cheese snobs and wine geeks, and I mean that in an affectionate way. And while they provide some of the most sophisticated flavor profiles, they are also some of the easiest preserves to make.

Mostarda first piqued my interest while I was working at Everest, a French restaurant that soars forty floors above the Chicago Stock Exchange. Much of the menu was grounded in classic French cuisine, but other influences inevitably popped onto the menu. In one dish, a refined pot-au-feu, we garnished the brothy, meaty braise with a spoonful of mostarda. French-born chef Jean Joho had spent time as a cook in Italy, where he had witnessed chefs finishing *bollito misto*, a dish of mixed boiled meats, with mostarda. Admiring the lift that the sweet, piquant condiment gave the rich meat, he began to implement the trick himself. Eventually I started making my own variations of mostarda. While it often has mustard or mustard seeds in it, "mostarda" doesn't mean "mustard" in Italian. The condiment's name derives from *mustum*, the Latin word for "grape must," the juice from freshly crushed grapes. Traditionally, pieces of fruit were simmered in grape must, then mixed with mustard and vinegar and cooked again. I'm loose with my definition: I call any preserve "mostarda" if I've added mustard or mustard seeds.

"Aigre-doux," the French term for sweet-and-sour, came into my repertoire later than mostarda did. During the preserving class I took with Christine Ferber at Chicago's French Pastry School, I sampled pears soaked in sweetened wine, the perfect foil for blue cheese. I have made my variation of her pear aigre-doux ever since.

While aigre-doux and mostarda are not interchangeable terms, both frequently mix fruit with wine, vinegar, and spices. While I like mostarda, I make aigre-doux more often. An aigre-doux can be turned into a vinaigrette, a pan sauce, a condiment, or a glaze. Often, the only effort involved is straining the liquid into a pot, reducing it, and stirring the fruit back in. Yet not all sweet-sour condiments need to be made with fruit. The white asparagus aigre-doux is one example that, instead of relying on the sweetness of the ingredient, draws out the subtle flavor in the vegetable with honey, orange, and sage. The cipollini aigre-doux is another example. Here, I make a caramel to mimic the flavor of caramelized onions.

Although I make most mostarda and aigre-doux in the summer, the best time to eat them is in the fall and winter. Out come the special occasion cheese plates and roasts. In fact, I use two of these recipes—Cranberry Aigre-Doux (page 99) and Butternut Squash Aigre-Doux (page 98)—on my table at Thanksgiving. There's also something about zingy currant mostarda mixed into a meat sauce that brightens a hearty winter meal more effectively than a splash of lemon juice. The one exception to this seasonal rule involves citrus preserves. In the summer, when green beans have arrived at the market, I'll pull out a jar of Meyer lemon aigre-doux from January and chop it up into a refreshing relish.

A WORD ON COOKING WINE

It's common for recipes to insist you cook with wine that you'd want to drink. It's a fine guideline but not always a realistic one. In many cases, simple, inexpensive table wines may serve recipes' needs better. All of my aigre-doux recipes require wine. In some cases, I've been specific, recommending aromatic Gewürztraminer to complement the fruit in Grape Aigre-Doux (page 94), for instance. In most cases, however, I've called for white or red table wine. These are neutral wines that serve as backdrops to the produce. With white wines, I prefer simple dry or off-dry wines that steer clear of oak. With red wine, a fruity bottle is much better than one with a web of bitter tannins.

WHITE ASPARAGUS AIGRE-DOUX

There are times when preserving makes economic sense. Then there are instances when a preserve flouts budget restrictions. This aigre-doux is more rarefied than others, because white asparagus doesn't come cheap. Thicker and smoother than green stalks, it's closer to hearts of palm in flavor. I find that oranges and aromatic herbs like sage and thyme complement its subtle earthiness. As a simple, elegant first course, I simmer the preserved spears gently in a splash of aigre-doux liquid and a knob of butter. This aigre-doux is so special that you don't need anything else.

Making this aigre-doux in quart jars allows for longer spears and less trimming. At Vie, we've even packed the aigre-doux into half-gallon jars when presented with very long asparagus. As with the Pickled Asparagus (page 21), if you have a lot of good-quality trimmings, include them in the total weight of asparagus and tuck them in the jars with the spears. Trimmed ends can be sliced into coins and added to salads or roasting vegetables.

makes 2 quarts

INGREDIENT	VOLUME	OUNCES	GRAMS	PERCENT
White asparagus	2 bunches	2 pounds	907 grams	42.5%
Champagne vinegar	1 1/3 cups	10 1/2 ounces	297 grams	14%
White table wine	1 1/3 cups	10 1/2 ounces	297 grams	14%
Honey	1 scant cup	10 1/2 ounces	297 grams	14%
Water	3/4 cup plus 1 tablespoon	7 ounces	198 grams	9.2%
Orange, juice and zest	1/2 cup plus 1 teaspoon	4 1/2 ounces	128 grams	6%
Kosher salt	1 tablespoon	1/4 ounce	8 grams	.3%
Thyme sprigs	4	—	—	—
Sage sprigs	4	—	—	—

1. With a vegetable peeler, gently peel the skin off the asparagus stalks, leaving the tips intact. Trim about 1/2 inch off the stem end and discard. Stand a spear in a quart jar to determine how much to trim, then trim the spears to fit the jar, saving any trimmings.

2. In a wide sauté pan with straight sides or a wide-bottomed pot, bring the vinegar, wine, honey, water, orange juice, zest, and salt to a boil. Lay the spears in the liquid, cover, and return to a boil. Remove from heat and keep warm.

3. Scald 2 quart jars in a large pot of simmering water fitted with a rack—you will use this pot to process the jars. Right before filling, put the jars on the counter. Meanwhile, soak the lids in a pan of hot water to soften the rubber seal.

4. In each jar, place 2 sprigs thyme and 2 sprigs sage. Pack the asparagus into the jars. Transfer the brine to a heat-proof pitcher and pour over the asparagus, leaving a 1-inch space from the rim of the jar. Check the jars for air pockets, adding more brine if necessary. Seal with lids and screw on the bands until snug but not tight.

5. Place the jars in a big pot fitted with a rack and add enough water to cover the jars by 1 inch. Bring the water to a boil and process the jars for 20 minutes (start the timer when the water reaches a boil). Turn off the heat and leave the jars in the water for a few minutes. Remove the jars from the water and let cool completely.

BLUEBERRY AIGRE-DOUX

Although I pack this aigre-doux away in July, when blueberries are inexpensive, I use it most often during the fall and winter months. Before using, I strain and reduce the liquid then add the blueberries back in. Prepared this way, the aigre-doux can be used as a vinaigrette with watercress and roasted nuts. It's just as phenomenal as a cheese condiment. For special occasions, I will grill a round of Camembert until it's about to burst, put it on a platter, and then pour the aigre-doux on top.

makes 5 half-pints

INGREDIENT	VOLUME	OUNCES	GRAMS	PERCENT
Red table wine	1 (750-ml) bottle	26 ounces	737 grams	44%
Sugar	2/3 cup	5 ounces	140 grams	8.5%
Red wine vinegar	1/3 cup	3 ounces	85 grams	5%
Lemon, juiced	1	1 ounce	28 grams	1.8%
Kosher salt	1/2 teaspoon	Less than 1/8 ounce	2 grams	.2%
Blueberries	4 1/2 cups	1 1/2 pounds	680 grams	40.5%

1. In a pot over high heat, mix together the wine, sugar, vinegar, lemon juice, and salt. Bring to a boil, then transfer to a heat-proof pitcher.

2. Scald 5 half-pint jars in a large pot of simmering water fitted with a rack—you will use this pot to process the jars. Right before filling, put the jars on the counter. Meanwhile, soak the lids in a pan of hot water to soften the rubber seal.

3. Pack the blueberries into the jars. Pour the wine mixture over the blueberries, leaving a 1/2-inch space from the rim of the jar. Check the jars for air pockets, adding more of the wine mixture if needed to cover the blueberries. Wipe the rims with a clean towel, seal with the lids, then screw on the bands until snug but not tight.

4. Place the jars in the pot with the rack and add enough water to cover the jars by about 1 inch. Bring the water to a boil and process the jars for 15 minutes (start the timer when the water reaches a boil). Turn off the heat and leave the jars in the water for a few minutes. Remove the jars from the water and let cool completely.

At the Table: THE TBD (PAGE 215)

CHERRY MOSTARDA

With heat from two different mustards and sweetness from juicy, sweet cherries, this mostarda is the perfect condiment for roasted meat, particularly pork and game birds. You also can use the mostarda in a sweet-and-sour glaze for roasts and ribs: just stir in another spoonful of mustard and brush the juices on the meat as it cooks.

makes 4 half-pints

INGREDIENT	VOLUME	OUNCES	GRAMS	PERCENT
Sugar	1 1/2 cups	10 2/3 ounces	300 grams	17.2%
Red wine vinegar	1/2 cup	4 ounces	113 grams	6.5%
Water	1/2 cup	4 ounces	113 grams	6.5%
Dijon mustard	1/4 cup	2 ounces	57 grams	3.3%
Coleman's English Mustard (not powdered)	2 tablespoons	3/4 ounce	21 grams	1.2%
Black mustard seeds	1 tablespoon	—	—	—
Kosher salt	2 teaspoons	1/4 ounce	6 grams	.3%
Sweet cherries, stemmed and pitted	6 3/4 cups	2 1/2 pounds	1134 grams	65%

1. In a pot over medium-high heat, mix together the sugar, vinegar, water, mustards, mustard seeds, and salt and bring to a boil. Add the cherries and continue to cook over medium-high heat until the cherries have softened, about 20 minutes.

2. Scald 4 half-pint jars in a large pot of simmering water fitted with a rack—you will use this pot to process the jars. Right before filling, put the jars on the counter. Meanwhile, soak the lids in a pan of hot water to soften the rubber seal.

3. Ladle the mostarda into the jars, leaving a 1/2-inch space from the rim of the jar. Check the jars for air pockets, packing in more mostarda if necessary to fill in gaps. Wipe the rims with a clean towel, seal with the lids, then screw on the bands until snug but not tight.

4. Place the jars in the pot with the rack and add enough water to cover the jars by about 1 inch. Bring the water to a boil and process the jars for 10 minutes (start the timer when the water reaches a boil). Turn off the heat and leave the jars in the water for a few minutes. Remove the jars from the water and let cool completely.

At the Table: PORK RILLETTES (PAGE 274)

CARAMEL CIPOLLINI AIGRE-DOUX

Italian cooks have long served these round, flat onions in sweetened vinegar as an antipasto. I'll eat them either straight out of the jar or warm them in a pan to serve with scallops or roast pork. To mimic the flavor of caramelized onions, I start the aigre-doux with caramelized sugar. When making this brine, wait for it to reach a deep golden brown color before adding the wine and vinegar. (For more on caramel in preserves, see Caramel Apple Jam, page 78.)

Peeling cipollini onions produces a lot of trimmings. Start with about 3¹/₂ pounds unpeeled cipollini for this recipe, selecting small onions when possible (large cipollini are more difficult to fit into the jars). You may have extra.

makes 5 pints

INGREDIENT	VOLUME	OUNCES	GRAMS	PERCENT
Sugar	1¹/₃ cups	8⁵/₈ ounces	245 grams	10.6%
White table wine	2²/₃ cups	19 ounces	540 grams	23.4%
Champagne vinegar	1¹/₃ cups	11¹/₄ ounces	318 grams	13.6%
Kosher salt	2¹/₂ teaspoons	³/₈ ounce	10 grams	.4%
Thyme sprigs	10	—	—	—
Bay leaves	5	—	—	—
Black peppercorns	2¹/₂ teaspoons	—	—	—
Cipollini onions, blanched and peeled	About 40	2 pounds, 10 ounces	1190 grams	52%

1. In a heavy-bottomed pot over medium-high heat, melt the sugar with a splash of water—just enough for the sugar to look like wet sand. Cook until the sugar begins to turn brown. Swirl the pan and continue to cook the sugar until it has reached a deep golden brown color, 5 to 7 minutes. Remove the pot from the heat and pour in the wine and vinegar. Be cautious: the liquids will splatter on contact with the sugar and the caramel will seize up and harden. Return the pot to the stove and cook over medium heat, stirring occasionally, until the caramel eventually dissolves. Stir in the salt and keep hot.

2. Scald 5 pint jars in a large pot of simmering water fitted with a rack—you will use this pot to process the jars. Right before filling, put the jars on the counter. Into each jar add 2 sprigs thyme, 1 bay leaf, and ¹/₂ teaspoon peppercorns. Pack in the onions. Meanwhile, soak the lids in a pan of hot water to soften the rubber seal.

3. Transfer the brine to a heat-proof pitcher and pour over the onions, leaving a ¹/₂-inch space from the rim of the jar. Check the jars for air pockets, adding more brine if necessary to fill in gaps. Wipe the rims with a clean towel, seal with the lids, then screw on the bands until snug but not tight.

4. Place the jars in the pot with the rack and add enough water to cover by about 2 inches. Bring the water to a boil and process the jars for 15 minutes (start the timer when the water reaches a boil). Turn off the heat and leave the jars in the water for a few minutes. Remove the jars from the water and let cool completely.

GRAPE AIGRE-DOUX

You can find red or green grapes at the grocery store year-round, but in late summer farmers start to bring more nuanced table grapes to market. Although it is easy to eat an entire bunch of the small, sweet goldenrod or round, purple canadice varieties that I buy from Mick and Cindy Klug in St. Joseph, Michigan, I make sure to save some for aigre-doux. To counter the inherent sweetness of these grapes, I add white wine and verjus, the tart juice of under-ripe grapes.

Like most recipes in this chapter, grape aigre-doux pairs effortlessly with cheese. But I also use it as the base of a vinai-grette for an updated Waldorf salad (page 229). In addition, this preserve can be turned into a simple, wine friendly sauce for pan-seared fish or roasted cauliflower. I simmer the liquid until reduced by half, whisk in butter until it's glossy, then swirl in the grapes. For best results, avoid cooking the grapes too long in the sauce—their thin skins break down quickly.

makes 4 half-pints

INGREDIENT	VOLUME	OUNCES	METRIC	PERCENT
White wine, preferably off-dry Gewürztraminer	1 1/2 cups	12 ounces	340 grams	31.6%
Verjus	1/2 cup	4 ounces	113 grams	11%
Champagne vinegar	1/4 cup	2 ounces	57 grams	5.4%
Sugar	1/2 cup	3 3/4 ounce	106 grams	9.8%
Kosher salt	1/2 teaspoon	less than 1/8 ounce	2 grams	.2%
Black pepper, ground	2 teaspoons	—	—	—
Vanilla bean	1	—	—	—
Small red or green grapes, such as canadice, goldenrod, Bronx, or Thompson seedless, stemmed	scant 4 cups	1 pound	454 grams	42%

1. In a pot over medium-high heat, mix together the wine, verjus, vinegar, sugar, salt, and pepper and bring to a boil. Split the vanilla bean in half and scrape out the seeds with the tip of a spoon. Mix in the seeds and bean and simmer for a minute more. Transfer to a heat-proof pitcher and remove the vanilla bean (reserve for another use, like Vanilla Melon Jam, page 77).

2. Scald 4 half-pint jars in a large pot of simmering water fitted with a rack—you will use this pot to process the jars. Right before filling, put the jars on the counter. Meanwhile, soak the lids in a pan of hot water to soften the rubber seal.

3. Pack the grapes into the jars, leaving about a 1/2-inch space from the rim of the jar. Check the jars for air pockets, pouring in more of the liquid if necessary to fill in gaps. Wipe the rims with a clean towel, seal with the lids, then screw on the bands until snug but not tight.

4. Place the jars in the pot with the rack and add enough water to cover the jars by about 1 inch. Bring the water to a boil and process the jars for 15 minutes (start the timer when the water reaches a boil). Turn off the heat and leave the jars in the water for a few minutes. Remove the jars from the water and let cool completely.

At the Table: WALDORF SALAD WITH APPLES, CANDIED WALNUTS, AND GRAPE AIGRE-DOUX DRESSING (PAGE 229)

MULBERRY AIGRE-DOUX

There's nothing like a little foraging to inspire canning activity. Vie's general manager, Jimmy McFarland, has a mulberry tree growing behind his house. When he gives the kitchen the head's up that the tree is ready to harvest, we pop over to collect buckets of the berries. By the end of the summer the tree is pretty well picked over, but our shelves are stocked with jars of the blackberrylike fruit suspended in red wine. This aigre-doux gives me a tart alternative to blueberry aigre-doux.

makes 4 half-pints

INGREDIENT	VOLUME	OUNCES	GRAMS	PERCENT
Red table wine	2 cups	16 ounces	454 grams	41.3%
Sugar	1/2 cup	3 3/4 ounces	105 grams	9.6%
Vinegar	1/3 cup	3 ounces	85 grams	7.7%
Kosher salt	1/2 teaspoon	less than 1/8 ounce	2 grams	.1%
Mulberries	4 cups	1 pound	454 grams	41.3%

1. In a pot over high heat, mix together the wine, sugar, vinegar, and salt. Bring to a boil, then transfer to a heat-proof pitcher.

2. Scald 4 half-pint jars in a large pot of simmering water fitted with a rack—you will use this pot to process the jars. Right before filling, put the jars on the counter. Meanwhile, soak the lids in a pan of hot water to soften the rubber seal.

3. Pack the mulberries into the jars. Pour the wine mixture over the mulberries, leaving a 1/2-inch space from the rim of the jar. Check the jars for air pockets, adding more of the wine mixture if needed to cover the mulberries. Wipe the rims with a clean towel, seal with the lids, then screw on the bands until snug but not tight.

4. Place the jars in the pot with the rack and add enough water to cover the jars by about 1 inch. Bring the water to a boil and process the jars for 15 minutes (start the timer when the water reaches a boil). Turn off the heat and leave the jars in the water for a few minutes. Remove the jars from the water and let cool completely.

At the Table: MIXED BERRY CRISP WITH GOAT CHEESE MOUSSE AND MULBERRY AIGRE-DOUX (PAGE 170)

CURRANT MOSTARDA

This preserve, which suspends mustard seeds and onion in a dark ruby-hued jelly, is one of the most visibly striking I make. I use any combination of red, black, or white currants, depending on what's available at the market. The season for fresh currants is fleeting, and they are available only for a few weeks in mid-summer. But winter menus are when the tartness of the berries really shines. A spoonful of the mostarda enlivens rich roasted meats, cured sausages, or nearly any kind of cheese. I also swirl spoonfuls into a reduction sauce, like roasted chicken jus, to brighten it with acidity.

This mostarda gets its body from homemade apple pectin (page 58). Because the pectin also adds sweetness to the preserve, substituting powdered pectin is not recommended.

makes 6 half-pints

INGREDIENT	VOLUME	OUNCES	GRAMS	PERCENT
Red currants, stems removed	about 6 pints	5 pounds	2270 grams	67%
Sugar	2 cups	1 pound	454 grams	13.4%
Sweet onion such as candy or Vidalia, diced	1	8 ounces	227 grams	6.8%
Pectin (page 58)	1 cup	8 ounces	227 grams	6.8%
Black mustard seeds	1/2 cup	2 3/4 ounces	75 grams	2.25%
Yellow mustard seeds	1/2 cup	2 3/4 ounces	75 grams	2.25%
Whole-grain mustard	1/4 cup	2 ounces	55 grams	1.5%

1. In a large pot over medium-high heat, bring the currants and sugar to a boil. Place a fine-mesh strainer over a pot. Pour the currants into the strainer and allow the fruit to drain overnight in the refrigerator, pushing gently on the solids occasionally to extract the currant juice.

2. Discard the currants. Mix the onions, pectin, mustard seeds, and mustard into the currant juice and cook over medium-high heat until the mostarda reaches about 210°F and has thickened, about 15 minutes.

3. Scald 6 half-pint jars in a large pot of simmering water fitted with a rack—you will use this pot to process the jars. Right before filling, put the jars on the counter. Meanwhile, soak the lids in a pan of hot water to soften the rubber seal.

4. Ladle the mostarda into the jars, leaving a 1/2-inch space from the rim of the jar. Wipe the rims with a clean towel, seal with the lids, then screw on the bands until snug but not tight.

5. Place the jars in the pot with the rack and add enough water to cover the jars by about 1 inch. Bring the water to a boil and process the jars for 10 minutes (start the timer when the water reaches a boil). Turn off the heat and leave the jars in the water for a few minutes. Remove the jars from the water and let cool completely.

At the Table: CHICKEN LIVER MOUSSE WITH ARUGULA, CURRANT MOSTARDA, AND GRILLED BREAD (PAGE 193)

BUTTERNUT SQUASH AIGRE-DOUX

Winter squash recipes are often for sweet dishes, like creamy soups and ravioli in brown butter sauce. If left unchecked, the sweetness can become cloying. This aigre-doux hits a balance between sweet and savory, with just enough maple syrup to curb the sharpness of the sherry and vinegar. For a simple side dish for Thanksgiving—or any winter feast—just pop off the lid and simmer the contents of the jar with a knob of butter.

makes 4 pints

INGREDIENT	VOLUME	OUNCES	GRAMS	PERCENT
Butternut squash, peeled, quartered lengthwise, seeded, and sliced $1/4$-inch thick	1 to $1^1/2$ squash	2 pounds, 4 ounces	1020 grams	46%
Sweet onion, such as candy or Vidalia	$1/2$ to 1 onion	4 ounces	115 grams	5%
Lustau East India Solera sherry	$2^1/2$ cups	1 pound, $1^3/4$ ounces	500 grams	22.5%
Maple syrup	$1^3/4$ cups	$14^3/4$ ounces	420 grams	19%
Kosher salt	$1/2$ teaspoon	less than $1/8$ ounce	2 grams	—
Freshly ground black pepper	$1/2$ teaspoon	less than $1/8$ ounce	1 gram	—
Sherry vinegar	$3/4$ cup	6 ounces	170 grams	7.5%

1. In a large pot over medium-high heat, mix together the squash, onion, sherry, maple syrup, salt, and pepper. Cover the pot and bring to a boil. Decrease to a simmer and cook until tender when pierced with a fork for 15 minutes. Season with additional salt and pepper to taste if needed.

2. Scald 4 pint jars in a large pot of simmering water fitted with a rack—you will use this pot to process the jars. Right before filling, put the jars on the counter. Meanwhile, soak the lids in a pan of hot water to soften the rubber seal.

3. Drain the squash, reserving the brine and pack the squash in the jars, using about $1^1/2$ cups per jar. In a pot, add the vinegar to the sherry-maple brine and bring to a simmer. Transfer to a heat-proof pitcher and pour the brine over the squash, leaving a $1/2$-inch space from the rim of the jar. Check the jars for air pockets, adding more liquid if necessary to fill in gaps. Wipe the rims with a clean towel, seal with the lids, then screw on the bands until snug but not tight.

4. Place the jars in the pot with the rack and add enough water to cover the jars by about 1 inch. Bring the water to a boil and process the jars for 10 minutes (start the timer when the water reaches a boil). Turn off the heat and leave the jars in the water for a few minutes. Remove the jars from the water and let cool completely.

At the Table: GLAZED BUTTERNUT SQUASH AIGRE-DOUX (PAGE 252)

CRANBERRY AIGRE-DOUX

Cranberry relishes vary widely, from straight from the can to overwrought creations that require at least twenty ingredients. This aigre-doux offers cranberry a middle ground, but because it spends time in the jar absorbing notes of star anise and vanilla bean, the cranberries taste nuanced and complicated, giving those other relish recipes a run for their money. It doesn't hurt that the aigre-doux also looks spectacular—deep red and glossy— at the table.

makes 4 pints

INGREDIENT	VOLUME	OUNCES	GRAMS	PERCENT
Red table wine	2 cups plus 3 tablespoons	17¹/₂ ounces	496 grams	29.6%
Honey	³/₄ cup plus 2 tablespoons	10¹/₂ ounces	297 grams	17.7%
Red wine vinegar	³/₄ cup plus 2 tablespoons	7 ounces	198 grams	11.8%
Kosher salt	2 teaspoons	¹/₄ ounce	7 grams	.4%
Vanilla beans, split in half with seeds scraped out with the tip of a spoon	2	—	—	—
Black peppercorns	2 teaspoons	—	—	—
Star anise	4	—	—	—
Fresh cranberries	6 to 7 cups	1¹/₂ pounds	680 grams	40.5%

1. In a large pot over medium-high heat, bring the wine, honey, vinegar, salt, and vanilla bean pod and seeds to a boil.

2. Scald 4 pint jars in a large pot of simmering water fitted with a rack—you will use this pot to process the jars. Right before filling, put the jars on the counter. Add ¹/₂ teaspoon peppercorns and 1 star anise to each jar. Extract the vanilla bean halves from the wine-honey liquid and place one in each jar. Pack in the cranberries, using about 6 ounces per jar. Meanwhile, soak the lids in a pan of hot water to soften the rubber seal.

3. Transfer the wine-honey liquid to a heat-proof pitcher and pour over the cranberries, leaving a ¹/₂-inch space from the rim of the jar. Check the jars for air pockets, adding more liquid if necessary to fill in gaps. Wipe the rims with a clean towel, seal with the lids, then screw on the bands until snug but not tight.

4. Place the jars in the pot with the rack and add enough water to cover by about 1 inch. Bring the water to a boil and process the jars for 15 minutes (start the timer when the water reaches a boil). Turn off the heat and leave the jars in the water for a few minutes. Remove the jars from the water and let cool completely.

At the Table: CRANBERRY AIGRE-DOUX RELISH (PAGE 252)

PEAR AND VANILLA AIGRE-DOUX

This was the first aigre-doux we made at Vie, and it remains a favorite: an amalgamation of sharp offset by honey, pears, and off-dry wine, its sweet-sour tang is perfect with rich blue cheeses. To turn a jar of this aigre-doux into the ultimate cheese condiment, strain its liquid into a small pot, reduce it down to a syrup, and then stir back in the pears.

makes 4 pints

INGREDIENT	VOLUME	OUNCES	GRAMS	PERCENT
White wine, preferably off-dry, like Gewürztraminer	1³/₄ cups	14 ounces	397 grams	18.25%
Champagne vinegar	1³/₄ cups	14 ounces	397 grams	18.25%
Honey	³/₄ cup plus 1 tablespoon	9¹/₂ ounces	272 grams	12.5%
Sugar	1 cup	7 ounces	200 grams	9.2%
Kosher salt	1 teaspoon	¹/₈ ounce	4 grams	.1%
Vanilla beans, split in half with seeds scraped out with the tip of a spoon	2	—	—	—
Black peppercorns	2 teaspoons	—	—	—
Bosc pears, peeled, cored, and quartered lengthwise	5 to 7 pears	2 pounds	907 grams	41.7%

1. In a large pot over medium-high heat, bring the wine, vinegar, honey, sugar, salt, and vanilla bean pod and seeds to a boil. Keep hot.

2. Scald 4 pint jars in a large pot of simmering water fitted with a rack—you will use this pot to process the jars. Right before filling, put the jars on the counter. Add ¹/₂ teaspoon peppercorns to each jar, then pack in the pears, using about 7 pieces per jar. Meanwhile, soak the lids in a pan of hot water to soften the rubber seal.

3. Transfer the liquid to a heat-proof pitcher. Remove the vanilla bean halves and divide among the jars. Pour the wine-honey liquid over the pears, leaving a ¹/₂-inch space from the rim of the jar. Check the jars for air pockets, adding more liquid if necessary to fill in gaps. Wipe the rims with a clean towel, seal with the lids, then screw on the bands until snug but not tight.

4. Place the jars in the pot with the rack and add enough water to cover by about 1 inch. Bring the water to a boil and process the jars for 15 minutes (start the timer when the water reaches a boil). Turn off the heat and leave the jars in the water for a few minutes. Remove the jars from the water and let cool completely.

At the Table: BLUE CHEESE WITH PEAR AND VANILLA AIGRE-DOUX AND ROASTED HICKORY NUTS (PAGE 238)

MANDARIN AIGRE-DOUX

I've always thought of red wine and orange as complementary. I most often use these flavors together as an accent sauce, folding puréed segments into reduced wine to finish a creamy parsnip soup (page 149), or a roasted duck breast. It is a beautiful sauce with rich seafood as well: just simmer the puréed segments and aigre-doux liquid, whisk in a knob of butter and spoon it over lobster or scallops. Using white wine instead of red makes an incredible sauce for lighter seafood.

makes 5 pints

INGREDIENT	VOLUME	OUNCES	GRAMS	PERCENT
Black peppercorns	5 teaspoons	—	—	—
Peeled mandarin segments	9 cups	3 pounds	1362 grams	55%
Red table wine	1 (750-ml) bottle	25 ounces	737 grams	30%
Red wine vinegar	³/₄ cup	6 ounces	170 grams	6.9%
Sugar	1 cup	7 ounces	200 grams	8%
Kosher salt	1 teaspoon	¹/₈ ounce	4 grams	.1%

1. Scald 5 pint jars in a large pot of simmering water fitted with a rack—you will use this pot to process the jars. Into each jar add 1 teaspoon peppercorns. Pack the mandarins into the jars, using 9 to 10 ounces per jar. Meanwhile, soak the lids in a pan of hot water to soften the rubber seal.

2. In a pot over medium-high heat, bring the wine, vinegar, sugar, and salt to a boil. Transfer to a heat-proof pitcher and pour over the mandarins, leaving a ¹/₂-inch space from the rim of the jar. Check the jars for air pockets, adding more liquid if necessary to fill in gaps. Wipe the rims with a clean towel, seal with the lids, then screw on the bands until snug but not tight.

3. Place the jars in the pot with the rack and add enough water to cover by about 1 inch. Bring the water to a boil and process the jars for 15 minutes (start the timer when the water reaches a boil). Turn off the heat and leave the jars in the water for a few minutes. Remove the jars from the water and let cool completely.

At the Table: SPRING-DUG PARSNIP SOUP WITH MANDARIN AIGRE-DOUX (PAGE 149)

MEYER LEMON AIGRE-DOUX

Fragrant and nearly sweet enough to eat raw, California's Meyer lemons are a treat in winter months. Marie Campagna, who grows Meyer lemons along with several other varieties of citrus at her family orchard outside San Diego, picks the fruit from December through March. When she has more than she needs (which is usually the case) she boxes the lemons up and mails them to us. You can tell a lemon is ready to be picked, she says, by how the stem bends. When it starts to droop, the lemon is ready.

Meyer lemon aigre-doux is extremely versatile. In the spring I make an emulsified vinaigrette to dress grilled asparagus or delicate butter lettuce leaves. Just pick out any visible seeds, blend the wedges and aigre-doux liquid until smooth, then drizzle in olive oil. The result has a texture as creamy as mayonnaise. In the summer I'll make a citrus relish to pair with fresh summer green and wax beans by dicing the wedges crosswise and mixing them with celery root slices, chives, and olive oil. Just like with Mandarin Aigre-Doux (page 101), you can be flexible with the wine. An aromatic Alsatian wine pairs well with the naturally floral fragrance of the lemons, but for more heft, make it with a medium-bodied red wine like Merlot.

makes 6 pints

INGREDIENT	VOLUME	OUNCES	GRAMS	PERCENT
White wine	2³/₄ cups	1 pound, 6 ounces	624 grams	23.7%
Champagne vinegar	1¹/₄ cup plus 1 tablespoon	11 ounces	312 grams	11.9%
Honey	1 cup	11¹/₂ ounces	330 grams	12.5%
Kosher salt	1 teaspoon	¹/₈ ounce	3 grams	.1%
Meyer lemons, each cut into about 6 wedges	11 to 12 cups	3 pounds	1362 grams	51.8%
Bay leaves	6	—	—	—
Thyme sprigs	6	—	—	—

1. In a pot over medium-high heat, bring the wine, vinegar, honey, and salt to a boil. Keep hot.

2. Scald 6 pint jars in a large pot of simmering water fitted with a rack—you will use this pot to process the jars. Right before filling, put the jars on the counter. Into each jar add 1 bay leaf and 1 thyme sprig. Pack the lemon wedges into the jars, using about 12 wedges per jar. Meanwhile, soak the lids in a pan of hot water to soften the rubber seal.

3. Transfer the brine to a heat-proof pitcher and pour over the lemons, leaving a ¹/₂-inch space from the rim of the jar. Check the jars for air pockets, adding more liquid if necessary to fill in gaps. Wipe the rims with a clean towel, seal with the lids, then screw on the bands until snug but not tight.

4. Place the jars in the pot with the rack and add enough water to cover by about 1 inch. Bring the water to a boil and process the jars for 15 minutes (start the timer when the water reaches a boil). Turn off the heat and leave the jars in the water for a few minutes. Remove the jars from the water and let cool completely.

At the Table: SPRING-DUG PARSNIP SOUP WITH MANDARIN AIGRE-DOUX (PAGE 149)

FERMENTING AND CURING: SAUERKRAUT, SALTED PRODUCE, AND CURED MEAT

If aigre-doux and mostarda are the wine and cheese snobs of the preserving world, then this chapter is the home-brewing mad scientist, the unpredictable genius in the corner of the room. Curing and fermenting is like that: even when you've done it several times, there's always that one batch that catches you by surprise. There can be failures, but the successes have the capacity to soar far beyond expectations.

I've been making sauerkraut with cabbage for ages, but it wasn't until six years ago that I started expanding into other kinds of sauerkraut, from batches made with savory Brussels sprouts to leafy, pungent ramps. Curing vegetables in salt isn't so far from curing meat. With the help of my chef de cuisine, Nathan Sears, we've developed a robust charcuterie program at Vie.

Fortunately, Nathan's cured meats pair seamlessly with most of our mostarda, aigre-doux, and pickles. Down the road, I'd like to expand into fermented fruit jams. For these jams, you mix fruit with salt, let it ferment, and then cook it into a jam with sugar. Yet we're still in the early days of those experiments.

What sugar is to fruit preserves, salt is to sauerkraut, cured meats, and preserved citrus rind. In fruit preserves, sugar attracts water molecules, dehydrating microorganisms. In curing, a similar effect takes place. Salt draws out moisture, making produce or meat inhospitable to spoilers. But it works slowly. While not hard to make, the preserves in this chapter require time—in some cases, a lot of it.

Fermentation is the other side of the story. While pickles need vinegar to stave off microbial activity, sauerkraut forms its own acidity. The trick hinges on the concentration of salt. You need enough to dehydrate and prevent the growth of undesirable bacteria, but not so much that you discourage the formation of *leuconostoc mesenteroides*, the bacteria that promotes the production of lactic acid. Generally, this amounts to a brine with a salinity level of 3 percent.

Making sauerkraut is straightforward. Mix shredded cabbage with salt and let it release water. Eventually, the cabbage starts to ferment, throwing off beneficial lactic acid. This not only gives sauerkraut its characteristic tang, but it also lowers the pH of the mixture. This is why a vat of sauerkraut will keep in the refrigerator for months without going rancid despite its funky smell. It is also why jars of sauerkraut can be processed in a water bath. Cabbage, a low-acid food on its own, becomes acidified through fermentation.

I've moved beyond cabbage to process a handful of other vegetables. When fermenting produce beyond cabbage, though, I have needed to make modifications. Ramps, for instance, never leach out enough water to form an adequate amount of brine on their own, so I mix water with salt to pour over the ramps. Even so, the vegetable sauerkrauts are similar enough, more variations on the classic than completely new recipes. Once you've mastered one, you can do them all.

With the exception of the pressed eggplant, the recipes in this chapter don't require specialized equipment. For sauerkraut, find a large container, preferably one that is taller than it is wide. It can be ceramic, enamel, or food-grade plastic. Once you have selected a container, rig a weight to fit inside the top. A weight will keep the produce—whether it's shredded cabbage, grated rutabagas, or lemon wedges—submerged in the brine. This is essential not only for successful fermentation but also to ensure the food stays free of contaminants.

To make a weight, I place a plate or a lid that covers most of the surface area on top of the salted or brined produce. I pour extra brine into a sealable plastic storage bag. (Using brine in the bag instead of plain water is a precaution against a leaky bag. If the bag of water seeped into the batch, the lower saline level could throw off the fermentation, opening the door to contaminants.) When placed on top, the bag effectively weighs down the plate or lid, keeping the vegetables submerged. Instead of plastic bags, Tony Porreca, our recipe tester, fills a half-gallon plastic tub with brine and covers it with a lid. If his sauerkraut dries out for any reason, he pours in some of the brine straight from the container. Once the weight is in place, take a look at how much of the top is exposed to air. If a lot of brine is exposed to the air, remove the weight, press a piece of plastic wrap on top of the surface, and put the weight back on. This will protect the brine from undesirable mold growth.

CERAMIC CROCKS

If you make sauerkraut at home often, consider investing in a German ceramic crock designed for making sauerkraut. These crocks come with a weight that fits snugly inside the container, providing consistent pressure to keep the vegetables submerged in brine as they ferment. Because we make much larger batches at the restaurant than most crocks can contain, I don't use one.

They can also be quite expensive. But a good one can give you more consistency at home—unless the pets take a liking to it: Some ceramic crocks require you to pour water between the weight and the lip of the container to seal it. One day Kate's friend found his cat sipping the brine from the crock lid. He now covers it with netting when he has a batch of sauerkraut in the works.

When you have a batch of sauerkraut fermenting, monitor changes in room temperature and watch the vegetables as they ferment. Periodically skim off bubbles and scum from the surface. During fermentation, you're likely to encounter funky smells, but those pungent aromas often overshadow more delicate, nuanced flavors. The brine might become cloudy, which is normal. If white mold appears around the edges, scrape it away and let the sauerkraut continue to ferment. If the brine becomes overtaken by mold, however, it is time to start over.

Before using sauerkraut or cured citrus rinds, you'll need to remove some of the salt by rinsing well under cool running water.

PICKLING SPICE MIX

It is handy to have a basic, all-purpose spice mix on hand when making a lot of pickles or sauerkraut. I occasionally use this mix with sauerkraut and use it with some—but not all—pickles. (If you use the same spices for all of your pickles, they start to taste the same.) While sauerkraut doesn't need spices, adding them can be a nice way to change up the flavor now and again. I like caraway seeds—especially in sauerkraut. If you are not a fan, leave them out.

makes about ¹/₂ cup

2 tablespoons coriander seeds
2 tablespoons mustard seeds

2 tablespoons caraway seeds
1 tablespoon fennel seeds

1 tablespoon black peppercorns
1 teaspoon dried red pepper flakes

Mix all the ingredients together and store in a cool, dry area. Before using, toast the spices in a dry sauté pan until aromatic. When using the spice mix in sauerkraut, add them when you add the salt.

CLASSIC SAUERKRAUT

The recipes that follow in this chapter offer ample evidence that plain old cabbage 'kraut isn't the only game in town. But it remains a classic for a reason. It's delicious, versatile, and easy to make. Not only is it good with a grilled bratwurst, it's also delicious braised in meat broth and served with sausages and potatoes for choucroute garnie, a classic Alsatian meal. I've even had luck frying sauerkraut into a crispy garnish—I just dust it in rice flour before plunging it into the deep fryer.

If making sauerkraut is new for you, this is a good place to start. Green cabbage is cheap and readily available; so is salt. I keep the seasonings neutral, but you could certainly add a tablespoon of Pickling Spice Mix (see above) for a mildly spiced version. If the cabbage doesn't release enough water to submerge it completely, you will need to add brine. You may also need extra brine if you plan on processing the sauerkraut in jars.

makes 6 pints

INGREDIENT	VOLUME	OUNCES	GRAMS	PERCENT
Green cabbage, sliced finely or shredded	24 cups	3 pounds, 12 ounces	1700 grams	97%
Kosher salt	¹/₄ cup plus 1 tablespoon, plus 3 tablespoons for making the weight	2 ounces, plus 1 ounce for making the weight	57 grams, plus 28 grams for making the weight	3% (not including the salt in the weight)

1. In a tall, large ceramic crock or food-grade plastic container, mix the cabbage with $^1/_4$ cup plus 1 tablespoon of the salt. Using a mallet, pound the cabbage to encourage it to release water. Or simply crush the salt into the cabbage with clean hands. (It may be easier to do this in a large, wide bowl.) Cover and set aside. It will take about 12 hours for the cabbage to release enough water to form a brine.

2. Once the brine forms, keep the cabbage submerged by making a weight. In a pot, simmer together $4^1/_2$ cups water with the remaining 3 tablespoons of salt. Cool to room temperature, then pour the brine into 1 or 2 heavy-duty resealable plastic storage bags. Place a plate or plastic lid on top of the cabbage and put the bag(s) on top. If you are using a ceramic crock for sauerkraut, it may come with a weight designed to fit inside the crock to weigh down the vegetables, eliminating the need for a makeshift weight. If this is the case, keep the extra brine in the refrigerator in case the sauerkraut looks dry or you need it for processing the jars.

3. Store the sauerkraut at a cool room temperature (60°F to 65°F) for 2 to 3 weeks, or until the fermentation stops. Bubbles on the surface will indicate that the fermentation is going strong. Periodically skim off foam with a ladle and scrape away any mold that may adhere to the sides of the container or surface of the brine. When bubbles no longer appear on the surface and the cabbage has a pleasant, tangy flavor, the fermentation is done. You will have about 12 cups of sauerkraut. At this point, the sauerkraut is ready to process. Alternatively, you can transfer the sauerkraut into a clean container and refrigerate it. If the cabbage stays submerged in the brine, the sauerkraut will keep for a few months in the refrigerator.

4. Scald 6 pint jars in a large pot of simmering water fitted with a rack—you will use this pot to process the jars. Right before filling, put the jars on the counter. Meanwhile, soak the lids in a pan of hot water to soften the rubber seal.

5. Strain the brine. Divide the sauerkraut among the jars, then ladle the brine over the top, leaving a $^1/_2$-inch space from the rim of the jar. Check for air pockets, adding more brine if necessary to fill in gaps. Wipe the rims with a clean towel, seal with the lids, then screw on the bands until snug but not tight.

6. Place the jars in the pot with the rack and add enough water to cover the jars by about 1 inch. Bring the water to a boil and process the jars for 15 minutes (start the timer when the water reaches a boil). Turn off the heat and leave the jars in the water for a few minutes. Remove the jars from the water and let cool completely.

VARIATION: You can use the same quantities of vegetables and salt to make a rutabaga sauerkraut. When rutabagas ferment, they become rich and subtly sweet. I use them as the foundation for improbably delicious latkes (page 271). To make rutabaga sauerkraut, grate the rutabagas with a box grater and follow the instructions for cabbage sauerkraut.

At the Table: DUCK FAT–POACHED WHITEFISH WITH DILL PICKLE VINAIGRETTE AND BRAISED SAUERKRAUT (PAGE 284); SMOKED STURGEON WITH RUTABAGA SAUERKRAUT LATKES AND CRÈME FRAÎCHE (271)

RAMP SAUERKRAUT

One of the best alternative sauerkrauts I've made is this one with slender, leafy ramps. Every spring I make gallons of this assertive, pungent variation. Some batches find a place on spring menus, while others are shelved for the fall to serve with dishes such as butter-roasted boudin blanc. If you've been fortunate enough to stumble upon an untapped forest of ramps in early spring, pounce on them, then come home and make this.

Unlike cabbage, which often releases enough water on its own after being salted to form a brine, ramps require a significant amount of water to adequately ferment. While all sauerkraut gives off a funky aroma while fermenting, the ramp sauerkraut smells especially strong. You may want to move it to the garage while it ferments, which takes about two weeks. The weight of the ramps in this recipe is based on trimmed ramps. To ensure you have enough for the recipe, start with 7 pounds before trimming.

makes 9 pints

INGREDIENT	VOLUME	OUNCES	GRAMS	PERCENT
Water	20 cups	160 ounces	4536 grams	65.5%
Kosher salt	scant 3/4 cup	4 ounces	113 grams	1.5%
Ramps, roots removed, washed well	—	5 pounds, 4 ounces	2380 grams	34%

1. In a large pot, bring the water and salt to a boil. Cool to room temperature.

2. Arrange the ramps in a tall, large ceramic crock or food-grade plastic container. Pour the brine over the top, completely submerging all of the ramps. (You should have some brine left over.)

3. The ramps will float unless weighted down. To ensure they stay submerged while they ferment, make a weight: Place a plate or plastic lid directly on top of the ramps. Pour the leftover brine into a resealable plastic storage bag and place it on top.

4. Ferment the sauerkraut according to the instructions for making Classic Sauerkraut (page 108).

BRUSSELS SPROUTS SAUERKRAUT

I'm surprised that sauerkraut made with Brussels sprouts isn't more common. After all, the sprouts themselves look like mini cabbages. I braise fermented Brussels sprouts in chicken stock to bring out their subtle sweetness—they are surprisingly mild prepared this way, but rich enough to stand up to roasted venison. For Thanksgiving, I also add chestnuts and bacon (page 248) to the braise, which round out the tang with sweetness, starch, and salt.

makes 10 pints

INGREDIENT	VOLUME	OUNCES	GRAMS	PERCENT
Water	16 cups	128 ounces	3630 grams	55.5%
Champagne vinegar	2 cups	16 ounces	454 grams	7%
Kosher salt	1 cup	5 ounces	142 grams	2%
Brussels sprouts, quartered	24 cups	5 pounds	2270 grams	35%
10 cloves garlic	¼ cup	1¼ ounces	35 grams	.5%
Bay leaves	5	—	—	—
Dried hot chile	1	—	—	—
Black peppercorns, cracked	1 teaspoon	—	—	—

1. In a large pot, bring the water, vinegar, and salt to a boil. Cool to room temperature.

2. In a tall, large ceramic crock or food-grade plastic container, mix the Brussels sprouts with the garlic, bay leaves, chile, and peppercorns. Pour the brine over the top, completely submerging all of the Brussels sprouts. (You should have some brine left over.)

3. The sprouts have a tendency to float. To ensure they stay submerged while they ferment, make a weight: Place a plate or plastic lid directly on top of the Brussels sprouts. Pour the leftover brine into a resealable plastic storage bag and place it on top.

4. Ferment according to the instructions for making Classic Sauerkraut (page 108).

At the Table: BRAISED FERMENTED BRUSSELS SPROUTS WITH CHESTNUTS (PAGE 248)

TURNIP SAUERKRAUT

Call me old-school, but I count The Lutèce Cookbook among the top tomes in my cookbook collection. Not only is it filled with the classic French dishes that earned the restaurant its decades-long reputation for being one of the best in the country, but it also documents legendary chef André Soltner's more personal food memories. It turns out that the guy had a passion for turnip sauerkraut.

In early fall, when the large white and purple-topped turnips started turning up at the market, Soltner made turnip sauerkraut for himself and good friends who appreciated the vegetable. I decided to try my hand at making turnip sauerkraut—and found it to be a delicious alternative to cabbage sauerkraut. It can be used interchangeably with other sauerkrauts, but I particularly like to braise it in chicken stock and finish it with cream.

Like rutabagas and cabbage, turnips release an adequate amount of water as they ferment, which means all you have to do is add salt. Yet the texture of a turnip is more fragile than that of a rutabaga. Instead of grating the vegetable, I slice it thinly so that the pieces don't fall completely apart as they ferment.

makes 5 pints

INGREDIENT	VOLUME	OUNCES	GRAMS	PERCENT
Turnips	about 20 cups (sliced)	3 pounds, 12 ounces	1700 grams	97%
Kosher salt	¼ cup plus 1 tablespoon, plus 3 tablespoons for making the weight	2 ounces, plus 1 ounce for making the weight	57 grams, plus 28 grams for making the weight	3% (not including the salt in the weight)

1. Halve the turnips and cut into ¼-inch slices. In a tall, large ceramic crock or food-grade plastic container, layer the turnip slices with 2 ounces of salt. Using a mallet, pound the turnips to encourage them to release water. It may take a few hours for the turnips to release enough water to form a brine.

2. Once the brine forms, keep the turnips submerged by making a weight: In a pot, simmer together 4½ cups water with the remaining 1 ounce salt. Cool to room temperature, then pour the brine into 1 or 2 resealable plastic storage bags. Place a plate or plastic lid on top of the turnips and put the bag(s) on top.

3. Ferment according to the instructions for making Classic Sauerkraut (page 108).

PRESSED EGGPLANT

We were well into developing recipes for this book when Tony Porreca, our tester, pulled out an experimental jar of salted, paper-thin slices of eggplant packed in olive oil. Undeniably savory with a subtle sour bite, the preserve was instantly addictive. For weeks Tony had been trying to re-create the preserved eggplant he ate while growing up in the Chicago suburbs. Every summer, his extended family came together to preserve the last of summer's eggplant by packing salted slices into large wooden food presses that expelled the water from the vegetable. Remaking the traditional preserve, which had been passed down through word of mouth only, wasn't easy. Tony first tried an iron press, which oxidized the eggplant. He then settled on a fruit press designed for crushing grapes into juice. Kosher salt wasn't salty enough, so he turned to iodized table salt. Since it was still missing the tang he remembered, he reached for a jug of plain white distilled vinegar and poured it over the salted pieces. The process—three days in the press, two days in vinegar, and two weeks smothered in olive oil—rendered the eggplant tender even though it had never been cooked. After several batches, Tony managed to replicate the tangy condiment for Italian cured-meat sandwiches. In doing so, he had preserved a nearly-lost family tradition.

The best time to make this preserve is in the late summer and early fall, when eggplants are cheap and large. Tony prefers mature globe eggplants because their seeds tend to contribute flavor. You will need a wooden fruit press for this recipe (one designed to press soft fruits, like grapes, works well).

Tony's family made a similar preserve with green tomatoes. The process was nearly the same, but the tomatoes didn't need to be pressed. Once salted, they could be seasoned with salt, soaked in vinegar for a few hours, and packed in oil.

makes 3 pints

CURING

INGREDIENT	VOLUME	OUNCES	GRAMS	PERCENT
Globe eggplants	6 medium	5 pounds	2270 grams	68%
Table salt	1/2 cup	5 1/3 ounces	150 grams	4.5%
White distilled vinegar	about 4 cups	about 32 ounces	about 907 grams	27.5%

1. Peel the eggplant and cut crosswise into 1/4-inch slices. Lay the slices out across a couple of baking sheets and season both sides evenly with the salt. Let sit for 30 minutes.

2. Set the press near a sink or area that provides a place for the eggplant liquid to drain. Pack the eggplant into the press in circular, overlapping layers (do not pat dry first). Put the top of the press on top of the eggplant and screw until there is just enough pressure to cause the eggplant to release some of its liquid. For the next 3 days, give the knob a three-quarter turn three times a day. Each time the press is tightened, more liquid will come out of the eggplant. When finished, all of the eggplant slices together will be no higher than a few inches.

{continued}

3. Remove the top of the press and peel apart the eggplant slices. They will be stuck together and will have taken on a slightly brownish color. Transfer them to a nonreactive container and pour in enough vinegar to cover completely, ensuring that both sides of each slice are coated. Let the eggplant soak for 2 days.

MARINATING

INGREDIENT	VOLUME	OUNCES	GRAMS
Extra-virgin olive oil	2 cups	12¹/₂ ounces	360 grams
Garlic cloves, thinly sliced (preferably with a mandoline)	9	³/₄ ounce	22 grams
Dried oregano	¹/₂ teaspoon	—	—
Red pepper flakes	1 teaspoon	—	—

1. In a pot of simmering water, scald 3 pint jars for a minute or two to ensure the jars are sterile (you do not need to process the jars once they are filled). Right before filling, put the jars on the counter.

2. Drain the eggplant slices and discard the vinegar. Stack the slices into piles about as big as a hamburger and lightly squeeze with your hands to remove any excess vinegar. (The slices will have soaked up the vinegar like a sponge.)

3. In a large bowl, mix ¹/₂ cup of the olive oil with the garlic, oregano, and red pepper flakes. Coat the eggplant in the oil and seasonings. Stack the eggplant slices into piles of 4 or 5, then slide them into the jars. Between each addition, drizzle more olive oil on top of the slices. Cover the eggplant with ¹/₂ inch of oil, making sure all the air pockets are removed. Cap the jars and leave at room temperature for 2 to 3 weeks before eating. This condiment will keep on the shelf as long as it remains covered in olive oil. Otherwise, it will last in the refrigerator indefinitely.

At the Table: CHARCUTERIE PLATTER (PAGE 221)

PRESERVED LEMONS

It's easy to understand why chefs across America have lemon rinds curing in their walk-in coolers: salt-cured lemons are not only easy to make, they also lend a lemony perfume to a dish without adding acidity. Morocco gets most of the credit for curing and cooking with citrus rinds, and rightly so. (What would a tagine be without preserved lemon rinds in the broth?) But the practice of curing lemons also has roots in America. In Housekeeping in Old Virginia, a household manual published in 1879, a recipe instructs cooks to coat lemons in "very dry salt," store them near a fire for seven days, and then cover them in boiling vinegar and spices. After a year in vinegar, they were ready to use.

My version of preserved lemons uses two parts salt to one part sugar. I also add a handful of herbes de Provence. *With this ratio, you can scale the recipe to cure more lemons. You also can use Meyer lemons or orange wedges, though I'd advise against grapefruit. Unfortunately, curing the rinds emphasized the grapefruit's bitter floral flavor, which I find more difficult to fold into savory meals than lemon or orange rind. When buying citrus to cure, opt for organic, unwaxed fruit. The wax on conventional store-bought lemons inhibits salt from soaking into the rind.*

To cook with preserved lemons, remove a few rinds and rinse them under cool running water for 15 minutes. Alternatively, soak them in several changes of cool water over the course of a few hours. Next, run a sharp knife between the rind and pith, removing as much pulp and pith as possible. I save the pulp to make compound butters like Preserved Lemon and Thyme Butter (page 246). Once the rind is clean, it is ready to be sliced or minced and added to stews, pan-seared fish, or sautéed vegetables. The lemons can be used after a month of curing, but I prefer to wait four months for the best results. After four months, store the lemons in the refrigerator. They will keep for more than a year.

makes about 2 pints

2 cups kosher salt, plus more if needed

1 cup sugar

¼ cup *herbes de Provence*

8 lemons

1. In a large bowl, mix together the salt, sugar, and *herbes de Provence.*

2. Slice off the ends of the lemons and cut smaller lemons into 4 wedges, larger lemons into 6 wedges. Coat the wedges generously in the cure. Layer some cure at the base of a ceramic or glass storage container (a wine bottle chiller or large Mason jar works well). Layer in the wedges, sprinkling more cure between each layer. Squeeze 1 or 2 of the lemons over the top, then coat the top layer generously with the remaining cure. If the lemons aren't completely covered, sprinkle a layer of salt over the top. Cover the container and set aside for 4 to 5 days.

3. In a few days, lemon juice will leach out of the wedges and mix with the salt, creating a brine. Check to see that the lemons are submerged. You might need to put a plastic lid on top of the lemons and put a weight, such as a ramekin, on the lid to prevent the wedges from bobbing to the surface, which inhibits proper curing. Place

{continued}

in a cool corner (preferably under 65°F), giving the lemons a periodic stir, and cure for at least 1 month but preferably 4 months. Once cured, the lemons will keep for at least a year in the refrigerator as long as they stay submerged in the brine.

At the Table: WARM WHEAT BERRY SALAD WITH PEAS AND PRESERVED LEMON VINAIGRETTE (PAGE 150); SCARLET TURNIPS WITH CRÈME FRAÎCHE AND PRESERVED LEMON (PAGE 249); PRESERVED LEMON AND THYME BUTTER (PAGE 246)

BEEF BACON

Every few weeks, we bring in half a steer from Dietzler Farms in Elkhorn, Wisconsin. My crew tackles the nearly 500 pounds of locally raised beef in a couple of hours. We butcher the beef into the obvious cuts, like strip steaks and fillets, but we also grapple with new ways to use less typical cuts, which is actually most of the animal. Since there is only so much ground beef that our restaurant can use, we find ways to bring out the best qualities in so-called lesser cuts, like the tongue, which we pickle; cheeks, which we braise; and bones, which we render into a rich, full-bodied stock (page 131). Making beef bacon from the belly was just a natural progression.

Although we cure and smoke it the same way that we make pork bacon, beef bacon has a chewier, more savory quality. Many people like maple syrup in their bacon cures. I prefer sorghum, a sweetener used in the Midwest when sugar was scarce. It's similar to molasses, adding hints of caramel that complement the smoke.

Beef belly is contained within the same primal cut—a large section of the animal that is later cut into smaller pieces—of beef that includes the rib eye. Acquiring a piece of it will take some doing, since you won't find this cut at an average butcher shop. I suggest getting familiar with a small butcher or a family like the Dietzlers, who sell their beef at Chicago's Green City Market in Lincoln Park. For me, the Dietzlers are ideal: the family-run operation is small enough that they can supply custom cuts as long as they have enough notice. If an operation can't get it for you, they might be able to suggest butchers in the area that buy whole animals and who can save you a belly.

Like the coppa recipe (page 118), the cure we use here is based upon the weight of the cut. Although we have ingredients measured for half of a belly in this recipe, if you have a whole belly (about 10 pounds), simply calculate the quantity of each ingredient based on the total weight of the beef. For more information on Insta Cure #1, often referred to as pink salt, see "Insta" Curing, page 118.

makes about one 4-pound slab of bacon

INGREDIENT	OUNCES	GRAMS	PERCENT
Beef belly	5 pounds	2270 grams	100%
Kosher salt	3 1/4 ounces	91 grams	4%
Sorghum	1 1/4 ounces	34 grams	1.5%
Freshly ground black pepper	.32 ounces	9 grams	.4%
Insta Cure #1	.2 ounces	6 grams	.25%

1. Halve the belly. Mix together the salt, sorghum, pepper, and Insta Cure #1 and spread the cure on the surface of a baking sheet. Press all sides of the belly pieces into the cure until evenly coated, then transfer to two 1-gallon resealable storage bags. Refrigerate the belly for 7 days. Each day, flip the bags over. (Water will start to leach out of the meat; don't throw it out or you will also be removing part of the cure.) After 7 days, the meat should feel firm, which means it is cured.

2. Prepare a smoker with hardwood charcoal and wood chunks (see The Draw of Smoke, page 197). Remove the belly from the cure and wipe dry with paper towels. Place the belly in the smoker and smoke until the meat reaches an internal temperature of 150°F, about 2 hours.

3. Remove the bacon and cool to room temperature. At this point, you can cut it into smaller slabs, wrap them in plastic wrap, and freeze or refrigerate until needed. The meat will keep for at least 2 weeks refrigerated and at least 6 months in the freezer.

At the Table: WOOD-GRILLED BURGERS WITH BEEF BACON (PAGE 175); BEEF CHILI (PAGE 265)

COPPA

An Italian cured meat, coppa is made from the pig's muscle that extends from the neck into the loin. Found in the shoulder, the coppa muscle is 3 inches wide and similar in shape to a loin but with more marbling. If you know a butcher who is familiar with Italian cured meat, you might get away with asking for fresh coppa (the cut is common in Italy). More realistically, you may have to acquire a whole pork shoulder and remove the coppa muscle yourself.

To find the muscle on the shoulder, locate the shorter, thicker side of the shoulder opposite the side where the ribs would be. Remove the muscle by cutting out a piece of meat that mirrors the shape of a loin. Since shoulder muscle tends to be forgiving, don't worry if the cut doesn't look perfect. The main point is acquiring a longish piece of shoulder meat no thicker than 4 inches.

To determine how much cure you need, weigh the meat. The weight will determine the quantities of the other ingredients, so using a scale is not optional for this recipe. Unlike most of the canning recipes, where the percentages of all the ingredients add up to 100, in this recipe the weight of the coppa is 100 percent. With some basic math, you can calculate the weight for other ingredients: simply multiply the ingredient's percentage by the weight of the coppa. For instance, if the recipe requires 5 percent salt and the meat weighs 5 pounds, you would multiply .05 by 5 pounds 80 ounces. So you'd need 4 ounces of salt.

It may take some experimenting to find the right conditions in your kitchen to cure coppa. Allocate at least six weeks—two for the refrigeration stage and four for the drying stage. It's not a bad idea to jot down the dates that you started the project, coated the coppa with a second coat of cure, and began aging the meat. These notes can be beneficial when you are evaluating results and determining what you would change next time.

"INSTA" CURING

We include Insta Cure #2—sodium nitrate, sodium nitrite, and salt—in the cure for coppa. It's different from Insta Cure #1—sodium nitrite and salt—but both products are often casually called pink salt. This generalization can be confusing, and misleading: while many cooks assume that pink salt is only needed to prevent meat from turning gray, sodium nitrite and nitrate serve a more important purpose. They stave off bacteria, especially botulism, from growing in the meat as it smokes or cures.

But they are designed for different purposes. Sodium nitrite becomes activated as soon as it touches meat. In contrast, sodium nitrate acts slowly, gradually converting itself into sodium nitrite over time. For this reason, Insta Cure #1 is more common with quickly cured meats that will be smoked or cooked, and Insta Cure #2 is used for aged meats that aren't cooked, like coppa. Both products are available from online sources, such as Sausagemaker.com. But if you don't want a heaping bucket of Insta Cure #2 for this recipe, politely ask a butcher who cures sausages if you can buy a cup.

1 (3 pound, 12 ounce) piece of fresh coppa will make about 3 pounds, 9 ounces of cured coppa

INGREDIENT	PERCENT
Coppa muscle	100%
Kosher salt	5%
Sugar	3%
Black pepper	.5%
Insta Cure #2	.25%
Garlic powder	.25%
Juniper berries, crushed with the side of a knife	10

1. Place the muscle in a large storage container. Mix together the salt, sugar, pepper, Insta Cure #2, garlic powder, and juniper berries. Coat the meat with half of the cure, cover, and refrigerate. After a few days, turn the meat over. Water will start to leach out of the meat; don't throw it out or you will also be removing part of the cure. After 1 week, rub the meat with the remaining cure, then cover and refrigerate for an additional week.

2. Remove the meat from the container and pat dry. At this point, you can approach the next step in two ways: hang the meat to dry in a cool room that consistently stays around 50°F to 60°F and 70 percent humidity (a wine cellar works well), or use your refrigerator.

3. If hanging the meat in a cool room, wrap it in a thin layer of cheesecloth, then twist the ends and tie tightly. Hang the coppa for about 4 weeks. When the coppa is ready, it will have lost about a third of its weight and feel firm when squeezed.

4. If you are using your refrigerator, line a rimmed baking sheet that will fit on a shelf in the refrigerator with a rack. Place the meat on top of it and let it age, uncovered, for 4 to 5 weeks (this method takes longer). Occasionally you may need to drain the baking sheet and rotate the meat to ensure even drying. (Never let the coppa sit in its juices.) When the coppa is ready, it will have lost about a third of its weight and feel firm when squeezed. If the coppa is still soft in the center after 4 to 4 1/2 weeks but its surface area is dry, wrap it tightly in plastic wrap and refrigerate it for another week. This will redistribute the moisture inside the meat, softening the exterior and drying out the middle.

5. Watch for mold as the meat ages. If you see white mold form, that's okay. It is a beneficial mold that will inhibit more deviant molds from growing. Any other mold will need to be removed. (Dry rot, which forms on meat when it cures in a cool room with low humidity, causes a hard shell to form on the outside, which creates a barrier that prevents moisture from evaporating in the center of the meat. The outside becomes rock-hard and the inside stays raw and mushy.) To remove unwanted mold, take a couple of cups of tepid water and mix as much salt into the water as it will hold. Using a clean cloth, wipe the surface of the coppa with the salt solution.

At the Table: CHARCUTERIE PLATTER (PAGE 221)

PRESSURE-CANNED PRESERVES

I don't pressure can often. When I do, it is for special occasions that warrant the effort, like a windfall of porcini mushrooms from the Pacific Northwest. Or for milk jam, which sweetens iced coffee superbly. Hard-neck garlic harvested in the summer also gets the pressure-canning treatment, its sweet pungency the ideal complement to pork belly (page 287). So this chapter may be short, but each recipe is worth the real estate.

First, some background. Low-acid foods for canning, such as unpickled vegetables, need to be processed at higher temperatures than acidic foods because they lack the acidity that inhibits the growth of botulism spores. While water boils at 212°F at sea level, it boils at much higher temperatures when under pressure. The steamy, high-pressure environment within a pressure canner drives the internal temperature of jar contents up to 248°F, which renders botulism spores inactive. In addition to higher temperatures, pressure canning also requires longer processing times.

To make the recipes in this chapter, you will need a pressure canner (not the same as a pressure cooker). More expensive than a regular canning pot, it has more bells and whistles. The lid clamps or twists on to secure to the pot, and a safety gauge controls the amount of pressure. Brands of pressure canners differ slightly, so read the manufacturer's instructions before trying these recipes.

The most important bobble on the canner is the gauge, which indicates the pressure within the canner. I use an easy-to-read dial gauge, but it can be thrown off from taking one too many knocks in the kitchen. If you're worried that your gauge is not accurate, have it tested at a county extension office. Your canner should also come with instructions on how to tell if it is effective. Some canners use a weighted gauge. It's not my preference, but it has advantages. A weighted gauge doesn't have the same calibration issues that a dial gauge does.

Unlike canning in a water bath, pressure canners need only a couple of inches of water at the bottom (the heat comes from steam, not water). The manufacturer's instructions will tell you the exact amount of water to add for your model, but I've provided general instructions. Like water-bath canning, you will also need a rack at the bottom to cushion the jars.

Before filling jars, you still need to scald jars in simmering water and soak the lids in a pan of hot water. (This step tempers the glass and softens the rubber seal in the lid; you do not need to sterilize the jars or lids.) But you won't fill the jars as high as you would if using a boiling water bath because pressure causes the contents of the jar to expand more. For a pint jar, leave 1 inch of space between the contents and the top of the jar.

Before securing the lid of the pressure canner, rub its underside with a light coat of vegetable oil. This prevents the lid from becoming stuck post-processing. Turn the heat to high and wait for a steady stream of steam to emerge from the open vent. Wait for seven to ten minutes for the canner to expel air and fill with steam, then put the weight or pressure gauge over the steam vent. Once the dial gauge reads the pressure level indicated in the recipe (for higher altitudes check with your university extension office), set the timer and process for the indicated amount of time.

When the processing has finished, let the pressure return to zero before you move the canner. There's a whole lot of pressure contained in that pot, and moving it around isn't very safe. It can result in broken jars.

If you don't have a pressure canner, you also could make these preserves and keep them in the refrigerator. Each recipe has suggestions on how to skirt the canning step, though the end result will be different.

GARLIC CONSERVA

Garlic cloves slowly cooked in olive oil are a classic Mediterranean condiment. The best time to make this conserva is in the summer, when heads of the hard-neck variety arrive at the market. These heads have fewer cloves, but the cloves themselves are large—up to three times as big as an average clove—which is a great thing when peeling a lot of them to make conserve. Summer cloves are also superior—nearly juicy compared with garlic I buy year-round. If you don't want to use a pressure canner, store the conserve under a layer of olive oil for up to a month in the refrigerator.

makes 4 half-pints

INGREDIENT	VOLUME	OUNCES	GRAMS	PERCENT
Extra-virgin olive oil	¹/₄ cup	2 ounces	55 grams	4.8%
Peeled garlic cloves	about 4 cups	1 pound, 14 ounces	800 grams	74.4%
Kosher salt	1 tablespoon	¹/₃ ounce	9 grams	.8%
Sugar	³/₄ cup	5 ounces	143 grams	12.5%
Champagne vinegar	¹/₃ cup plus 1 tablespoon	3 ounces	86 grams	7.5%

1. In a large, wide pot over medium-high heat, warm the olive oil. Stir in the garlic and salt, decrease the heat to medium, and cook until the garlic begins to turn golden brown 8 to 10 minutes. Stir in the sugar and cook another 2 minutes until the garlic and sugar begin to caramelize. Deglaze the pan with the vinegar and continue to cook until the garlic is completely tender, about 2 minutes. (You may need to add some water to the pan to keep the garlic from scorching.)

2. Scald 4 half-pint jars (you will not be using this pot to process the jars). Right before filling, put the jars on the counter. Pack the conserve into the jars, leaving a 1-inch space from the rim of the jar. Wipe the rims with a clean towel, seal with the lids, then screw on the bands until snug but not tight.

3. Place a rack in the bottom of the pressure canner and rub the bottom of the lid with vegetable oil to prevent the lid from becoming stuck after processing. Add about 2 inches of warm water and put the jars in the canner. Follow the instructions on the pressure canner for securing the lid. Remove the pressure gauge from the steam vent and place the canner over high heat. Allow the steam to vent for 7 minutes for a small pressure canner, 10 minutes for a large pressure canner. Once vented, put the pressure gauge over the steam vent and wait for the gauge to read 10 psi (pounds per square inch). Once it reaches 10 psi, adjust the heat to ensure that the canner maintains the same pressure. Process for 10 minutes, starting the timer once the gauge reaches 10 psi.

4. Turn off the heat and let the pressure return to zero. Carefully take off the lid. Remove the jars and let cool.

At the Table: SLOW-ROASTED PORK BELLY WITH GARLIC CONSERVA AND GLAZED PICKLED SUMMER BEANS (PAGE 287)

MILK JAM

Gooey, with a mild caramel flavor, milk jam is, essentially, homemade condensed milk. The jam's lengthy cooking time on the stove draws out some sweetness from the milk solids, but the real magic happens in the pressure canner, where the jam turns from off-white to light caramel. Out of the jar, it can be stirred into iced coffee or spooned over desserts, such as clafoutis (page 189). Or cook the jam down further into an amber dulce de leche. Both goat's milk and cow's milk can be used in this recipe. If you notice the liquid has separated from the solids after the jars have been processed, the jam is still fine; just give it a good stir before using.

makes 4 pints

INGREDIENT	VOLUME	OUNCES	GRAMS	PERCENT
Whole milk	1 gallon	136 ounces	3780 grams	78%
Heavy cream	2 cups	19 ounces	460 grams	10%
Granulated sugar	3 cups	1 pound, 4 ounces	567 grams	12%
Baking soda	1/2 teaspoon	—	—	—

1. In a heavy-bottomed pot over medium-high heat, bring the milk, cream, sugar, and baking soda to a gentle simmer. Cook, stirring frequently, until the jam reaches 215°F, about 2 hours.

2. Scald 4 pint jars (you will not be using this pot to process the jars). Right before filling, put the jars on the counter. Meanwhile, soak the lids in a pan of hot water to soften the rubber seal.

3. Transfer the jam to a heat-proof pitcher and pour into the jars, leaving about a 1-inch space from the rim of the jar. Wipe the rims with a clean towel, seal with the lids, then screw on the bands until snug but not tight.

4. Place a rack in the bottom of the pressure canner and rub the bottom of the lid with vegetable oil (this will prevent the lid from becoming stuck after processing). Add about 2 inches of warm water and put the jars in the canner. Follow the instructions on the pressure canner for securing the lid. Remove the pressure gauge from the steam vent and place the canner over high heat. Allow the steam to vent for 7 minutes for a small pressure canner, 10 minutes for a large pressure canner. Once vented, put the pressure gauge over the steam vent and wait for the gauge to read 10 psi (pounds per square inch). Once it reaches 10 psi, adjust the heat to ensure the canner maintains the same pressure. Process for 20 minutes, starting the timer once the gauge reaches 10 psi.

5. Turn off the heat and let the pressure return to zero. Carefully take off the lid. Remove the jars and let cool.

At the Table: CHERRY CLAFOUTIS WITH MILK JAM (PAGE 189); SWEET MILK PUNCH (PAGE 213); ICED COFFEE WITH MILK JAM (PAGE 224)

PRESERVED PORCINI MUSHROOMS

In early summer and late fall, we receive shipments of porcini mushrooms from Jeremy Faber, a Seattle-based chef turned forager. Jeremy's porcini, found growing in the woods of the Pacific Northwest, are a special addition to the menu when they are fresh. When we have the good fortune to acquire more than we can use, we preserve them.

Because mushrooms are a low-acid food and this preserve isn't acidified with vinegar, this preserve must be processed in a pressure canner. If you would rather not use a pressure canner, you can abandon the quantities dictated in this recipe. Simply buy the porcini that you can find (or afford), grill them, pack them in a storage container, and cover them with a layer of olive oil, which will slow them from spoiling. Stored in the refrigerator, the mushrooms will keep for a couple of weeks.

makes 4 pints

GRILLING

INGREDIENT	VOLUME	OUNCES	GRAMS
Porcini mushrooms	—	2¹/₂ pounds	1133 grams
Olive oil, for grilling the mushrooms	—	—	—
Kosher salt	—	—	—

1. In a colander under cool running water, give the mushrooms a good rinse. Blot them dry with a towel and trim off the tough ends of the stems. Halve the mushrooms, place in a large bowl, and toss with a splash of olive oil and a pinch of salt until coated evenly.

2. Prepare a fire in a grill using a mix of hardwood charcoal and wood chunks, spreading the coals evenly for direct-heat cooking. Arrange the mushrooms on the grill and sear, turning occasionally, until they are lightly charred, about 3 minutes. (They do not have to be cooked through.)

INGREDIENT	VOLUME	OUNCES	GRAMS	PERCENT
Porcini mushrooms, grilled	6¹/₂ cups	2 pounds, 4 ounces	1020 grams	56%
Water	3¹/₂ cups	28 ounces	794 grams	43.6%
Kosher salt	2 teaspoons	¹/₄ ounce	8 grams	.4%

1. Scald 4 pint jars (you will not be using this pot to process the jars). Right before filling, put the jars on the counter.

{continued}

2. Bring the water to a boil. Pack the mushrooms into the jars. Add $^1/_2$ teaspoon salt to each jar, then pour in the water, leaving a 1-inch space from the rim of the jar. Wipe the rims with a clean towel, seal with the lids, then screw on the bands until snug but not tight.

3. Place a rack in the bottom of the pressure canner and rub the bottom of the lid with vegetable oil. Add about 2 inches of warm water to the bottom and put the jars in the canner. Follow the instructions on the pressure canner for securing the lid. Remove the pressure gauge from the steam vent and place the canner over high heat. Allow the steam to vent for 7 minutes for a small pressure canner, 10 minutes for a large pressure canner. Once vented, put the pressure gauge over the steam vent and wait for the gauge to read 10 psi (pounds per square inch). Once it reaches 10 psi, adjust the heat to ensure the canner maintains the same pressure. Process for 45 minutes, starting the timer once the gauge reaches 10 psi.

4. Turn off the heat and let the pressure return to zero. Carefully take off the lid. Remove the jars and let cool.

Pressure gauge

PART TWO

At the Table

Now that I have a gleaming jar of aigre-doux, what do I do with it? It's a question that I am often asked, and one that this half of the book seeks to address. Throughout the year I work preserves into sauces, glazes, and condiments. In the process of juxtaposing seasonal produce with pickles, jams, and sauerkraut in my pantry, I have found pairings that never fail me. Sliced pickled asparagus with crème fraîche come together as one of my favorite light sauces for spring. In the fall, a jar of rutabaga sauerkraut can quickly be made into tangy, addictive latkes. Trimmings that are often discarded also get put to use. For instance, I blend the pulp from preserved lemons into butter to pair with rolls at my Thanksgiving table. In these simple ways, I gently cheat nature, prolonging the seasons with an arsenal of preserves. The menus that follow inspire you to do the same.

Stocking Up

Making stock has been such a regular occurrence in my restaurant life that it is hard to think about cooking without a ladleful handy. While you may have your favorite method, here I've provided instructions for how I make mine.

I never want a stock to dominate a dish, preferring it instead to be a flavor carrier. So I stay basic with seasonings—no garlic, some *herbes de Provence*—and go for body. Body comes from gelatin, the protein thickener extracted from the connective tissues in animal bones. It's what makes a well-made stock quiver like jelly when cold. While many different kinds of bones can be used to make stock, the best are necks, feet, shins, and backs, which have plenty of connective tissue. Bones and water simmered in a pot will give you stock, but the meaty flavor is better when balanced by *mirepoix*, the standard issue of onions, carrots, and celery. Cut the mirepoix in large chunks so the vegetables don't disintegrate as the stock simmers.

Another crucial thing needed to make stock is a tall pot. These recipes are cut back to fit into a standard 10-quart stockpot. For best results, choose a stockpot that is taller than it is wide. This allows you to cover the bones and vegetables in just enough water to simmer the stock without diluting it. Choose bones that will fit in your pot.

To avoid burning yourself, wait about ten minutes before ladling a finished stock through a strainer into a fresh pot or container. Then taste it. I often find that a strained stock needs to reduce a bit to reach a balance between a savory flavor and good body. If the stock tastes too light, simmer it for ten to twenty minutes, or until it has achieved a greater depth of flavor.

AT THE TABLE

SPRING

EARLY SIGNS

LEMON-PICKLED TURNIPS
WITH BABY LEEKS AND
PICKED HERBS • 134

BRAISED CHICKEN LEGS IN PEARL
PASTA WITH SWISS CHARD AND
PICKLED STEMS • 135

POUND CAKE WITH DEHYDRATED
STRAWBERRY JAM AND
SWEETENED CRÈME FRAÎCHE • 137

{ this *Menu* serves 4 }

Spring arrives slowly in Chicago. It isn't unusual for a late-season snow to come along, dusting the daffodils and hitting the pause button on the season completely. This is a restless time for chefs. By March, we've grown weary of hard winter squashes and gnarled, mature root vegetables, yet we still have to wait a month or two before spring produce really cuts loose.

Our discontent is pushed aside once the first box of baby vegetables arrives in the kitchen. To complement their crisp, delicate flavors, I turn to soft herbs, like chervil, chives, parsley, and tarragon. (Hard herbs, such as rosemary or sage, can taste overpowering this time of the year.) I also favor citrus juice and zest to keep flavors lively and clean.

I take a lighter approach to main courses, preferring broths to creamy sauces and vegetable oils to heaps of butter. But while early spring is the time to sweep away rich winter dishes in favor of fresher flavors, it can still deliver bone-chilling days. Warming main courses, like braised chicken thighs with quick-pickled chard stems, help us brace against the cold that's bound to linger for a few more weeks.

LEMON-PICKLED TURNIPS *with* BABY LEEKS *and* PICKED HERBS

Poached leeks dressed with vinaigrette, a classic French bistro preparation, inspired this simple salad. Here, the sharpness of lemony salad turnips is countered by the sweetness of baby leeks glazed in butter—truly a spring treat. But since spring produce is as unpredictable as spring weather, tender baby leeks aren't always easy to find. If unavailable, use green onions (scallions), which are about as thin as baby leeks. Pictured on pages 132 and 133.

1/2 pound baby leeks	1 cup raw white salad turnips, shaved crosswise	2 cups loosely packed fresh herbs (such as tarragon, parsley, and sliced chives)
2 tablespoons unsalted butter		
Kosher salt	2 tablespoons pickling liquid from Lemon-Pickled Turnips	Extra-virgin olive oil, for coating
1 cup Lemon-Pickled Turnips (page 22)		

1. Slice off the root ends of the leeks, keeping as much of the white end intact as possible. Trim away the dark green tips and slice the leeks into 3-inch pieces. For each piece, make an incision lengthwise halfway through the leek. Pry the leek open and run it under water, fanning the layers to remove any residual dirt.

2. Put the leeks in a small pot, pour in just enough water to cover, and bring to a simmer over medium-high heat. Swirl in the butter and season with salt. Decrease to a simmer and cover. Cook until the leeks are tender, 2 to 3 minutes. Uncover and cook until most of the water has evaporated and the butter glazes the leeks, 1 minute.

3. In a bowl, toss the pickled and fresh turnips with the pickling liquid, herbs, and enough olive oil to coat the turnips evenly. Taste, adding more pickling liquid, if desired. For each portion, arrange the leeks on the plate and spoon the turnips on top.

BRAISED CHICKEN LEGS *in* PEARL PASTA *with* SWISS CHARD *and* PICKLED STEMS

When friends come over for a casual meal, this dish is a nearly fail-safe main course. The chicken stays moist, even if you set it aside to accommodate an extended cocktail hour or a guest's late arrival. With easy-to-find ingredients, it's also casual enough for a weekday dinner. Pearl pasta—either Israeli couscous or Italian fregola pasta will do—added near the end of the cooking time absorbs most of the broth, giving the dish its own built-in pilaf.

4 chicken legs, thighs attached
Kosher salt and freshly ground
    black pepper
Grapeseed oil
2 stalks celery, chopped
1 yellow onion, diced

1 carrot, chopped
5 garlic cloves, smashed with the blunt
    side of a knife
1 cup white wine
2¹/₂ cups chicken stock (page 130)
1 tablespoon *herbes de Provence*

1 cup pearl pasta
Chopped fresh dill or sprigs of chervil
Swiss Chard and Pickled Stems
    (recipe follows)

1. Place an oven rack on the lowest level in the oven and remove the other rack. Preheat the oven to 325°F.

2. Season the chicken with salt and pepper. In a large Dutch oven or heavy-bottomed pot over high heat, warm about 1 tablespoon oil. In two batches, brown the chicken on both sides and transfer to a platter. Pour off some of the fat from the pan, leaving about 1 tablespoon. (Don't worry if there are some brown bits of chicken remaining in the pot—they will add flavor to the braise.)

3. Stir in the celery, onion, carrot, and garlic and cook over medium heat until the onion has softened, about 4 minutes. Pour in the wine, using a spoon to dislodge any brown bits from the bottom of the pot, and simmer until the wine has reduced by half. Return the chicken to the pot and pour in the stock. Bring to a boil, stir in the *herbes de Provence*, cover, and transfer to the oven.

4. Braise for 1 hour. Remove the lid and check the chicken: it should be tender when pierced with a fork. If not, return the lid and cook for another 15 minutes. When tender, stir in the pearl pasta and return to the oven, uncovered, for 10 minutes. To serve, divide the pasta among 4 bowls. Place a chicken leg and thigh on top, and garnish with dill or chervil. Spoon some chard alongside the chicken.

Swiss Chard and Pickled Stems

While chard stems can be forgettable when raw, they are dynamic when pickled, providing a sharp contrast to wilted chard leaves. Unlike the pickles in the first half of this book, this is essentially a quick pickle, meant to be consumed soon after it is made. The stems can be pickled up to a week or two before serving.

makes about 3 cups

¹/₂ cup champagne vinegar	¹/₂ teaspoon kosher salt
¹/₂ cup water	1¹/₂ pounds Swiss chard
1 shallot, minced	2 tablespoons extra-virgin olive oil
2 tablespoons honey	

1. In a 4- to 6-quart pot, simmer the vinegar, water, shallot, honey, and salt until the honey and salt have dissolved.

2. Tear the leaves off the stems. Trim off the tough ends and dice the stems into ¹/₄-inch pieces. Add the stems to the pot. (If the brine doesn't cover the stems completely, that's okay. The stems will soften in the brine.) Bring to a simmer and cook, stirring occasionally to ensure all the stem pieces absorb some brine, for 5 minutes. Let the stems cool completely in the brine. If you are not planning to serve them right away, cover and refrigerate for up to 2 weeks.

3. In a large pot over high heat, warm the olive oil. Stir in the leaves and a pinch of salt and sauté until they begin to wilt. Using a slotted spoon, add the pickled stems to the pot, then spoon in half of the pickling liquid. Cook until the chard leaves are soft and most of the liquid is evaporated. Taste, adding more pickling liquid if you prefer a sharper taste.

POUND CAKE *with* DEHYDRATED STRAWBERRY JAM *and* SWEETENED CRÈME FRAÎCHE

My mom's mom, Rita, a fourth-generation Missourian, baked a mean pound cake. She used confectioners' sugar instead of granulated for a cake with a finer crumb. It's the perfect neutral base for showing off homemade preserves. If I'm still waiting for local strawberries, I serve the cake with strawberry jam to curb my craving. But if the pantry is perilously low on strawberry preserves, I opt for Kumquat Marmalade (page 83) instead.

makes 1 loaf cake

1 cup unsalted butter, softened
1²/₃ cups confectioners' sugar, sifted
2 teaspoons pure vanilla extract
1¹/₂ teaspoons baking powder

¹/₂ teaspoon kosher salt
4 large eggs, at room temperature
2¹/₂ cups all-purpose flour
¹/₂ cup whole milk, at room temperature

Sweetened Crème Fraîche
  (recipe follows)
Dehydrated Strawberry Jam (page 63)

1. Preheat the oven to 325°F. Butter a 9¹/₄ by 5¹/₄-inch or 1¹/₂ quart loaf pan.

2. In a stand mixer fitted with the paddle attachment, cream the butter and sugar on medium-high speed until fluffy. Beat in the vanilla, baking powder, and salt. Add the eggs one at a time, mixing well between each addition. On low speed, stir in one-third of the flour, then pour in half of the milk. Repeat, scraping down the sides between additions, until all the flour and milk are incorporated.

3. Pour the batter into the prepared pan and bake until a skewer inserted in the center of the cake comes out clean, about 1 hour.

4. To serve, cut the cake into ¹/₂-inch slices and serve with a dollop of crème fraîche and a generous spoonful of jam.

Sweetened Crème Fraîche

makes 1¹/₄ cups

1 cup Crème Fraîche (page 17)
3 tablespoons confectioners' sugar
1 teaspoon pure vanilla extract

1. In a bowl, whisk together the crème fraîche, confectioners' sugar, and vanilla until the cream reaches the consistency of pudding.

SPRING SUPPER

GRILLED AND PICKLED ASPARAGUS
WITH PROSCIUTTO AND
FRIED EGGS • 141

ROASTED LAMB MEATBALLS WITH
TOMATO-BEAN RAGOUT AND
GREEN GARLIC • 142

RHUBARB SUMMER PUDDING WITH
KUMQUAT MARMALADE • 145

{ this *Menu* serves 4 to 6 }

ROASTED LAMB MEATBALLS *with*
TOMATO-BEAN RAGOUT *and* GREEN GARLIC

Although these meatballs are made primarily with lamb, I like to grind a little pork fatback into the mix. It's more neutral than lamb fat (which has a strong, gamey taste that isn't for everyone) and helps yield tender meatballs. A stand mixer with a meat-grinding attachment makes quick work of the grinding process. If you don't have a grinder, buy ground lamb and ask the butcher to grind some fatback for you. In a pinch, you can cube the fat into small pieces and then pulse it in a chilled food processor until the fat is roughly the same size as the ground lamb. If green garlic isn't available, finish the dish with two cups of sliced green onions instead.

1 large egg

$^1/_2$ cup whole milk

$^1/_2$ cup fresh bread crumbs

$^1/_4$ cup grated Parmigiano-
    Reggiano cheese

1 teaspoon fennel seeds

1 pound lamb shoulder, trimmed,
    cut into cubes, and ground in
    a meat grinder

4 ounces pork fatback, cut into cubes
    and ground in a meat grinder

3 cloves garlic, finely chopped

1 tablespoon smoked sweet paprika

$^1/_2$ teaspoon kosher salt

Pinch of red pepper flakes

Tomato-Bean Ragout (recipe follows)

1 tablespoon extra-virgin olive oil

1 cup sliced green garlic (white and
    light green parts only)

1 lemon, for zesting

1. Preheat the oven to 400°F. Oil a rimmed baking sheet. In a small bowl whisk together the egg, milk, bread crumbs, and cheese. Let sit for 15 minutes.

2. In a dry sauté pan over medium heat, toast the fennel seeds until aromatic. In a large bowl, combine the lamb, fatback, garlic, paprika, fennel seeds, salt, and red pepper flakes. Pour in the egg mixture. Using your hands, mix the ingredients together until evenly distributed. The mixture will feel sticky. Form into 18 to 20 balls about $1^1/_2$ inches in diameter and place on the prepared baking sheet. Bake until lightly browned, about 15 minutes.

3. Meanwhile, bring the ragout to a gentle simmer. Using tongs, transfer the meatballs into the ragout, cover, and simmer for at least 5 minutes.

4. Heat the olive oil in a sauté pan over high heat. Add the green garlic and sauté until soft, about 30 seconds. Spoon the bean ragout into 4 warmed bowls, ensuring that each portion has 3 to 5 meatballs. Top with a spoonful of green garlic. Grate lemon zest over each bowl to finish.

AN
EARTH DAY
GESTURE

SPRING-DUG PARSNIP SOUP WITH
MANDARIN AIGRE-DOUX • 149

WARM WHEAT BERRY SALAD
WITH PEAS AND PRESERVED
LEMON VINAIGRETTE • 150

SORREL-CHÈVRE FRITTATA
WITH SMOKED SPRING ONION
SALSA VERDE • 152

WHOLE-WHEAT SHORTBREAD
WITH RAINIER CHERRY JAM
AND YOGURT • 153

{ this *Menu* serves 6 }

WARM WHEAT BERRY SALAD *with* PEAS *and* PRESERVED LEMON VINAIGRETTE

Salted lemon, fresh mint, and fennel shake up wholesome wheat berries. Some wheat berries are quite large; I prefer small kernels, like the ones I buy from Heritage Prairie Farm, for their lighter texture. If you see similar wheat berries for sale at the farmers' market, try them out. Curly pea shoots and pops of sweet peas sweeten the deal. When I can find it, I also like to stir in anise hyssop, a licorice-flavored herb.

I have another neat trick to separate this dish from weightier whole-grain salads. I dehydrate some of the cooked wheat berries, then fry them until crisp. To do so, set up a dehydrator or preheat the oven to 135°F and oil a baking sheet. Remove ¹/₂ cup of the cooked wheat berries and spread out onto the baking sheet. Dehydrate them for five hours. To fry the wheat berries, heat ¹/₂ inch of oil in a wide pot or straight-sided sauté pan over medium-high heat. Once the oil begins to shimmer, scatter the wheat berries into the pot and fry until crisp, about 1 minute. Drain the wheat berries on paper towels and season with salt. While the dynamic texture is worth the effort, you can skip this step without compromising the flavor of this honestly good—and good for you—salad.

---

2 cups wheat berries
Kosher salt
4 wedges Preserved Lemons (page 115)
¹/₂ sweet onion (like candy or Vidalia),
    finely diced

Grated zest and juice of 1 lemon
3 tablespoons champagne vinegar
2 tablespoons honey
Freshly ground black pepper
¹/₂ cup extra-virgin olive oil

2 cups peas, freshly shucked or frozen
¹/₄ cup coarsely chopped fresh mint
¹/₄ cup coarsely chopped fresh fennel
    fronds or anise hyssop
6 cups pea shoots

---

1. To prepare the wheat berries, rinse them under cold water. Place in a medium pot and cover with 2 inches of water. Bring the pot to a boil and season with a big pinch of salt (about ¹/₂ teaspoon). Cover and simmer over low heat until tender but still chewy, about 1 hour. Drain the wheat berries (if any excess water remains). You should have about 6 cups of wheat berries.

2. To make the vinaigrette, run the lemon wedges under a stream of cool running water for 15 minutes to rinse away excess salt. You also can soak the wedges in a generous amount of water overnight. Drain the wedges, remove the pulp, and cut away as much pith as possible without losing any of the rind. (You may save the pulp for lemon butter, page 246.) Mince the rind. In a small bowl, mix the rind with the onion, lemon zest and juice, vinegar, and honey. Season gently with salt and pepper (the rind will be salty), then whisk in the olive oil.

3. To make the salad, if using fresh peas, blanch them in a pot of boiling salted water for 2 minutes, then drain. If using frozen peas, rinse them briefly under running water. Fold the peas into the wheat berries, followed with all but 2 tablespoons of the vinaigrette. Mix in the mint and fennel fronds, then taste, seasoning with salt if needed. Keep warm.

4. To serve, in a large bowl toss the pea shoots with salt, pepper, and the remaining 2 tablespoons of vinaigrette. Lay a bed of pea shoots on a serving platter. Spoon the warm wheat berries on top.

SORREL-CHÈVRE FRITTATA *with* SMOKED SPRING ONION SALSA VERDE

If you tasted sorrel blindfolded, you'd be excused if you thought that someone had slipped you lemon-infused spinach. A pucker-inducing dark-green leaf, sorrel is spinach's acerbic cousin, but its acidity plays well against rich ingredients like eggs and cheese. If sorrel is out of reach, use spinach and squeeze some lemon juice over the frittata after you pull it from the oven.

3 tablespoons extra-virgin olive oil
2 cups coarsely chopped fresh sorrel
8 large eggs

4 ounces fresh goat cheese,
   at room temperature
1/4 cup Crème Fraîche (page 17)
1/2 teaspoon kosher salt

Freshly ground black pepper
1 tablespoon unsalted butter
Smoked Spring Onion Salsa Verde
   (recipe follows)

1. Preheat the oven to 400°F. Heat 1 tablespoon of the olive oil in an ovenproof 10-inch cast-iron skillet or sauté pan over medium-high heat. Stir in the sorrel and sauté briefly, about 1 minute, just until wilted. Pour the sorrel into a colander to drain out any excess water. Wipe out the skillet—you will use it to cook the frittata.

2. In a food processor, purée the eggs, goat cheese, crème fraîche, salt, and pepper. Add the sorrel and pulse to form a coarse purée.

3. Heat the butter and the remaining 2 tablespoons olive oil in the skillet over medium heat, swirling the fats to combine. Pour in the egg purée and stir gently for about 2 minutes. Transfer the frittata to the oven and bake until set, about 12 minutes. Invert the frittata onto a cutting board and cut into 6 wedges. Place the wedges on warmed plates. Spoon the salsa verde over each wedge or serve on the side.

Smoked Spring Onion Salsa Verde

makes about 2 1/2 cups

1 cup Smoked and Pickled Spring
   Onions (page 24)
1/2 cup coarsely chopped fresh
   Italian parsley

1/4 cup coarsely chopped fresh tarragon
1/4 cup coarsely chopped fresh chervil
2 tablespoons chopped capers

1/4 cup extra-virgin olive oil
Kosher salt and freshly ground
   black pepper

1. Drain the spring onions, reserving the pickling liquid. Coarsely chop the onions and transfer to a mixing bowl. Whisk in the pickling liquid followed by the parsley, tarragon, chervil, and capers. Whisk in the olive oil, taste for seasoning, and adjust with salt or pepper if needed.

WHOLE-WHEAT SHORTBREAD *with* RAINIER CHERRY JAM *and* YOGURT

Nutty whole-wheat shortbread cookies—which are really like indulgent graham crackers—complement the tang in this jam while creamy yogurt adds a tangy finish. This shortbread makes an ideal accompaniment for Buttermilk Ice Cream with Brandied Peaches (page 161) as well.

makes about 2 dozen shortbread

1 cup unsalted butter, cubed, at room temperature
3/4 cup confectioners' sugar

1 teaspoon kosher salt
1 cup all-purpose flour
1/2 cup whole-wheat flour

1 cup whole-milk plain yogurt, for serving
1/2 cup Rainier Cherry Jam (page 76), for serving

1. In a stand mixer fitted with the paddle attachment, mix the butter, sugar, and salt on medium-low speed until barely mixed. Add the flours and mix on low speed just until the dough comes together. Place the dough on a lightly floured surface and knead a few times. Shape the dough into a 6-inch-diameter round patty, wrap in plastic wrap, and refrigerate for at least 2 hours or overnight.

2. Preheat the oven to 300°F. Line two baking sheets with parchment paper. On a lightly floured surface, roll the dough out roughly 1/4-inch thick. Cut into 3 by 1-inch rectangles and place on the prepared baking sheets. Bake the shortbread until golden brown, about 25 minutes. Cool on the parchment until the shortbread firms up.

3. For each serving, place 2 heaping tablespoons of yogurt in a bowl. Spoon a dollop of the jam on top of the yogurt and serve with a couple of shortbread cookies.

AT LAST, AL FRESCO

ROASTED SUNCHOKES WITH
MAPLE–BLACK WALNUT BUTTER
AND PARSLEY • 157

RAINBOW TROUT WITH CREAMED
RAMPS AND MORELS • 159

ROASTED PORK SHOULDER WITH
GARLIC MUSTARD CHIMICHURRI
AND SPRING SPINACH • 160

BUTTERMILK ICE CREAM WITH
BRANDIED PEACHES • 161

CHEESE AND CRACKERS WITH
CARAMEL APPLE JAM • 163

{ this *Menu* serves 6 }

I'm convinced that sunlight has a seasoning effect on food. Whether served under bright noon rays or a waning evening light, meals eaten outside can taste earthy, fresh, and savory.

That these opportunities are rare in my world of commercial kitchens is what makes them all the more valuable. As soon as the thermostat stays above 60°F consistently, Chicago restaurants turn cracked sidewalks into makeshift dining rooms decked with flowerpots—a city requirement for all outdoor dining spaces. Inevitably, lines form of people willing to wait for a patio spot. No one seems to mind the diesel trucks and city buses roaring by. During the window of opportunity when eating outdoors is comfortable and mostly bug-free, a spot in the sun is a destination worth waiting for.

The first outdoor meal of the year also marks the end of spring, but not before I have a chance to serve up the season's best ingredients. By late spring, it's a convergence of sunchokes, morels, ramps, and wild garlic. This menu highlights those flavors. Earthy sunchokes are augmented by similarly earthy black walnuts, while lean trout is enriched by a creamy ramp and morel sauce. Roasted pork shoulder kicks up the meal's richness factor, enlivening the table with a zesty garlic mustard chimichurri sauce. Meanwhile, a course of cheese and crackers encourages guests to linger outside longer before dessert, a fresh buttermilk ice cream paired with last year's peaches. Prepare the menu in its entirety, or choose your own adventure, putting together dishes that suit your tastes. No matter which direction you go, remember that this is a visceral meal, one that doesn't pretend to be refined or clever, just good. And these dishes, while they take some time in the kitchen, are worth waiting for, just like a seat on the patio.

ROASTED SUNCHOKES *with* MAPLE–BLACK WALNUT BUTTER *and* PARSLEY

Sunchokes taste like artichokes, but with their thin, paper-bag skins, and crunchy texture, they are sweeter and earthier. This is one of the reasons they pair so well with black walnuts. I take the pairing one step further in this warm salad, whipping together a creamy dressing sweetened by maple and black walnut butter. Some chefs advocate peeling sunchokes, but I prefer to give them a good scrub instead. If you like watercress, serve the sunchokes on a bed of the peppery greens.

1/4 cup plus 2 tablespoons grapeseed oil
1 1/2 pounds sunchokes, scrubbed and cut into bite-size chunks
2 tablespoons unsalted butter

Kosher salt and freshly ground black pepper
1/2 cup Maple–Black Walnut Butter (page 84), at room temperature

1/4 cup buttermilk
2 tablespoons sherry vinegar
2 cups loosely packed Italian parsley leaves

1. Preheat the oven to 425°F. Heat 2 tablespoons of the oil in a large ovenproof sauté pan over medium-high heat. Scatter the sunchokes in the pan and sear until they start to caramelize, 2 to 3 minutes. Transfer the pan to the oven and roast until the sunchokes are cooked through but a little bit of crunch remains in the center, about 5 minutes. Swirl in the unsalted butter, season with salt and pepper, and keep warm.

2. In a small bowl, whisk together the flavored butter with buttermilk and vinegar. Whisk in the remaining 1/4 cup of oil and season with salt and pepper.

3. Pour the vinaigrette over the sunchokes. Sprinkle the parsley on top and toss to combine. Serve warm.

RAINBOW TROUT *with* CREAMED RAMPS *and* MORELS

With their distinct honeycomb texture that appears to be designed to absorb flavor, morels are one of my favorite mush-
room varieties. I like to pair them with ramps, which provide a wild-onion edge to the creamy sauce that drapes the trout.

Like other wild mushrooms, morels need to be washed well to remove the dirt and pine needles that get trapped in
their porous surface and hollow center. It's best to wash the mushrooms the day before you plan to cook them so most
of the water has time to evaporate (wet mushrooms won't sear effectively). I submerge the mushrooms in the water,
lift them out of the water, and let them dry on a cooling rack set on top of the oven. Later, I refrigerate the mushrooms,
uncovered, until needed. If you can't find morels, make this recipe with a mix of chanterelles, black trumpets, oyster
mushrooms, or other wild and cultivated varieties.

Since this dish is part of a multicourse menu, I advise serving a smaller portion of trout to guests than you would if it
were the main course. One large trout should yield four portions, a small trout two. Pictured on pages 154 and 155.

---

1 pound morel mushrooms

6 tablespoons grapeseed oil

3 tablespoons unsalted butter

1/2 cup diced sweet onion (such as
  candy or Vidalia)

Kosher salt and freshly ground
  black pepper

1/4 cup brine from Pickled Ramps
  (page 23)

1 cup Pickled Ramps (page 23), chopped

1/2 cup Crème Fraîche (page 17)

3 tablespoons chopped mixed fresh
  herbs (such as parsley, tarragon,
  and chives)

6 (3- to 4-ounce) skin-on rainbow
  trout fillets

---

1. To clean the morels, fill a large, deep bowl with water. Halve the larger morels lengthwise but keep the smaller
    morels whole. Submerge the morels in the water and agitate the water to shake away pine needles or bits of dirt.
    Line a baking sheet with a rack and scatter the morels in one layer on top. Let them air dry in a warm corner of
    the kitchen for at least a couple of hours. Once the morels are dry, refrigerate them uncovered unless you plan to
    use them that day.

2. To cook the morels, heat 2 tablespoons of the oil and 1 tablespoon of the butter in a large sauté pan over high
    heat until the butter starts to bubble. Add the morels and onion and sear until the morels start to crisp and the
    onion becomes tender, 5 to 8 minutes. Season lightly with salt and pepper. Pour in the ramp pickling liquid to
    deglaze the pan, then stir in the ramps. Cook until the pan is nearly dry. Remove the pan from the heat and mix
    in the crème fraîche and herbs. The sauce should be lightly creamy, with large pieces of morels. Taste, seasoning
    with more salt and pepper, if needed. Keep warm. You will have about 2 cups.

3. To cook the fish, season the fillets on both sides with salt and pepper. Cook the fish in 2 sauté pans to avoid
    crowding. Heat about 2 tablespoons of the oil and 1 tablespoon of the butter in each pan. Once the butter begins
    to bubble, place the trout portions, skin side down, into the pan and cook until the skin is crispy, about 3 min-
    utes. Flip the fish over and briefly sear the other side until cooked through, 30 seconds to 1 minute.

4. To serve, place one portion of fish, skin side up, in the center of each plate. Spoon the sauce over the top to finish.

ROASTED PORK SHOULDER *with*
GARLIC MUSTARD CHIMICHURRI *and* SPRING SPINACH

All cuts of pork are good carriers for flavorful condiments, but among the shanks to the loin, the shoulder stands out. It might have to do with the cut's near-perfect ratio of meat to fat, which cries out for a piquant, acidic counterpart. In this recipe the condiment comes in the form of a pungent chimichurri made with garlic mustard tops and spring garlic. Green, with round, scalloped leaves, garlic mustard is an invasive species multiplying rapidly throughout Midwestern forests and backyards. But it is edible—good, actually, particularly in sauces. In late April I can take a stroll around the neighborhood and come back with enough of the weed to make this chimichurri. If garlic mustard hasn't invaded a forest near you, use a combination of mustard greens and parsley instead.

When buying pork, ask the butcher to tie it in twine for you. This helps hold the shape of the pork shoulder while it cooks, making for a better presentation. Allow at least one day to brine the pork before roasting.

8 cups water	1 yellow onion, sliced	Kosher salt
1/2 cup sorghum molasses	1 carrot, diced	Extra-virgin olive oil
1/4 cup kosher salt	1 head garlic, halved crosswise	6 ounces baby spinach, thick
1 tablespoon black peppercorns	1 lemon, halved	stems removed
1 tablespoon coriander seeds	1 (3-pound) boneless pork shoulder	Garlic Mustard Chimichurri
2 teaspoons hot smoked paprika	roast, tied with butcher's twine	(recipe follows)
5 allspice berries	6 radishes, sliced thinly	

1. To make the brine, in a large pot over medium-high heat, whisk together the water, molasses, salt, peppercorns, coriander, paprika, and allspice. Stir in the onion, carrot, and garlic. Squeeze the lemon juice into the pot, then add the halves. Bring to a boil, then remove from the heat and cool completely over an ice bath. Once cold, submerge the pork in the brine and refrigerate overnight or up to 2 days.

To cook the pork, preheat the oven to 425°F. Remove the pork from the brine, pat dry, and bring to room temperature. Place the pork in a roasting pan fitted with a rack. Roast until the meat starts to caramelize, about 30 minutes. Decrease the heat to 300°F and continue to roast until the pork reaches an internal temperature of 145°F, about 1 1/2 hours. Remove the pork from the oven and loosely cover with aluminum foil. Let the pork rest for 30 minutes.

2. To serve, in a small bowl toss the radishes with a few pinches of salt. Heat a thin film of olive oil in a large pot or sauté pan over medium-high heat. Add the spinach and sprinkle with salt. Cook the spinach briefly, just until it starts to wilt, then transfer to a warmed platter. Slice the meat crosswise into 1/2-inch slices. Lay the slices on top of the spinach and scatter the radishes alongside. Spoon the chimichurri over the slices and serve extra chimichurri at the table.

Garlic Mustard Chimichurri

For the brightest color, make the sauce no more than two hours before serving. The chimichirri will keep in the refrigerator for about a week.

makes about 1 cup

2 cups garlic mustard tops, or 1¹/₂ cups mustard greens or parsley or a mixture of both, coarsely chopped	2 sprigs spring garlic, coarsely chopped Grated zest and juice of 1 lemon 2 tablespoons red wine vinegar	1 teaspoon smoked hot paprika ¹/₂ teaspoon kosher salt ³/₄ cup extra-virgin olive oil

1. Put the garlic mustard, spring garlic, lemon zest and juice, vinegar, paprika, and salt in a food processor. Pulse a couple of times just to combine (you aren't looking for a smooth purée). With the processor running, drizzle in the olive oil and blend just until incorporated. Taste, adjusting with more salt or paprika if desired.

BUTTERMILK ICE CREAM *with* BRANDIED PEACHES

Unlike classic ice cream, which is made from a base of crème anglaise, this ice cream is made from a sabayon, a frothy custard made by whisking egg yolks with Marsala wine in a bowl over simmering water. The reason I make sabayon instead of crème anglaise is the buttermilk. To avoid the risk of making ice cream with lumps of curdled milk, I stir the buttermilk in only after the sabayon is thick enough to drip off a whisk in shiny ribbons. Since the ice cream isn't very sweet on its own, I like topping it with brandied peaches. You could also use brandied cherries or a spoonful of strawberry jam. If you're so inclined, a few shortbread cookies (page 153) add welcome crunch.

makes 1¹/₂ pints

6 large egg yolks ¹/₂ cup sugar	¹/₄ teaspoon kosher salt 2 cups buttermilk	1 cup Brandied Peaches (page 70), for serving

1. To make the ice cream base, whisk together the egg yolks, sugar, and salt in the top pan of a double boiler or in a heat-proof bowl over a pot of barely simmering water, ensuring that the water does not touch the bowl. Continue to whisk until the sabayon changes from loose and frothy to thick and pale, falling into ribbons when the whisk is lifted from the bowl, about 4 minutes. It should register about 160°F on a thermometer.

2. Pour the sabayon into the bowl of a stand mixer fitted with the whisk attachment and whip on medium speed for about 1 minute until it has cooled slightly. Fold in the buttermilk and chill over an ice bath. Refrigerate for at least a couple of hours or overnight.

{continued}

3. To freeze the ice cream, give the base a good stir, then pour into an ice cream maker. Churn according to the manufacturer's instructions and store in a chilled container in the freezer.

4. To serve, strain the peach brandy syrup into a small pot and simmer over medium-low heat until the liquid has thickened. Stir in the peaches. Serve slightly warm over scoops of the ice cream.

CHEESE AND CRACKERS *with* CARAMEL APPLE JAM

I don't know many people who can resist jam served with a soft, bloomy-rind cheese and homemade crackers. Thin and crisp, these pepper-flecked crackers echo the savory flavors in the caramel apple jam. To roll out the crackers to the optimal thinness, you will need a pasta machine. Alternatively, roll the dough as thin as you can with a rolling pin. The dough may seem dry at first, but after resting for a couple of hours it becomes softer and easily passes through the pasta rollers. To make the crackers even more savory, add a teaspoon of mustard seeds to the dough, then sprinkle with sea salt. Instead of baking the crackers, you can opt to pan-fry them in vegetable oil for a crispy chiplike cracker.

3¹/₂ cups all-purpose flour
1 teaspoon kosher salt
¹/₄ teaspoon freshly ground black pepper
1 cup buttermilk

1 large egg, lightly whisked
4 tablespoons unsalted butter, melted
1 (6- to 8-ounce) round cow's or sheep's milk soft-rind cheese

1 half-pint jar Caramel Apple Jam (page 78)

1. In a stand mixer with the paddle attachment, mix together the flour, salt, and pepper on low speed. With the mixer running, pour in the buttermilk, egg, and butter and mix until a coarse dough forms. The dough may appear dry, but it will hydrate as it rests. Wrap in plastic wrap and refrigerate for at least 2 hours or overnight.

2. Remove the dough from the refrigerator and let it come to room temperature. Preheat the oven to 400°F. Oil a couple of baking sheets.

3. Attach the pasta roller attachment to a stand mixer and set the rollers on the widest setting. If using a hand-cranked pasta machine, attach it to the counter or table next to the workspace. Unwrap the dough and cut it into 4 pieces. Flatten the dough until it is thin enough to fit through the rollers. Guide the dough through the rollers. Fold the dough in overlapping thirds (like a letter) and pass it through again. Switch to the next narrow-est setting and guide the dough through twice. Guide the dough through the next few settings until it has passed through the rollers' third-thinnest setting.

4. Lay the sheet on a floured work surface and cut crosswise into 1-inch-thick strips. Transfer the crackers to the baking sheets. Bake until the crackers are golden brown, 8 to 10 minutes. Remove the crackers and let cool. Repeat with the rest of the dough. You will have about 60 crackers.

5. Serve the crackers alongside the cheese and jam. Extra crackers keep in a sealed container for about 1 week.

SUMMER

LAZIER DAYS

PRESERVED GAZPACHO • 167

GRILLED SKIRT STEAK
WITH FENNEL PANZANELLA
SALAD • 168

MIXED BERRY CRISP WITH
GOAT CHEESE MOUSSE AND
MULBERRY AIGRE-DOUX • 170

{ this *Menu* serves 6 }

It's not easy for chefs to put on the brakes. We often mean to, but even when we're mired under the weight of an insane prep list, we will still contemplate adding one more component to a plate. Part of it is bravado—we like to show off—but another part of it is for pure fun. Pushing ourselves to conjure new creations is why many of us got into the business in the first place.

These sorts of culinary fireworks are entirely out of place in the heat of summer, when a glass of iced tea forms beads of condensation in a matter of minutes. Kitchens are always hot places, but the temperature can turn withering in July and August. This is the time of year when an extra garnish makes us look like we are trying too hard. It also is when a dirty term like "convenience food" starts to sound like an acceptable, even an attractive, option.

This menu is a chef's version of convenience food. It works when your homework—the canned tomatoes and pickled peppers and fennel—has been done in advance. The hard part out of the way, a simple pop of a lid provides the makings for an entire batch of gazpacho or the vinaigrette for a bracingly refreshing panzanella salad.

Dessert is easy too. Summer is the season of fruit crisps, when little needs to be done to accentuate in-season berries other than piling them high in a baking dish and covering them with a buttery, crumbly topping. On this menu, dessert is the one place where I've caved to one chef-y addition: goat cheese mousse. In all fairness, though, it is simple, coming together when you fold together whisked goat cheese and cream into tempered egg yolks. In fact, the mousse alone is a fine dessert with a spoonful of Mulberry Aigre-Doux (page 95).

True convenience is eating leftovers pulled straight from the refrigerator. In this regard, this menu scores high. The gazpacho improves when chilled overnight, and the panzanella salad holds up brightly the next day tossed with a few fresh greens.

PRESERVED GAZPACHO

Cold temperatures generally dull flavors, but the vinegar and spicy peppers add pep to the broth of this refreshing gazpacho. For the most flavorful result, make it the day before you plan to serve it. The canned tomatoes we make at Vie tend to be more watery than grocery-store brands. If you don't have your own canned tomatoes, use juicy fresh ones instead: core the tomatoes, blanch them in boiling water to loosen the skins, shock them briefly in ice water, and then pass them through a food mill. It won't feel as lazy, but it will taste delicious.

4 cups Canned Tomatoes (page 46)
1 cup chopped Grilled and Pickled Sweet
   Peppers (page 39)
1/2 cup chopped Grilled and Pickled Hot
   Peppers (page 37)

1 cucumber, peeled, seeded, and diced
   (about 1 cup)
1/2 sweet onion (such as candy or
   Vidalia), minced (about 1 cup)
5 cloves garlic, minced

Kosher salt and freshly ground
   black pepper
1/2 cup extra-virgin olive oil, plus more
   for finishing
2 tablespoons red wine vinegar

1. In a bowl, mix together the tomatoes, sweet and hot peppers, cucumber, onion, and garlic. Season with salt and pepper, then whisk in the olive oil and red wine vinegar. Taste, adjust the seasoning with more vinegar or salt, and refrigerate for at least 30 minutes before serving. You will have about 7 cups of gazpacho.

2. Before serving, taste, adding more vinegar or salt if needed. Ladle the soup into chilled bowls and finish each serving with a drizzle of olive oil.

GRILLED SKIRT STEAK *with* FENNEL PANZANELLA SALAD

Chunks of toasted bread softened with the juices of ripe tomatoes, panzanella salad is the stuff of Tuscan dream vacations. But a great bread salad doesn't have to mean tomatoes. For this rendition I've featured another favorite Italian ingredient: fennel, both fresh and pickled. While the fresh fennel lends refreshing crunch, the pickled fennel adds crucial sharp-sweet balance to the salad. Marinated skirt steak, grilled and served in slices on top of the bread, takes this from side salad to main course. If grilling in the cold is your thing, the same salad translates well to fall and winter. Use roasted root vegetables in place of corn and shave pecorino cheese over the top. Leftover vinaigrette is terrific over roasted carrots or grilled fish.

1/2 cup extra-virgin olive oil

3 cloves garlic, minced

1 teaspoon red pepper flakes

Juice of 1 lemon

Kosher salt and freshly ground
   black pepper

8 ounces day-old rustic country bread
   (to make about 3 cups croutons)

6 sprigs thyme

1/2 fennel bulb

2 pounds skirt steak, trimmed of
   excess fat

3 ears corn, husked

4 ounces arugula

About 1 cup Fennel Vinaigrette
   (recipe follows)

1. To make the marinade, in a bowl whisk together 1/4 cup of the olive oil, the garlic, red pepper flakes, lemon juice, and about 1 teaspoon salt and 1/2 teaspoon pepper. Place the steak in a storage container and coat in the marinade. Cover and refrigerate overnight or up to 2 days.

2. Prepare a fire in the grill, spreading the coals evenly for direct-heat cooking. As the grill heats up, make the croutons. Preheat the oven to 400°F. Tear the bread into large bite-size pieces. In a large bowl, mix the bread with the remaining 1/4 cup olive oil and the thyme, then season with salt and pepper. Spread the croutons across a baking sheet and toast until golden and crisp but not completely dry, 8 to 10 minutes.

3. To prepare the fennel, cut the 1/2 fennel bulb in half and cut out the core. Using a sharp knife or a mandoline, shave the fennel lengthwise into thin slices.

4. To cook the steak, season the meat lightly with salt and pepper and grill over high heat until medium-rare, 2 to 4 minutes per side, depending on the thickness of the cut. Let rest at least 5 minutes. Meanwhile, rub the corn with a little olive oil and season lightly with salt and pepper. Grill over high heat for about 6 minutes, rotating the ears a few times, until some of the kernels are pleasantly blistered. When cool enough to handle, cut the kernels off the cob.

5. To serve, in a large bowl, toss together the croutons, corn, shaved fennel, arugula, and just enough vinaigrette to coat the ingredients evenly (about 1 cup, depending on how much the bread soaks up). Divide the salad between 6 plates or spoon onto a large platter. Cut the skirt steak into 5- to 6-inch pieces, then slice across the grain into 1/2-inch strips. To serve, drape the steak on top of the salad.

GRILL OUT

VERBENA SLING • 175

WOOD-GRILLED BURGERS WITH
BEEF BACON • 175

GRILLED AND PICKLED SUMMER
SQUASH SALAD • 179

PICKLED CELERY ROOT
REMOULADE • 180

HOT PEPPER SAUCE • 181

SUMMER BERRY SODA
FLOATS • 181

{ this *Menu* serves 6,
but could be extended to serve 10
with additions of grilled sausage,
chicken, or fish }

Summer grilling sessions are enmeshed into the Virant family DNA. When we were younger, my siblings and I gathered at our parents' house outside of St. Louis every Fourth of July. The day was purposefully lazy, involving little beyond lounging by the pool and catching up with family news. The only real action took place on my parents' large outdoor grill. Once the grill was fired up, the effort required by the cook was minimal. Yet the effects—wood smoke licking the meat and vegetables, imparting its signature char—were complex, and completely intoxicating.

I've always had a wood grill on the line at Vie, and we use it often to impart smoke to everything from sturgeon to spring onions. It's even easier to leverage the power of a grill when cooking at home. Burgers, sausages, or fish can take up part of the grill while the remaining space is used to char slices of zucchini or peppers. What sets a memorable grilling session apart from an average effort, however, is the selection of condiments. Here pickles play an important role. A purée of lime juice, cilantro, and pickled hot peppers adds instant zip to grilled vegetables or acts as a potent salsa, while a cooling celery root remoulade is terrific on burgers or mixed into potato salad.

In fact, the condiments are the most important part of the menu; everything else is negotiable. If you've reached your burger limit, you could just as easily grill up a whole lake trout or side of salmon and serve it with the same condiments. Or add a few chicken thighs or vegetable kebabs, if that suits you better. What isn't negotiable when grilling in the summer is having ample refreshment. I've provided two options: verbena slings for the adults and soda floats for the kids.

VERBENA SLING

Mike Page, the bartender at Vie, composed this cocktail to leverage the bright green verbena cordial we make at the restaurant. A dry, juniper-rich gin, like North Shore #11 or Death's Door, plays off the floral cordial, making for a summery alternative to a gin and tonic. While this recipe makes one cocktail, you also could mix together several servings at once in a pitcher. Pictured on pages 172 and 173.

makes 1 cocktail

1 ounce Lemon Verbena Cordial
(page 214)
¾ ounce gin
2 ounces lemonade

Dash grapefruit cocktail bitters
(such as Fee Brothers)
Soda water

In a tall glass, mix together the cordial, gin, lemonade, and bitters. Fill the glass with a few large ice cubes, then top with a splash of soda water.

WOOD-GRILLED BURGERS *with* BEEF BACON

We always save some of the beef we buy from Dietzler Farm for Vie's signature burger, served on house-made buns. I don't go crazy with lettuce, onions, and tomatoes, preferring to limit toppings to a nice piece of cheese, a couple of crisp pieces of beef bacon, and slices of dill pickle. Feel free to embellish.

6 to 12 slices Beef Bacon (page 116) or
pork bacon
2 pounds ground grass-fed beef
6 slices aged Cheddar or smoked
Jack cheese

6 Burger Buns (recipe follows)
1 dill pickle (page 30), halved
or quartered

1. Heat a sauté pan over medium heat. Cook the bacon until the fat has rendered and the meat is crisp. Using a slotted spoon, transfer the bacon to paper towels to drain.

2. Divide the beef into 6 portions, just over 5 ounces each. Pat each portion into a ½-inch patty and season with salt and pepper.

{continued}

3. Prepare a fire in the grill, spreading the coals evenly for direct-heat cooking. Grill the burgers over medium-high heat until cooked to your liking, 3 to 4 minutes per side for medium-rare. In the last minute of cooking, put a piece of cheese on each patty. Meanwhile, toast the buns briefly until slightly charred.

4. Place the burgers on the bun bottoms and top with 1 or 2 beef bacon slices. Serve with a dill pickle on the side.

Burger Buns

Made from dough enriched with butter and milk, this recipe yields buns with a soft, chewy texture and small crumb. You could easily use the same recipe to make dinner rolls for other occasions. I weigh the ingredients and the portions of dough for the most consistency, but I have provided volume measurements as well for convenience. And while I opt for fresh yeast (also called cake yeast)—which many bakers say is the most reliable form of commercial yeast—I've also provided instructions for using active dry yeast. If you do buy fresh yeast, which is sold in blocks at some specialty grocery stores, it needs to be stored in the refrigerator.

makes 10 buns

1 ounce / 30 grams fresh yeast
(or 2 teaspoons active dry yeast)
11^1/$_4$ ounces / 320 grams / 1^1/$_4$ cups milk, at room temperature (70°F)
10^2/$_3$ ounces / 303 grams / 2^1/$_2$ cups bread flour

8^2/$_3$ ounces / 246 grams / 2 cups cake flour
1^1/$_3$ ounces / 39 grams / ^{1}/$_8$ cup plus 2 tablespoons sugar
1 tablespoon kosher salt

2^2/$_3$ ounces / 75 grams / 5^1/$_2$ tablespoons unsalted butter, cubed, at slightly colder than room temperature (60°F)
1 large egg, lightly beaten with a splash of water

1. In the bowl of a stand mixer, stir the fresh yeast into the milk until dissolved. (If using active dry yeast, add the yeast to the milk. Do not stir. Let stand 5 minutes.)

2. In a separate mixer bowl, mix together the flours and sugar. Add about one-third of the flour mixture to the yeast slurry and mix on low speed with the dough hook until a paste forms. Stir in the rest of the flour and the salt and mix on medium-low speed for 4 minutes or until smooth.

3. Turn the mixer to low speed and gradually add the cubes of butter to the dough as it mixes. Once all the butter has been added, continue to mix on low speed until the dough is smooth and pulls away from the sides of the mixing bowl, about 5 minutes. Remove the dough hook and cover the mixing bowl with plastic wrap. Let the dough rise at room temperature until doubled in size, about 1^1/$_2$ hours.

4. Lightly oil 2 baking sheets or line them with parchment paper.

5. Transfer the dough to a lightly floured counter. Using a knife or bench scraper and a scale, portion the dough into 3^1/$_2$-ounce pieces, around the size of a heaping ^{1}/$_2$ cup. To form each ball, cup the palm of your hand around the top of the piece of dough and move your hand in a circle until the friction of the counter and your hand

shape the dough into a ball. (Too much flour on the counter will make it difficult for enough friction to form between the dough and the counter. If this happens, wipe the counter with a damp cloth.)

6. Place on the prepared baking sheet, 5 dough balls per sheet. Cover with slightly damp kitchen towels or linen napkins and let the balls rise at room temperature until they have grown by about a third in size, about 35 minutes.

7. Preheat the oven to 350°F. Gently press the balls to flatten them slightly, then brush the tops with the egg wash. Bake, rotating the baking sheets halfway through, until the tops are evenly browned and the bread is baked through, about 30 minutes. Cool for at least 30 minutes. The buns will keep, sealed in a plastic bag, for 3 days at room temperature. Alternatively, slice them in half and freeze for future use.

GRILLED *and* PICKLED SUMMER SQUASH SALAD

With casual menus, I like to offer vegetable side dishes that can be left on the table for nibbling while the rest of the meal comes together. This is an ideal place to pair fresh vegetables with their pickled counterparts. The acidity and flavor from the vinegar and the smoke from the grilled squash are lively enough to stand out at room temperature.

1 pound assorted summer squash (such as zucchini and yellow squash), halved lengthwise

Kosher salt and freshly ground black pepper

Extra-virgin olive oil, for drizzling

2 cups Pickled and Spiced Summer Squash (page 43), drained and pickling liquid reserved

1 cup loosely packed mixed fresh herbs (any combination of picked chervil, wood sorrel, mint, and parsley leaves)

1/3 cup crumbled sheep's milk feta cheese

1. Prepare a fire in the grill, spreading the coals evenly for direct-heat cooking. Place the fresh summer squash halves on a baking sheet and season with salt and pepper. Drizzle with enough olive oil to lightly coat the vegetables, then grill over medium-high heat until lightly charred and al dente, 3 minutes per side. Once the vegetables are cool enough to handle, slice them into 1/2-inch pieces and transfer to a bowl.

2. Slice the pickled summer squash into pieces roughly as big as the grilled squash. Add to the bowl with the grilled squash and drizzle with a few tablespoons of olive oil until the pickled and grilled vegetables are lightly coated. Add 1 to 2 tablespoons of the pickling liquid and the herbs and mix together. Taste the salad and adjust the seasoning with more salt, pepper, or pickling liquid as needed. Sprinkle the feta on top.

PICKLED CELERY ROOT REMOULADE

You can think of this condiment as a kind of tartar sauce made with mild pickled celery root. It is terrific on burgers but also makes a nice accompaniment to a side of grilled salmon. You could also mix it with sliced boiled potatoes and diced fennel for a sophisticated potato salad. When making the remoulade, it's important to start with a thick mayonnaise base. Once the celery root and brine have been mixed in, the condiment thins out.

makes about 2¹/₂ cups

1 large egg
1 large egg yolk
2 cloves garlic
Juice and grated zest of ¹/₂ lemon
2 tablespoons pickling liquid from
   Pickled Celery Root (page 51)

About 1¹/₂ cups grapeseed oil
Kosher salt and freshly ground
   black pepper
2 cups Pickled Celery Root (page 51),
   drained

¹/₂ cup minced Dill Pickles (page 30)
1 cup loosely packed mixed fresh herbs
   (any combination of chives, dill
   sprigs, tarragon, and parsley leaves),
   coarsely chopped

1. In a food processor blend together the egg, yolk, garlic, lemon juice and zest, and pickling liquid. While the processor is on, gradually drizzle in 1 cup of the oil until it becomes thick. If it is still on the looser side, drizzle in an additional ¹/₄ cup oil. (The oil and egg will bind together to form an emulsion. If the emulsion breaks and the mixture loses its creamy consistency, pour the mixture in a liquid measuring cup, add another egg yolk to the food processor, and drizzle in the broken mixture as if it were oil.) Season with salt and pepper. You will have more than 2 cups of mayonnaise.

2. Transfer the mayonnaise to a bowl. Using a spatula, fold in the pickled celery root, dill pickles, and herbs. Taste and adjust the seasoning with salt, pepper, or more pickling liquid. Refrigerate until ready to serve.

HOT PEPPER SAUCE

A dab of this hot sauce will enliven just about anything off the grill. Along with lime juice and cilantro, it's also a great condiment to have on hand when making tacos.

makes 1³/₄ cups

1 cup drained Grilled and Pickled Hot
    Peppers (page 37)
¹/₂ cup loosely packed cilantro sprigs
Juice and grated zest of 2 limes

¹/₂ cup grapeseed oil
Kosher salt
Freshly ground black pepper (optional)

In a food processor or blender, pulse together the peppers, cilantro, and lime juice and zest. While the processor is running, drizzle in the oil until the ingredients form an emulsified dipping sauce. Adjust the seasoning with a few pinches of salt and pepper, if desired.

SUMMER BERRY SODA FLOATS

Grill-outs are all about simple pleasures, and what's not to like about a soda float on a hot afternoon? For a more adult version, I use more soda and less cream. Leftover berry syrup will keep in the refrigerator for about a month.

3 pounds berries (raspberries,
    blackberries, sliced strawberries,
    or a combination), plus extra berries
    for garnish

¹/₂ cup granulated sugar
1 cup heavy cream
2 tablespoons confectioners' sugar

About 12 ounces soda water
About 1 quart vanilla ice cream

1. Refrigerate 6 tall glasses. In a large heavy-bottomed pot over medium-high heat, mix together the berries and the granulated sugar. Bring to a boil, cover, and decrease to a brisk simmer. Cook until the fruit has released its juices and forms a syrup, about 7 minutes for smaller berries and 10 minutes for strawberries. Strain the berries through a fine-mesh strainer and let the syrup cool.

2. With a whisk or using a stand mixer fitted with the whisk attachment, whip the heavy cream with the confectioners' sugar until it forms soft peaks. Keep chilled.

3. To assemble the floats, pour ¹/₄ cup berry juice into each glass, followed by ¹/₄ to ¹/₂ cup soda water and 1 to 2 scoops vanilla ice cream. Top with the whipped cream and garnish with fresh berries.

A MIDSUMMER MEAL

PICKLED AND FRESH SUMMER
BEAN SALAD WITH PRESERVED
TOMATO VINAIGRETTE • 185

FRIED CHICKEN WITH CHERRY
BOMB PEPPER SAUSAGE GRAVY
AND DROP BISCUITS • 186

CHERRY CLAFOUTIS WITH
MILK JAM • 189

{ this *Menu* serves 4 }

Everyone has that one meal that makes regular, welcome appearances on the table. Some have meatloaf, others have stir-fry. When I was growing up, we had fried chicken.

Once a month or so, my mom would pull out the sturdy cast-iron pan, dredge buttermilk-marinated chicken in flour, and fry up pieces until they were crisp and golden. On extremely hot days, she'd fry the chicken the day before and serve it cold. Other days, she'd stir up a simple gravy with a bit of flour and some pan drippings. Served either way, her fried chicken always had me coming back for seconds.

I've since adapted my mom's basic recipe to incorporate pickles. I soak the chicken overnight in a marinade of buttermilk mixed with the summer bean pickling brine, which gives the meat slightly more tang than buttermilk alone. Sausage gravy may sound heavy for summer eating, but not when it's balanced by sweet, piquant cherry bomb peppers. I make my own sausage mix for the gravy, which is easier than it sounds with the help of a meat grinder. To sop up excess gravy, I serve a batch of simple drop biscuits. But I don't change my mom's method for frying: a cast-iron pan, which conducts heat effectively, allows me to get that irresistible crunchy coating.

You might think that the bean salad is on this menu to make me feel better about serving fried chicken, but it's a lot more than a requisite serving of vegetables. Using pickled and fresh versions of the same ingredient is something I do often, but it is an especially good way to serve green and wax beans. The sharpness of the pickled beans gives life to the tame fresh beans, and the zingy tomato vinaigrette is a standout on its own. When paired with the rich chicken, the beans add balance to the plate.

When the table is cleared of dinner plates, it's time to bring out the clafoutis. Light, easy to make, and an ideal vehicle for fruit, a classic clafoutis is practically an essential summertime dessert. I use preserved fruit, such as brandied cherries, but a handful of blackberries or pitted fresh cherries is just as satisfying.

PICKLED *and* FRESH SUMMER BEAN SALAD
with PRESERVED TOMATO VINAIGRETTE

I'm picky about beans, but the local tender green and wax varieties sold in the summer are a true treat. More delicate than the tough-skinned versions that hang out year-round at the grocery store, these mild vegetables readily soak up seasonings. They're also crowd pleasers, even among pickier eaters.

This recipe makes more tomato vinaigrette than you need for the salad, but the vinaigrette keeps well in the refrigerator for about a week. I often use it on green salads or with grilled zucchini and roasted peppers. Pictured on pages 182 and 183.

1 cup Sweet Pickled Cherry Tomatoes (page 44), in pickling liquid
1 cup extra-virgin olive oil
Kosher salt and freshly ground black pepper

1 pound summer beans (preferably a combination of green and wax beans), ends trimmed
1 pint Pickled Summer Beans (page 42), drained, pickling liquid reserved for the fried chicken marinade (page 186)

2 cups loosely packed fresh herbs (such as chervil, tarragon, parsley, and sliced chives)
Block of pecorino cheese, for shaving

1. To make the vinaigrette, in a blender or food processor, blend the cherry tomatoes and pickling liquid. Blend in the olive oil and season with salt and pepper. Taste, adjusting with more pickling liquid or seasoning if needed. This makes about 2 cups of vinaigrette, which is more than you will need for this recipe.

2. To cook the beans, bring a large pot of salted water to a boil. Blanch the beans for 4 minutes, drain, and spread onto a baking sheet to cool to room temperature.

3. To assemble the salad, in a large bowl, mix the cooked beans with the pickled beans, herbs, and enough vinaigrette to coat the beans evenly (about ¼ cup). Transfer the salad to a large serving bowl. Using a vegetable peeler, shave a few pieces of pecorino over the top.

FRIED CHICKEN *with* CHERRY BOMB PEPPER SAUSAGE GRAVY *and* DROP BISCUITS

I use a whole bird for fried chicken. When butchering the bird, I keep part of the breast bone and ribs attached to the breast portions so the meat doesn't dry out as much when it fries. Still, I prefer dark meat for fried chicken, so I sacrifice one of the breasts for the sausage gravy. When I'm frying chicken for a crowd, I occasionally set up a smoker or wood-fired grill. After the chicken has been seared on both sides, I put the pieces in the smoker or grill to finish cooking while I sear the remaining pieces. The chicken won't be quite as crispy, but it absorbs delicious smoky flavors.

2¹/₂ cups buttermilk
About 1 cup pickling liquid from
 1 pint jar of Pickled Summer Beans
 (page 42)
1 (4- to 5-pound) roasting chicken, cut
 into pieces (2 wings, 2 thighs, 2 legs,
 and 2 breasts)

2 cups all-purpose flour
1 tablespoon smoked sweet paprika
1 teaspoon dried tarragon
1 teaspoon garlic powder
1 teaspoon freshly ground black pepper
Vegetable oil, for frying
Kosher salt

Cherry Bomb Pepper Sausage Gravy
 (recipe follows), for serving
Drop Biscuits (recipe follows), for serving

1. In a large bowl, mix the buttermilk and pickling liquid together. Coat the chicken in the marinade, cover, and refrigerate overnight.

2. In a large bowl mix together the flour, paprika, tarragon, garlic powder, and black pepper. Drain the chicken. Set aside 1 breast for the gravy. Cut the remaining breast in half and transfer, along with the remaining pieces, to the bowl. Coat the pieces in the flour mixture, patting off any excess, and place in a single layer on a baking sheet.

3. Preheat the oven to 350°F. Meanwhile, heat the frying oil. Pour 1 inch of oil into a large cast-iron pan over medium-high heat. Once the oil begins to shimmer on the surface, fry the chicken pieces in batches to avoid crowding the pan. Once the pieces are brown and crispy on one side, about 3 minutes, using tongs turn the pieces over and brown the other side, another 2 minutes. If the oil drops significantly between batches, add more oil and let it heat up before adding more pieces. Transfer the fried chicken to a baking sheet, season with salt, and bake until the chicken is cooked through, about 20 minutes.

4. To serve, place the fried chicken on a platter and spoon the gravy over the top. Serve with a basket of warm biscuits on the side.

Cherry Bomb Pepper Sausage Gravy

Although this gravy is not complicated, it takes some preparation. The weight of the chicken breast used will determine how much bacon you need for the sausage. Have about five ounces on hand, though you might not need all of it. You can also use pork fatback instead of bacon for a subtler flavor. The sausage won't be stuffed into a casing, but you will need a grinder to grind the meat and seasonings together. (A meat grinding attachment for a stand mixer will do the job.) You also can elect to grind the chicken heart and liver into the sausage mixture. Before grinding, ensure that all of the ingredients are thoroughly chilled. After grinding, it's important to knead the ground meat briefly to give the lean breast meat an opportunity to bond with the fat.

makes about 3 cups

1 (6 to 9-ounce) chicken breast, boned, skinned, and cubed

4¹/₂ ounces bacon or pork fatback

1 chicken heart (optional)

1 chicken liver (optional)

1 clove garlic, minced

1 tablespoon chopped fresh sage

1 teaspoon fennel seeds, toasted in a dry pan and ground

¹/₂ teaspoon freshly ground black pepper

¹/₂ teaspoon kosher salt

2 tablespoons grapeseed oil

2 tablespoons all-purpose flour

1 sweet onion (such as candy or Vidalia), chopped

1 cup Chicken Stock (page 130)

1 cup whole milk

¹/₄ to ¹/₂ cup Pickled Cherry Bomb Peppers (page 36), sliced

1. Weigh the cubed breast meat—it should be between 6 and 9 ounces. Weigh out half as much bacon and dice it. In a bowl toss the breast cubes and bacon with the heart and liver (if using), garlic, sage, fennel, black pepper, and salt. Fit the meat grinder with a coarse plate and pass the mixture through the grinder into a mixing bowl. Using your hands, knead the mixture until it is tacky to the touch, about 2 minutes.

2. In a large cast-iron pan or Dutch oven over medium heat, warm the grapeseed oil. Brown the sausage, breaking the meat into small pieces with a spoon until nearly cooked through, about 7 minutes. Stir in the flour and cook, stirring often, for 3 minutes until a light roux forms. Mix in the onion and cook 1 minute more. Whisk in the chicken broth and milk. Bring to a boil, decrease to a simmer, and cook until the gravy has thickened and has lost the starchy texture from the flour, about 15 minutes. To finish, stir in the cherry bomb peppers (fewer if you want a mild gravy, more if you like spice) and season with more salt and pepper if needed.

Drop Biscuits

makes 30 biscuits

2³/4 cups plus 1 tablespoon
    all-purpose flour
²/3 cup cornmeal
2 tablespoons minced fresh sage

1 tablespoon baking powder
2 teaspoons baking soda
¹/2 teaspoon kosher salt
¹/2 cup cold unsalted butter, cubed

¹/4 cup lard (or an additional ¹/4 cup
    cold butter, cubed)
1¹/2 cups buttermilk, plus a few extra
    tablespoons to brush on top

1. Preheat the oven to 400°F. Oil 2 baking sheets or line with parchment paper.

2. In a large bowl, whisk together the flour, cornmeal, sage, baking powder, baking soda, and salt. Using your fingers, rub the butter and lard into the flour until it forms a coarse, crumbly mixture. Stir in the buttermilk and mix briefly, just until a tacky, stiff dough forms.

3. Using a large spoon, drop 1-ounce portions (about 2 heaping tablespoons) of dough onto the prepared pans. Brush the tops with buttermilk and bake until the biscuits are golden brown and baked through, about 16 minutes.

CHERRY CLAFOUTIS *with* MILK JAM

Almond meal yields a slightly denser clafoutis than an all flour version. Like crepe batter, I let the clafoutis batter sit overnight in the refrigerator before baking.

makes 1 clafoutis

1 cup heavy cream
3 large eggs
¹/4 cup sugar
1 or 2 vanilla beans

1 cup almond meal
¹/4 cup all-purpose flour
¹/2 teaspoon kosher salt

12 ounces Brandied Cherries (page 68)
1 cup Milk Jam (page 124)

1. In a bowl, whisk together the cream, eggs, and sugar. Split the vanilla beans in half and scrape out the seeds with the tip of a spoon. Mix in the seeds, then whisk in the almond meal, flour, and salt. Add the vanilla bean pods, cover, and refrigerate overnight.

2. Preheat the oven to 325°F. Butter an 8-inch round ceramic baking pan or pie pan. Remove the vanilla bean pods. Give the batter a good stir and pour half into the prepared pan. Dot with cherries, then pour in the remaining batter. Bake until the batter has set and the top is nicely brown, 35 to 40 minutes.

3. To serve, cut the clafoutis into wedges. Whisk the milk jam and spoon over each serving.

ON THE FARM

CHICKEN LIVER MOUSSE WITH
ARUGULA, CURRANT MOSTARDA,
AND GRILLED BREAD • 193

WHITEFISH ESCABECHE
WITH EGGPLANT-TOMATO
VINAIGRETTE • 195

TOMATO JAM–GLAZED
BARBECUED GOAT • 198

BRAISED LIMA BEANS • 200

CRISPY KALE • 200

PEACH SORBET WITH LEMON
VERBENA CORDIAL • 201

RASPBERRY BROWN BUTTER CAKE
WITH YOGURT ICE CREAM AND
ELDERFLOWERS • 202

{ this *Menu* serves 6 }

Midwesterners never take summer for granted. When you spend almost half of the year under a canopy of snow, the months of June, July, and August take on special significance. During the summer months, an entire population, from Missouri to Michigan, takes to the outdoors, colonizing rivers and lakes and stocking up on enough vitamin D to get them through the following winter.

When I was growing up, summer meant the usual activities: fishing, hiking, and grilling. At Vie, summer is our season for farm dinners. We shut down operations for a day, pack our knives, and pay a visit to our sources of ingredients—and inspiration. Our destinations have varied, from Elkhorn, Wisconsin, where the Dietzlers raise the beef we serve, to Champaign, Illiniois, and Prairie Fruits Farm, where our goat's and sheep's milk cheeses come from.

Though casual, these aren't paper-plate affairs. Real plates and glassware adorn place settings. There might even be tablecloths. On the Dietzler's property one year, I set up a fully functioning kitchen in the middle of an alfalfa field. A change of venue has its advantages. I often find cooking on a farm ideal for preparations that I don't serve often at Vie, like slow-cooked goat glazed with tomato jam. I can afford to be bold, offering tangy vinegar-marinated fish, chicken liver mousse with grilled bread, and freshly shucked lima beans. I will even supply freshly churned ice cream if I have access to a freezer.

Maybe it's because food tastes better outside, but these farm dinners always seem to magnify the flavors of ingredients. Arugula tastes more peppery, raspberries sweeter. There is also the fun of spending time with staff away from our kitchen. We play fast and loose with menu ideas, and we interact with the crowd, becoming a more significant part of the meal than when we stay planted behind a kitchen door. With a long table set in the field, hardwood charcoal smoldering in a grill, and cicadas buzzing in the clover, cooking on a farm is about as close as one can get to summer culinary nirvana.

These are not necessarily complicated meals, but they are meant to show thought and respect for the surroundings. The dishes on this menu also can be mixed and matched to suit the event. If a light lunch is the goal, the whitefish escabeche served with sides of lima beans and crispy kale suffices. If a hearty meal is warranted, serve the chicken liver mousse followed by the tender, smoky goat. If goat isn't your thing, make fried chicken (page 186) instead. But when it comes to dessert, don't skip the brown butter cake—it is delicious for almost any occasion.

CHICKEN LIVER MOUSSE *with* ARUGULA, CURRANT MOSTARDA, *and* GRILLED BREAD

Silky and rich, this recipe takes chicken livers and gussies them up with a spoonful of currant mostarda. The most complicated part of this recipe is tracking down fatback. Since we buy whole hogs at Vie, we usually have more than enough to go around. So should a good butcher. Some butchers will sell fatback trimmed from the loin or shoulder if you ask.

When you have fatback in hand, plan on working a few days ahead. First, soak the livers overnight in milk to draw out some of the blood. The next day, marinate the livers. On day three, blend the livers and marinade with blanched fatback, eggs, and cream. For easy serving, bake the mousse in ramekins, allowing about four hours for the mousse to set up. When I bake this mousse in a terrine, I add pink salt to prevent the slices from turning gray. I've omitted the pink salt here since slicing isn't necessary. This chicken liver mousse goes well with several other preserves. Try it with Grape Aigre-Doux (page 94): strain the liquid into a small pot, reduce the liquid by half, and then mix in the grapes. Pictured on page 194.

1 pound chicken livers	1/4 teaspoon ground cinnamon	6 slices country bread
Whole milk, for marinating	1/4 teaspoon ground nutmeg	1/4 sweet onion, preferably candy or
1/3 cup port	1 large egg	Vidalia (optional)
2 shallots, minced	1 large egg yolk	4 ounces arugula
1 teaspoon kosher salt, plus extra	5 ounces heavy cream	1 cup Currant Mostarda (page 96)
for finishing	5 ounces fatback, cubed	
1/2 teaspoon freshly ground black pepper	Extra-virgin olive oil	

1. Trim the veins and any discolored patches from the livers with a sharp paring knife. Put the livers in a bowl and pour in just enough milk to cover. Cover the livers and refrigerate overnight. The next day, drain the livers (discarding the milk), then mix them with the port, shallots, 1 teaspoon of the salt, the pepper, cinnamon, and nutmeg. Cover and refrigerate overnight.

2. Preheat the oven to 300°F. Line a 16-ounce loaf pan with plastic wrap or lightly oil six 1-cup ramekins.

3. Place the livers, marinade, egg, and yolk in a food processor. In a small pot, bring the cream to a simmer and remove from the heat. In a pot of boiling water, blanch the fatback for 1 minute. Drain and transfer to the food processor. Pulse the livers and fat together until a coarse purée forms. While the food processor is running, drizzle in the cream and continue to blend until smooth.

4. Using a spatula, pass the mousse through a fine-mesh strainer and spoon into the loaf pan or ramekins. Cover the loaf pan or the ramekins with aluminum foil and place in a deep roasting pan. Fill the pan with water halfway up the sides of the loaf pan or ramekins and bake until set, about 1 1/2 hours for the loaf pan, 40 minutes for

{continued}

the ramekins. (To check for doneness, uncover a ramekin or a corner of the loaf pan and insert a thermometer into the center. It should register 155°F.) Remove from the roasting pan and let cool completely. Refrigerate overnight, or until the mousse is firm.

5. To serve the mousse, brush olive oil evenly on both sides of the bread. If you have access to a grill, preferably one that is wood-fired, you can grill the bread over medium-low heat, about 1 minute per side. Otherwise, preheat the oven to 450°F. Arrange the bread on a baking sheet and toast until golden, 3 to 5 minutes.

6. To serve, using a mandoline or a very sharp knife, shave the onion into thin slices and season with a pinch of salt (if using). Divide the arugula among 6 plates and top with the onion slices. Place a piece of toasted bread on each plate, followed by a spoonful of mostarda. If using the loaf pan, invert the pan onto a cutting board and remove the pan and plastic wrap. Warm a sharp knife under hot water and dry it off. Slice into ¹/₂-inch pieces and divide among the plates. If using ramekins, place a ramekin on each plate.

WHITEFISH ESCABECHE *with* EGGPLANT-TOMATO VINAIGRETTE

Escabeche, a Mediterranean preparation in which the fish is first fried and later marinated, provides a simple way to serve fish as an appetizer. It works well with mild whitefish from the Great Lakes but it also is a great way to prepare sea bass as well as oily fish such as mackerel and sardines (while I remove the skin from whitefish or sea bass, for mackerel or sardines I recommend leaving the skin on). Not only can the fish be served at room temperature, it also can be made a day ahead of time. The key is the flavor of the marinade. I reach for a jar of eggplant-tomato relish, which has enough vinegar, garlic, and herbs to be pleasantly pungent, even when served at cooler temperatures. Pictured on page 196.

1¹/₂ pounds skinned lake whitefish fillets or sea bass	¹/₄ cup vegetable oil	1 pound green and wax beans, trimmed
¹/₂ teaspoon kosher salt	1 cup Eggplant-Tomato Relish (page 32)	A handful of fresh basil leaves, larger ones torn
²/₃ cup rice flour	1 cup extra-virgin olive oil	

1. To make the fish, first line a plate with paper towels. Season the fish with salt, then dredge through the flour. Shake off any excess. In a large sauté pan over medium-high heat, warm about 2 tablespoons of the vegetable oil. Fry half of the fish until cooked through, about 2 minutes per side, and transfer to the prepared plate. Add the remaining 2 tablespoons oil to the pan and fry the remaining fish. Transfer the fish to a rimmed platter.

{continued}

2. In a small bowl, whisk together the relish and the olive oil. Taste, adding more salt if needed. Pour the relish over the fish and let marinate. Alternatively, cover and refrigerate the escabeche, then serve the following day after bringing it to room temperature.

3. To prepare the beans, bring a large pot of salted water to a boil. Blanch the beans for 4 minutes, drain, and spread onto a baking sheet to cool to room temperature. Season the beans with salt and pepper, then drizzle with some of the juices from the eggplant.

4. To serve, divide the fish among 6 plates, spooning the beans, basil, and relish on top of each piece.

THE DRAW OF SMOKE

Vie has never pretended to be a barbecue restaurant. While I might prepare the occasional slow-smoked pork shoulder for a special dinner, I primarily use smoke as a flavoring agent for meat, fish, and vegetables. I wouldn't go so far as to say that smoke acts as a preservative the way I apply it, but I like the way it lends a sweet, earthy flavor to foods I preserve, like beef bacon or pickled onions. In the past I used a stovetop smoker for smaller projects, but I wanted an effective way to infuse smoke into ingredients on a slightly bigger scale. To get the right rig for the job, I turned to two experts: my brother Tom, and Gary Wiviott, the author of *Low & Slow: Master the Art of Barbecue in 5 Easy Lessons.*

My brother Tom lives in North Carolina, where sauce is tomato-free and applied sparingly. Visiting Tom means eating smoky meat with perfect bark—the dark, crispy, caramelized crust that forms on the best barbecues.

Both Gary and Tom agreed that an inexpensive Weber Smokey Mountain would meet my smoking needs at Vie. The short cylindrical contraption, which looks as high tech as a homemade spaceship, is practical for a few key reasons. It's easy to assemble. Once it is up and smoking, there's no need to baby it. And it is capable of smoking for several hours. If I plan it right, I can smoke ingredients in succession, from onions to sturgeon to bacon, in one afternoon. I've even made magic with top round by smoking it for a couple of hours.

The smoker comes in three parts. The bottom charcoal basin holds the hardwood lump charcoal and the wood pieces (charcoal briquettes aren't happening here). The tall cylindrical center fits a metal bowl for water and a top and bottom grate. A domed lid covers the top. To get started, you build a fire in a chimney starter with a mix of newspaper and charcoal, then you dump the smoldering coals on top of more charcoal and a few wood pieces. After putting the center cylinder over the charcoal basin, you need to fill the bowl with water and wait about 10 minutes for the smoke to settle down. Then you add your meat, fish, or vegetable, cover the smoker with a lid, and make sure that both vents (the top one on the lid and the bottom one in the charcoal basin) are open. In Tomato Jam–Glazed Barbecue Goat (page 198), I include more detailed set-up information.

There are several other fine barbecue-enabling contraptions out there, and Gary shares tips for rigging a regular kettle grill for smoking in his book. For the recipes in this book, you can use any smoking device you'd like. But since I am most familiar with the Weber Smokey Mountain, my instructions for slow smoking (which are based on Gary's recommendations) are tailored to its specifications. Make adjustments to the process to best suit your smoker.

TOMATO JAM–GLAZED BARBECUED GOAT

This recipe is something of a hybrid: it takes guidance from classic slow-cooked barbecue, but it is finished in the oven. Goat meat responds well to both smoke and slow cooking, and its lean muscles abandon any stringy toughness after four hours in a smoker. But since it's much leaner than pork shoulder or brisket, it also benefits from being finished in an oven with a tangy glaze to prevent it from becoming too dry. The smoky, lip-smacking goat and sweet glaze only get better when served with a side of braised lima beans.

Cooking meat this way takes time and care, but it is not difficult once you have the smoker set-up down. Allow three days to make this recipe. On day one, season the leg with the rub. On day two, smoke and then braise the leg. On the last day, finish the leg in the oven with the sauce. To slow-cook the goat in a smoker, you will need hardwood lump charcoal, which is available at some grocery stores and most hardware stores, as well as 3- to 5-inch chunks of untreated wood, like cherry, apple, or hickory, also available at hardware stores. For more on barbecue, see The Draw of Smoke, page 197.

GOAT
1 teaspoon fennel seeds
1/2 teaspoon black peppercorns
1 allspice berry
1 dried red Indian chile or 2 or 3 dried
  Mexican pequin chiles
1 1/2 teaspoons kosher salt

1 teaspoon mustard powder
1 teaspoon sweet smoked paprika
1 teaspoon sumac
1 teaspoon garlic powder
1 (4-pound) bone-in goat leg, shank
  removed, trimmed of visible silverskin

GLAZE
1 cup apple cider vinegar
1 sweet onion (such as candy or Vidalia),
  thinly sliced
2 cups Tomato Jam (page 48)
Kosher salt

1. To make the spice rub for the goat, in a dry sauté pan over medium-low heat, toast the fennel seeds, peppercorns, allspice berry, and dried chile until fragrant, about 1 minute. In a spice grinder or in a mortar with a pestle, grind the spices together. Mix in the salt, mustard powder, paprika, sumac, and garlic powder. Rub the goat leg with the spices, then cover and refrigerate overnight or up to 3 days.

2. Prepare a smoker: Remove the lid and the large center cylinder. Open the vent in the charcoal basin, ensuring that the holes aren't blocked by bits of charcoal or ash. Place the center ring down and the charcoal chamber on top of it. Fill the chamber halfway up with hardwood charcoal.

3. Set up the chimney starter: Put about 3 sheets of crumpled newspaper at the base of a heavy-duty chimney starter. Place the chimney on a grate or a heat-proof surface that allows air to flow into its base (a spare kettle grill works well) and light the paper on about 3 sides. After 5 to 10 minutes, the charcoal should start to catch fire, begin to glow red, and turn ashen around the edges.

4. Dump the hot contents of the chimney over the unlit charcoal and use metal tongs to pick up any pieces that stray to the sides. Once the smoke subsides, place three 3- to 5-inch wood chunks on the charcoal.

5. Reassemble the smoker: Return the center cylinder (which should be fitted with a water bowl and two grates) on top of the charcoal basin. With a heat-proof pitcher or watering can, gently pour water through the grates into the bowl, trying not to splash the coals underneath, until it is nearly full. Once the smoke has subsided, about 5 minutes later, put the goat on the top grate and cover with the lid, ensuring that the vent is open.

6. Smoke the goat for about 4 hours between 225°F and 250°F, checking only periodically to ensure the coals are still burning (the less you open the lid, the more smoke stays with the meat). If, for any reason, the charcoal goes out too soon, start another chimney of charcoal. If the pan dries up, leave it alone—the temperature may get a little hotter, but it will be fine for the time the goat is in the smoker. After 4 hours, the goat should be dark brown, slightly crispy on the edges, and tender but not falling part when pierced with a fork.

7. To continue cooking the goat, preheat the oven to 300°F. Line a roasting pan with a rack. Transfer the goat to the prepared pan and add about 2 cups of water to the pan (just enough to cover the bottom of the pan by about $^1/_2$ inch). Cover with aluminum foil and bake until the meat is nearly falling off the bone, 2 to 3 hours. Cool the goat leg in its juices (you should have $1^1/_2$ to 2 cups of juice) and refrigerate overnight to allow the meat to marinate in the juices and soak up flavor.

8. To prepare the glaze, preheat the oven to 350°F. In a saucepan reduce the apple cider vinegar with the onion until almost dry. Remove the goat leg from its juices and pour the juices into the saucepan. Reduce the glaze by half, then stir in the tomato jam. Continue to simmer until the glaze coats the back of a spoon, a few minutes. Season with salt, if needed.

9. To finish the goat, transfer the goat leg to a roasting pan and brush half of the glaze generously over the top. Cover with aluminum foil and bake until the meat is hot all the way through, about 35 minutes. Remove the foil, increase the oven temperature to 400°F, and roast until the tomato jam is caramelized, 5 to 8 minutes. Brush the rest of the glaze on top and transfer to a platter to serve family-style (on or off the bone).

BRAISED LIMA BEANS

Baked in tomato sauce and cheese, lima bean casseroles used to be common. At some point, though, limas became old news, crowded out by garbanzos, cannellini, fava, and cranberry beans. Yet I still like the way this flat, starchy legume can hold its own in a sturdy side dish. When fresh shelling beans start arriving at the market in early summer, I keep an eye out for limas. When shucked right out of the pod and cooked soon after, they have a creamy texture that absorbs the flavor of fresh herbs. Although adding a Parmesan rind or two to the pot is optional, a hint of cheese is a pleasant throwback to those classic casseroles.

I buy up fresh limas when they're available, freezing extra shucked beans for use down the road. If fresh beans are nowhere to be found, you can make the same dish with dried. Use 1 cup of dried beans and slowly simmer them in 4 cups of water until cooked through. Drain the beans, reserving 1 cup of water. Next, follow the recipe, using that reserved cup of water instead of the 2 cups of stock called for below.

1/4 cup extra-virgin olive oil	5 cloves garlic, sliced	2 cups chicken stock (page 130),
2 tablespoons unsalted butter	1 teaspoon chopped fresh thyme	vegetable stock, or water
1 sweet onion (such as candy or	1 teaspoon chopped fresh sage	1 to 3 rinds Parmesan cheese (optional)
Vidalia), diced	2 bay leaves	Kosher salt and freshly ground
1 carrot, diced	2 pounds fresh lima bean pods, shelled	black pepper
1 stalk celery, diced	(about 2 cups shelled beans)	

Warm the olive oil and butter in a pot over medium heat. Stir in the onion, carrot, celery, and garlic and cook until softened, about 3 minutes. Add the thyme, sage, and bay leaves and simmer a minute more. Stir in the lima beans and cook 2 minutes more. Pour in the stock, add the Parmesan rinds, and bring to a boil. Decrease to a simmer and cook until the lima beans are tender (the mixture will be brothy). Season to taste with salt and pepper. Remove the Parmesan rinds before serving.

CRISPY KALE

There are two ways to achieve this addictive, crispy kale. The first is frying, which is the best way to get evenly crisp, crinkly leaves. The second is baking, which makes the cleanup much easier. I've supplied both methods below. Both versions need to be served immediately.

2 bunches Tuscan kale
Vegetable or olive oil
Sea salt

1. Using your hands, tear the leaves away from the tough stems. Slice the stems into thin disks.

2. To fry the kale, first line a plate with paper towels. In a shallow pot over medium heat, warm 1 inch of vegetable oil until it shimmers, about 350°F. In batches, fry the leaves until they become crisp, about 30 seconds. Using a wire skimmer, transfer the leaves to the prepared plate and season with salt. Add the stems and fry until they soften. Using a slotted spoon or wire skimmer, transfer the stems to the same plate and season with salt.

3. If baking the kale instead, preheat the oven to 400°F. Using your hands, mix the kale leaves thoroughly with about 1/4 cup olive oil. Distribute the leaves evenly between 2 baking sheets and bake, rotating the pans once, until the leaves are crispy, 12 to 15 minutes. Once crisp, season with salt. To cook the stems, in a sauté pan over medium-high heat, warm 1 tablespoon olive oil. Saute the stems until soft, about 5 minutes, and season with salt. Serve with the crispy leaves.

PEACH SORBET *with* LEMON VERBENA CORDIAL

A spoonful of peach sorbet melting in a splash of lemon verbena cordial is a pretty ideal way to transition a summer meal into dessert. When cooking the sorbet base, I keep the skins on the peaches—they add color and impart a slight bitterness that balances the sugars in the fruit (though you could remove the skins if you prefer a lighter, sweeter result). Either fresh or frozen peaches work in this sorbet. Make the purée the day before freezing; this allows time for the flavors to deepen.

makes about 1 quart

1 pound, 4 ounces peach slices
1/2 cup honey
1/2 cup water

Juice of 1/2 lemon
Lemon Verbena Cordial (page 214),
    for serving

1. Place the peaches in a medium pot over medium heat. Stir in the honey, water, and lemon juice and bring to a simmer. Cover, decrease the heat, and cook until the peaches are tender, about 20 minutes. Pour the peaches and juices into a blender and purée until completely smooth. Refrigerate overnight.

2. Pour the sorbet base into an ice cream maker. Churn according to the manufacturer's instructions and store in a chilled container in the freezer until ready to serve.

3. To serve, spoon the sorbet into chilled cups and drizzle the cordial over the top.

RASPBERRY BROWN BUTTER CAKE *with* YOGURT ICE CREAM *and* ELDERFLOWERS

What separates this cake from similar creations is brown butter. It gives the cake a savory edge countered by the sweetness of vanilla bean, which is infused into the hot butter. While delicious with tart, fresh raspberries, you also can make this cake with frozen cranberries and lemon zest in the fall and winter. A spoonful of summer berry jam added to the batter also works as a stand-in for fresh fruit.

makes 1 cake

3/4 cup salted butter	1 1/2 cup fresh raspberries, plus about
1 vanilla bean	1/2 cup for garnish
1 cup sugar	Yogurt Ice Cream (page 205)
1/2 cup all-purpose flour	Elderflower Syrup (page 205)
3 large eggs	

1. Preheat the oven to 350°F. Butter a 9-inch round or 8-inch square cake pan.

2. Melt the butter in a pot over medium heat. Split the vanilla bean in half lengthwise and scrape out the seeds with the tip of a spoon. Mix in the seeds and bean and continue to cook the butter until it browns. (It will turn amber in color and smell like toasting nuts.) Immediately take off the heat to prevent the butter from scorching. Remove the bean and reserve for another use. Cool the butter to room temperature.

3. In a medium bowl mix the sugar and flour together. Whisk in the eggs, and then drizzle in the butter. Scatter half of the raspberries in the bottom of the cake pan and pour the batter on top. Scatter the remaining raspberries on top. Bake until a toothpick inserted into the center comes out clean and the top no longer looks raw, about 35 minutes.

4. To serve, cut or spoon portions of cake onto plates. Top with a spoonful of the ice cream. In a small bowl, mix together the remaining raspberries with the elderflower syrup and drizzle the berries and syrup over the ice cream.

Yogurt Ice Cream

Like Buttermilk Ice Cream (page 161), yogurt ice cream has tang that tames the richness of the cake. Since there's no cus-tard to make, the ice cream comes together easily. Once you've made the honey-sugar syrup, just whisk, chill, and churn.

makes about 1¹/₄ quarts

¹/₂ cup sugar
¹/₃ cup water
¹/₄ cup honey
1 quart whole-milk plain yogurt
1 cup heavy cream

1. In a pot over high heat, whisk together the sugar, water, and honey and bring to a boil. Remove from the heat and chill until ice cold.

2. In a bowl, whisk together the yogurt, cream, and sugar syrup. Pour the base into the ice cream maker and churn according to the manufacturer's instructions. Store in a chilled container in the freezer.

Elderflower Syrup

Elderflower bushes grow along the highway from Chicago to Champaign, Illiniois. If I spot a bush within reach, I will pull off the highway and trim a bouquet to make this syrup. Elderflowers have a delicate, mildly anise like flavor that works well in cocktails—try this syrup in a gin and tonic, for instance—as well as with fresh berries. I like to gloss fresh raspberries with a few spoonfuls of this syrup to garnish desserts in the summer.

makes about 1 cup

¹/₂ cup sugar
¹/₂ cup water
3 to 4 large clusters elderflowers, pulled off the stem

Dissolve the sugar in water over medium heat. Stir in the elderflowers and let infuse for at least a couple of hours or refrigerate overnight. Strain and use within a month.

HAPPY HOUR INTERLUDE

A bar in a restaurant isn't unusual. But when you're the first place in town to offer a proper watering hole since the 1920s, you've earned some bragging rights.

Vie was the second business in Western Springs to obtain a liquor license post-Prohibition (the first went to a chain grocery store), and we have never taken the bar for granted. On some nights, regular customers guest bartend. On others, we host dinners featuring local brewers and distillers. Through trial and error, we've also worked out ways to leverage preserves on the cocktail menu.

When you make as many jams and pickles as we do, you're bound to end up with a few odd bits—extra pickling brine, say, or a lonely jar of brandied cherries. A few late nights at the restaurant, a bit of experimentation, and it's only a matter of time before someone pours brine into a martini. Just like that, the dirty martini à la pickled ramps was born. Mike Page, our bar manager, is a good sport about it all, often taking jars off our hands to conjure seasonal punches, smashes, and slings. The jar-to-bar connection continues at my second restaurant in Chicago, Perennial Virant, where bartender Matty Eggleston accents cocktails with aigre-doux liquid, yielding a similar effect as a shrub—a fruit and vinegar syrup added to drinks for tartness.

These days both bars are stocked year-round with house-made concoctions, from the beer jam that laces the Manhattan to more fleeting items, like gooseberries in a summer cocktail or milk jam in winter sweet milk punch. And even though we don't serve them regularly, I can attest to the healing properties of canned local tomatoes when applied to a Bloody Mary. When it makes sense to do so, we also turn to local spirits, like Death's Door, a racy gin distilled from wheat grown on and around Washington Island in Wisconsin, and nuanced Buffalo Trace Bourbon, made with Kentucky and Indiana corn.

With apologies to Brussels sprouts sauerkraut, not all preserves are meant to make it into a cocktail. But more can be put to work at the bar than you might imagine. Think of a cocktail as a balancing act between acidity, bitterness, and sweetness. When experimenting on your own, start gradually—a dab of kumquat marmalade in a mimosa, for example—then go bold, mixing pumpkin butter into a shandy (a cocktail typically made with beer and soda) or a whole jar of brandied peaches into a punch bowl for white sangria. The cocktails that follow serve as a starting point for bartending alchemy.

PICKLED RAMP MARTINI *with* PICKLED RAMP–STUFFED OLIVES

Don't limit yourself to ramps in this homemade dirty martini. The brine from pickled fennel or dill pickles also makes a mean drink. Or add some heat with some of the juice from Pickled Cherry Bomb Peppers (page 36). The recipe below yields one cocktail. Ramp-stuffed olives, which are optional, make enough for eight drinks. Or just float a single pickled ramp on top. Pictured on page 206 and 207.

makes 1 cocktail

1/8 cup finely chopped Pickled Ramps
(page 23)
8 gordal or other large green olives, pitted
3 ounces gin

1 ounce vodka
3/4 ounce brine from Pickled Ramps
(page 23)

1. Press the ramps into the hollow of the olives and refrigerate until needed.

2. In a cocktail shaker filled with ice, mix together the gin, vodka, and brine. Shake, then strain into a chilled martini glass. Garnish with a stuffed olive.

BEER JAM MANHATTAN

Ask our bartender, Mike, about the popularity of this drink year-round; he's shaken his fair share. The biggest difference between our version and a traditional Manhattan is the splash of syrupy beer jam, which takes the place of vermouth. Brandied sour cherries are the best garnish with this drink, but brandied sweet cherries are a fine, if sweeter, addition. Pictured on page 210.

makes 1 cocktail

3 1/2 ounces bourbon (such as
Buffalo Trace)
1 ounce brandied sour cherry juice
(page 68)

3/4 ounce Beer Jam (page 60)
Dash of orange bitters
(such as Peychaud's)
1 brandied sour cherry

In a cocktail shaker filled with ice, mix together the bourbon, cherry juice, and beer jam. Shake, then strain into a chilled martini glass. Garnish with a sour cherry.

happy hour interlude

RHUBARB NORMANDY

The Manhattan was addictive enough to give way to a second beer jam. This is a take on a Normandy, a classic cocktail made with Calvados, in which the sharp tang of rhubarb takes the place of cranberries. Although rhubarb is most often consumed in spring, this cocktail's apple accents make it perfect for fall. The rhubarb's flavor is complemented by Chartreuse, an herbal French liqueur, and cane syrup, a thick sweetener made from evaporated sugar cane juice.

makes 1 cocktail

1 ounce Calvados (preferably Coeur de Lion)
1 ounce apple liqueur (such as Berentzen)

1 ounce Rhubarb Beer Jam (page 61)
$1/2$ ounce yellow Chartreuse
$1/4$ ounce cane syrup (such as Depaz)

In a cocktail shaker filled with ice, mix together the Calvados, apple liqueur, beer jam, Chartreuse, and cane syrup. Shake, then strain into a chilled tumbler or pilsner glass.

GOOSEBERRY SMASH

Muddling citrus fruits in a glass starts many a great cocktail. Here, tart gooseberries complement fresh lime for a lighter, more food-friendly take on a Dark and Stormy.

makes 1 cocktail

1 tablespoon Gooseberry Jam (page 71)
2 thin slices lime
$1^1/2$ ounces dark rum
$1/2$ ounce triple sec

Dash of orange bitters (such as Peychaud's)
2 tablespoons soda water
1 tablespoon ginger ale or ginger beer

In a lowball glass, muddle the gooseberry jam with the lime. Pour in the rum and triple sec and add a dash of bitters. Mix well, add ice, and top with the soda water and ginger ale. Stir again.

KENTUCKY BURNT APPLES

Our smoked apple butter is such a natural for a bourbon-based cocktail that it was only a matter of time before our bar manager, Mike Page, came up with this example. Here, bourbon and smoked apples are topped off with a spicy wheat beer. Pictured on page 211.

makes 1 cocktail

1¹/₂ ounces bourbon (such as
  Buffalo Trace)
³/₄ ounces apple liqueur
  (such as Berentzen)
¹/₂ ounce cane syrup (such as Depaz)

1 ounce lemonade
1 tablespoon Smoked Apple Butter
  (page 79)
Wheat beer

In a tumbler or pilsner glass, stir the bourbon, apple liqueur, cane syrup, lemonade, and apple butter well. Top with a splash of beer and a few ice cubes.

SWEET MILK PUNCH

Like many punches, this one is deceptively potent. Caramel and hazelnut notes from the milk jam and Frangelico mask the impact of the bourbon, making it appropriately warming for our winter cocktail menu. Though this recipe serves one, several servings can be mixed together in a punch bowl for a party.

makes 1 cocktail

1 ounce bourbon infused with vanilla
  (such as Buffalo Trace)
1 ounce triple sec (such as
  Luxardo Triplum)
2 ounces whole milk

1 ounce water
³/₄ ounce Frangelico
1 tablespoon Milk Jam (page 124)
Brandied cherries for garnish (page 68)

In a cocktail shaker or tall glass, stir together the ingredients well, being sure to blend in the jam. Strain into a dessert wine glass, top with ice cubes, and garnish with a brandied cherry.

LEMON VERBENA CORDIAL

Made by steeping fruits or herbs in a grain alcohol, cordials provide another way to preserve seasonal ingredients, but with more kick. Aromatic herbs, like lemon verbena, are ideal for these infusions. Over several weeks, the alcohol extracts the flavors of the slender green leaves until it has absorbed their aroma, taking on their bright green color. Once diluted and sweetened, this cordial gives a homemade stamp to cocktails, like the Verbena Sling (page 175), and offers a heady finish to fruit desserts, such as Peach Sorbet (page 201).

When making cordials, pick a neutral 192-proof grain alcohol, which is 95 percent alcohol by volume. We use Polmos Piritus Rektvfikowany, (piritus rektvfikowany is Polish for rectified spirit) but any similar grain alcohol will do. Don't let this part throw you—once the infusion is completed, the base is diluted to a proof similar to vodka. While the high alcohol levels in infusions make them shelf-stable, over time the flavors dull and color oxidizes. This is especially true with green cordials like this one, which is best consumed within a year of making it.

makes about 1¹/₂ quarts

INFUSION	SIMPLE SYRUP
¹/₂ cup sugar	1 cup sugar
1 ounce fresh lemon verbena leaves	1 cup water
3 cups 192-proof rectified spirit or similar premium grain alcohol	Purified water, for diluting

1. To make the infusion, place the sugar and lemon verbena in a 1-quart Mason jar. Pour in the spirit and cap with a lid. Shake once daily for 3 weeks. Store in a cool, dark place in between shakes.

2. Strain the infusion slowly through a paper coffee filter into a clean jar, allowing the liquid to drain slowly for a less cloudy finished product.

3. Meanwhile, make the simple syrup. In a small pot, mix together the sugar and tap water. Bring to a simmer and cook until the sugar has dissolved, a few minutes. Cool completely.

4. To make the cordial, measure the strained infusion. Add an equal amount of purified water to dilute the alcohol. Stir in simple syrup until the cordial tastes balanced (you may not use all of the simple syrup). If the cordial still tastes too alcoholic, pour in a few more splashes of purified water. Store the cordial in a cool, dark place and use within the year.

THE TBD

During the soft opening of my second restaurant, Perennial Virant, our bartender, Matty Eggleston, created a cocktail with juices from our blueberry aigre-doux. With spicy ginger juice complementing the sweet-tart syrup from the aigre doux, it was immediately thirst quenching. I couldn't wait to put it on the menu, but there was a hitch: Matty didn't have a name for it. We started calling it the TBD—"to be determined"—assuming that eventually we'd come up with a real name. Instead, the name stuck, and so did the cocktail's popularity.

At the restaurant, Matty uses a juicer to juice fresh ginger and then mixes it with equal parts sugar. For smaller batches, you can get by grating fresh ginger, then straining the juice through a fine-mesh strainer. This cocktail requires simple syrup. To make simple syrup, follow the instructions provided in the Lemon Verbena Cordial (page 214). Pictured on page 211.

makes 1 cocktail

2 inches fresh ginger root, peeled
Sugar
1 1/2 ounces vodka, such as Zubrowka
3/4 ounces Blueberry Aigre-Doux liquid
    (page 91), plus blueberries
    for garnish

1/2 ounce freshly squeezed lime juice
1/4 ounce simple syrup
1 drop pure vanilla extract

1. To make the ginger syrup, using a Microplane zester to grate the ginger. Put the grated ginger in a fine-mesh strainer and press firmly against the pulp to extract as much juice as possible. Stir in equal parts sugar to the juice (you will have only a small amount of juice).

2. In a cocktail shaker filled with ice, pour in the vodka, aigre-doux liquid, and lime juice. Add 2 healthy dashes of ginger syrup, pour in the simple syrup, and add a small drop of vanilla. Shake, then strain into a highball glass filled with ice. Garnish with the blueberries.

FALL

A DAY OF CANNING

{ this *Menu* serves 4 to 6 }

The inspiration for this menu, a lazy afternoon in early fall spent canning with a few friends, is idyllic. It is also—in my experience—improbable.

Canning isn't a lazy activity, especially during the time of year where late summer tomatoes and eggplant converge at the market with winter squashes and Brussels sprouts. At Vie, it takes some choreography to ensure we pack as many fresh tomatoes away in jars as possible while not forgoing fall favorites, like the rutabagas we ferment for latkes or the spiky green romanesco florets that I pack into giardiniera. Steam fills the air as water baths work overtime to process countless jars. To say the least, it's an industrious time in the kitchen.

This menu, most of which can be prepared ahead of time, provides a way to reward a small group of friends who have volunteered (with some arm-twisting, perhaps) to help preserve the last bit of summer produce. They will need energy, so ply them with iced coffee sweetened with milk jam. They will get hungry, so keep them on task by frying up green tomatoes served with basil mayonnaise. Serve pickled tongue crisped in a pan along with prosciutto and coppa for a few savory bites. And for a sweet snack while the last jars boil away, pass out a plate of thumbprint cookies.

Just as it is necessary to keep your kitchen helpers contented during your canning party, it is also important to distract the less helpful from veering too close to the kitchen. I recommend that you strategically place the food away from the action to keep others out of your way.

FRIED GREEN TOMATOES *with* BASIL MAYONNAISE *and* LOCAL LETTUCES

Late into tomato season, the last few green tomatoes on the vine are likely to encounter frostbite before they can ripen. I don't take chances, picking them green rather than leaving them for the compost heap. When the tomatoes are fried and served with basil-flavored mayonnaise, this decision doesn't taste like a compromise at all. Seasoning the tomatoes at least an hour before you fry them gives time for the salt to soak in. When choosing lettuces, I go for a mix of baby chard, tatsoi, dandelion greens, and red oak, but any mix of tender greens will do. Pictured on pages 216 and 217.

GREEN TOMATOES
2 green tomatoes, sliced about 1/2 inch
   thick (about 8 slices)
Kosher salt and freshly ground
   black pepper

1/2 cup all-purpose flour
1 large egg, lightly beaten
1/2 cup bread crumbs
Grapeseed oil, for frying
1 tablespoon unsalted butter

SALAD
4 ounces mixed local lettuces
1/2 sweet onion (such as candy or
   Vidalia), shaved
Juice of 1/2 lemon
2 tablespoons extra-virgin olive oil
Kosher salt and freshly ground
   black pepper
Basil Mayonnaise (recipe follows)

1. To prepare the tomatoes, season the tomato slices on both sides with salt and pepper and let sit at room temperature for 1 hour.

2. Line a plate with paper towels. Dredge the tomatoes in the flour, followed by the egg and bread crumbs. In a large, shallow pan over medium-high heat, add enough grapeseed oil to generously coat the bottom of the pan. In two batches, fry the tomatoes until golden and crisp, 1 to 2 minutes per side. When nearly done with the first batch, swirl in half of the butter. Transfer the tomatoes to the prepared plate and wipe the pan clean. Repeat for the second batch.

3. Meanwhile, to make the salad, in a large bowl, toss together the lettuces, onion, lemon juice, and olive oil. Season with salt and pepper.

4. To serve, place the salad on the plate. Distribute the fried tomatoes on top of the salad and spoon the basil mayonnaise over the tomatoes.

Basil Mayonnaise

makes about 1³/₄ cups

1 large egg

1 large egg yolk

2 cloves garlic

1 cup coarsely chopped fresh basil leaves

Juice of ¹/₂ lemon

¹/₄ cups grapeseed oil

Kosher salt and freshly ground
   black pepper

In a food processor, blend together the egg, yolk, garlic, basil, and lemon juice. While the processor is running, gradually drizzle in 1 cup of the oil until it becomes thick. If it is still on the loose side, drizzle in more oil until it reaches the right consistency. (The oil and egg are binding together to form an emulsion. If the emulsion breaks and loses its shape, pour the mixture in a liquid measuring cup, add an egg yolk to the food processor, and drizzle in the broken mixture as if it were oil.) Season with salt and pepper and refrigerate until needed. This mayonnaise will keep for about a week and makes more than you need for this recipe.

CHARCUTERIE PLATTER: NATHAN'S COPPA, FRIED PICKLED TONGUE, PROSCIUTTO, VANILLA MELON JAM, PICKLED WATERMELON RIND, *and* WATERCRESS

Thanks to Vie's resident meat-curing expert (and chef de cuisine), Nathan Sears, we serve an evolving selection of cured meats on our charcuterie plate. Not only does this allow us to show off Nathan's superlative coppa, pastrami, and other projects, but it also makes good use of our pickles and preserves. Present a plate of cured meats and condiments to a group and guests can pick their own favorite meat-and-preserves combination.

Making cured meats takes time and dedication. Serving them, however, is easy. The recipe that follows is more of a serving suggestion than a real recipe. While I offer recipes for Nathan's coppa and pickled tongue, you can instead buy admirable cured meats, such as the prosciutto from La Quercia in Norwalk, Iowa. If you happen to have slices of pressed eggplant packed in olive oil (page 113), now is the time to eat them—they are excellent with on bread with cured meat. And if you prefer pickled vegetables with cured meat, pull out a jar of Giardiniera (page 34). Pictured on page 222.

PLATTER

4 ounces Pickled Beef Tongue (recipe follows), lightly crisped

4 ounces Coppa (page 118), thinly sliced

2 to 4 ounces thinly sliced prosciutto

CONDIMENTS

1/2 cup Vanilla Melon Jam (page 77)

1 shallot, minced

2 tablespoons fresh lemon juice

2 tablespoons extra-virgin olive oil, plus extra for the watercress

Kosher salt and freshly ground black pepper

1/2 cup Pickled Watermelon Rind (page 49)

Strong mustard

4 ounces watercress

1 loaf country bread, sliced

1. For the platter, fan out slices of tongue, coppa and prosciutto.

2. For the condiments, in a small bowl, mix together the melon jam, shallot, lemon juice, and the 2 tablespoons olive oil. Season to taste with a pinch of salt and pepper and transfer to a small bowl. Place on or next to the platter, along with a small bowl of pickled watermelon rind and a small bowl of mustard. In a small bowl, mix the watercress with a drizzle of olive oil and a pinch of salt. Garnish the platter with watercress and serve the bread alongside.

Pickled Beef Tongue

The smack of vinegar from pickled tongue wakes up a platter of cold cuts, especially when the tongue is eaten with a dab of hot mustard. When making this recipe, plan accordingly. The first day, soak the tongue overnight. The next day, braise it, then peel away the outer skin and let it cool completely in its braising liquid. Finally, slice the tongue and cover it in a vinegary broth, where it can be stored, refrigerated, for a few weeks.

1 (2¼-pound) beef tongue
Kosher salt and freshly ground
    black pepper
1 onion, diced
1 carrot, peeled and diced

1 celery, diced
3 bay leaves
3 sprigs thyme
1 tablespoon mustard seeds
1 tablespoon coriander seeds

1 teaspoon red pepper flakes
1 teaspoon black peppercorns
1 cup red wine vinegar
Grapeseed oil

1. Soak the tongue overnight in ice water and about ¹/₂ teaspoon salt.

2. Drain the tongue, transfer to a pot, and top with the onion, carrot, celery, bay leaves, thyme, mustard seeds, coriander seeds, red pepper flakes, black peppercorns, and a pinch of salt. Cover with about 1 inch of water. Bring to a boil, decrease to a gentle simmer, and cook until the tongue is tender and the tough outer membrane has loosened, 3 to 4 hours. (If the pot becomes dry before the meat is ready, add up to 4 cups more water and continue to simmer.) Remove the tongue and place on a baking sheet. Strain and reserve the broth. You will have about 8 cups of broth. When the tongue is cool enough to handle but still warm, peel away and discard the membrane (this is difficult to do when the tongue is cold). Return the tongue to the broth and refrigerate overnight.

3. Remove the tongue from the broth and slice crosswise into ¹/₄-inch pieces. Place in a heat-proof storage container. In a pot, bring the broth to a boil. Decrease to a simmer and cook, skimming away fat with a ladle, until the broth has reduced to about 1 cup, about 45 minutes. Stir in the vinegar and pour the hot mixture over the tongue. Weigh the pieces of tongue down with a plate or a heavy-duty storage bag filled with water and refrigerate for at least a few hours or up to 3 weeks.

4. Before serving, pat the tongue dry between 2 paper towels. In a large sauté pan over medium heat, warm a tablespoon of grapeseed oil. Add the slices of tongue and cook until crisp, about 1 minute per side. Season with salt and pepper and transfer to a platter.

ICED COFFEE *with* MILK JAM

Anyone who has seen the collection of coffee-making equipment on my kitchen counter could label me something of a coffee fanatic. It's true. I worry about water temperature and the grind of the beans. I experiment equally with espresso and drip coffee. Most of all, I drink it—a lot of it. This iced coffee drink appeals to my inner coffee geek because cold-brewed coffee imparts a gentler flavor profile than hot-brewed, chilled coffee. It also satisfies afternoon coffee cravings, because few things quell discontent in a hot kitchen like iced coffee sweetened with caramelized milk.

4^1/$_2$ cups cold water
1 cup ground coffee
1 cup Milk Jam (page 124)
Ice

1. In a bowl, stir together the water and coffee. Cover and refrigerate for 12 to 24 hours. Strain through a fine-mesh strainer. (The concentrate can be refrigerated for about a week.)

2. In a pitcher, mix the coffee and the jam together. You will have about 44 fluid ounces. To serve, pour over tall glasses filled with ice.

THUMBPRINT COOKIES

People who make jam also make thumbprint cookies—for obvious reasons. These homey cookies offer a way to show off preserves. Still, these wouldn't be worth mentioning if they also didn't also taste so good. Pecans ground into the flour make a sturdy base that pairs well with summer fruit preserves, such as apricot, plum, or blackberry. This recipe makes a big batch. I like to freeze half of the dough to save for a quick batch of cookies down the road, but you also could halve the recipe.

makes about 8 dozen cookies

4 cups pecans
4 cups all-purpose flour
^{1}/$_4$ cup whole-wheat flour
1 teaspoon salt
1 pound unsalted butter,
    at room temperature

1 cup sugar
1 to 2 cups Apricot Jelly (page 65),
    Rainier Cherry Jam (page 76) or
    other fruit preserves

1. Preheat the oven to 325°F. Butter 2 baking sheets.

2. In a food processor, grind the nuts with 1 cup of the all-purpose flour until nearly smooth. In a large bowl, whisk together the nut mixture with the remaining flours and the salt.

3. In a stand mixer fitted with the paddle attachment, cream the butter and sugar until smooth and creamy. In batches, add the flour mixture, mixing on low speed until the dough comes together.

4. Using your hands, roll the dough into small balls (about ½ ounce each, about half the size of a golf ball) and place on the prepared baking sheets in 4 rows of 3. Press your thumb in the center to create the thumbprint, but do not flatten the ball because the cookie will spread as it bakes. Transfer to the oven and bake 10 minutes, rotating the baking sheets once. Remove the sheets from the oven, add a dab of jam into each thumbprint, and bake until the cookies are golden brown, an additional 5 minutes. Transfer the cookies to a cooling rack and ready the next batch of cookies (if baking all of the dough, plan on baking in several batches).

FALL: a day of canning

FIRST FROST

WALDORF SALAD WITH APPLES,
CANDIED WALNUTS, AND GRAPE
AIGRE-DOUX DRESSING • 229

CHICKEN-FRIED STEAK WITH
SMOKED SPRING ONION RELISH
AND SLOW-COOKED KALE • 230

PUMPKIN BUTTER BARS • 233

{ this *Menu* serves 4 }

It is no revelation that cold weather triggers cravings for richer, more filling foods. The first day we have to scrape ice off the car is probably the last day we will think about grilling a plate of zucchini. But fall is also an exciting time—a period when Halloween costumes, politicians, and football teams are assessed, often with equal levels of excitement. When that first frost hits, it suddenly feels okay to leave tomatoes behind and migrate into winter squashes and kale.

This menu acts as a transition between the warm days of early fall and the bitingly cold days that inevitably follow. It's a warming, comforting menu of familiar flavors with a few updated additions. A Waldorf salad with grape aigre-doux offers a light start to the meal, while the chicken-fried steak and a smoked spring onion relish drive home the comfort-food effect. But the best comes last: simple spiced pumpkin butter bars, a perfect, homey end to the meal.

WALDORF SALAD *with* APPLES, CANDIED WALNUTS, *and* GRAPE AIGRE-DOUX DRESSING

Composed of apples, celery, mayonnaise, and walnuts served on a bed of lettuce, this classic American salad from the Waldorf-Astoria Hotel in New York City has long inspired imitators. I prefer to think of my version as an update. Curry oil and the liquid saved from tangy grape aigre-doux give the mayonnaise twenty-first-century relevance. So does the contrast between Honeycrisp apples and preserved grapes. Occasionally I augment the fresh celery with Pickled Celery Root (page 51), but I'll leave that call up to you.

While this salad has a few components, most of them can be made ahead of time. The curry oil in the dressing can be made as much as a week ahead, the candied walnuts will stay crisp for at least five days as long as they are stored in an airtight container, and the dressing will keep in the refrigerator for about five days. This recipe makes more dressing than you need, but extra is terrific served with plain mixed greens. Pictured on pages 226 and 227.

¹/₂ cup apple cider

Juice of ¹/₂ lemon

1 tablespoon Madras curry powder

1 cup grapeseed oil

1 large egg

2 tablespoons Crème Fraîche
   (page 17)

¹/₂ cup liquid strained from Grape
   Aigre-Doux (page 94)

Kosher salt

1 cup toasted walnuts

¹/₂ cup sugar

Freshly ground black pepper

2 cups shredded iceberg lettuce

2 stalks celery, sliced

1 apple (preferably Honeycrisp),
   thinly sliced

¹/₂ cup drained grapes from Grape
   Aigre-Doux (page 94)

1. To make the dressing, in a small pot, reduce the apple cider, lemon juice, and curry powder until almost dry, about 5 minutes. Stir in the grapeseed oil and cook until the oil is too hot to touch, about 2 minutes. Cool the oil to room temperature.

2. In a food processor, blend the egg, crème fraîche, and aigre-doux liquid. While the processor is on, gradually drizzle in the curry oil until it becomes thick. (If the emulsion breaks and loses its shape, pour the mixture in a liquid measuring cup, add an egg yolk to the food processor, and drizzle in the broken mixture as if it were oil.) Season with salt and refrigerate until needed. You will have about 2 cups.

3. To make the candied walnuts, line a baking sheet with parchment paper or a silicone baking mat. In a cold pan, combine the sugar with just enough water to create a mixture that resembles wet sand. Place the pan over high heat and cook the sugar until it begins to brown, about 5 minutes. Decrease the heat to medium and stir in the walnuts. Season with a few pinches of salt and pepper and cook, stirring constantly, until a frosty coating covers the walnuts. Pour onto the prepared baking sheet and let cool completely.

4. To serve the salad, combine the lettuce, apples, and celery. Spoon just enough dressing to coat the ingredients evenly (about ¹/₄ cup) and add a pinch of salt and pepper. Toss and garnish with the candied walnuts and grapes.

CHICKEN-FRIED STEAK *with* SMOKED SPRING ONION RELISH *and* SLOW-COOKED KALE

As with the fried chicken I serve in the summer (page 186), I add pickling brine to kick up the acidity in the buttermilk marinade for the steak. But rather than serve the steak with gravy, I take a different approach, turning to slowly cooked kale, a side dish gleaned from chef Suzanne Goin's cookbook, Sunday Suppers at Lucques. *Deglazing kale a few times with water gives the vegetable time to develop a deep, caramelized flavor, giving it enough substance to stand up to steak. An easy relish of smoked spring onions served on the side balances both components with an acidic accent.*

4 (6-ounce) thin slices beef sirloin or round steak
Kosher salt
1 cup buttermilk
¼ cup pickling liquid strained from Smoked and Pickled Spring Onions (page 24)

2 cups all-purpose flour
1 tablespoon smoked sweet paprika
1 teaspoon dried tarragon
1 teaspoon garlic powder
1 teaspoon freshly ground black pepper
Grapeseed oil, for frying
2 tablespoons unsalted butter

1 cup drained Smoked and Pickled Spring Onions (page 24)
½ cup extra-virgin olive oil
1 cup loosely packed fresh parsley, chopped
¼ cup chopped fresh chives
Slow-Cooked Kale (recipe follows)

1. Place each steak between 2 pieces of plastic wrap and pound to about ¹/₂ inch thick with a mallet. Season both sides with salt. Mix the buttermilk and the pickling liquid. In a separate bowl, combine the flour, paprika, tarragon, garlic powder, and black pepper. Dip each steak into the buttermilk followed by the seasoned flour.

2. Preheat the oven to 200°F. In a large cast-iron pan over medium-high heat, pour in 1 inch of oil. Heat the oil until it begins to shimmer on the surface. In two batches to avoid crowding the pan, fry the steaks until brown and crispy on one side, about 2 minutes. Using tongs, carefully turn the steaks over and brown the other side, another 2 minutes. Transfer the fried steaks to the oven to keep warm. If the oil level drops significantly between batches, add more oil and let it heat up before frying the second batch. Pour off the excess oil, place the steaks back in the pan, and baste with butter for an additional minute. Transfer the steaks to a warmed serving platter.

3. Mix together the pickled onions and olive oil. Stir in the parsley and chives and serve alongside the steak with a side of kale.

Slow-Cooked Kale

2 pounds Tuscan kale

1/4 cup diced bacon

1 sweet onion (preferably candy or
    Vidalia), sliced

5 cloves garlic, sliced

1 1/2 cups water

Kosher salt

1. With a sharp knife, remove the center ribs from the kale leaves. Slice the leaves and stems thinly and blanch in a pot of boiling, salted water for 2 minutes. Drain.

2. In a Dutch oven or heavy-bottomed pot over medium-low heat, render the bacon. Once nearly crisp, stir in the onion and garlic and sweat until the onion slices are translucent, about 3 minutes. Add the kale, cover, and cook 10 minutes. Uncover and reduce the liquid until the pan is dry and the kale begins to crisp. Deglaze the pan with about 1/2 cup of the water and cook until the pan is dry and the kale once again begins to caramelize. Deglaze with another 1/2 cup water and cook until the pan is nearly dry. Deglaze a third time with the remaining 1/2 cup water and cook until the pan is nearly dry. Season with salt and keep warm until ready to serve. The whole process will take about 20 minutes.

PUMPKIN BUTTER BARS

Move over pumpkin pie. With a shortbread base and creamy pumpkin top, these simple bars are a perennial autumn hit. Served with Yogurt Ice Cream (page 205) or whipped Crème Fraîche (page 17), they cap this seasonal meal. But they are also just as pleasant with my third (or fourth) cup of coffee of the day.

makes 20 bars

CRUST

1 cup unsalted butter, at room
temperature

$1/2$ cup granulated sugar

2 tablespoons brown sugar

2 cups all-purpose flour

$1/4$ teaspoon kosher salt

$1/8$ teaspoon cinnamon

FILLING

12 ounces cream cheese, at room
temperature

$1/2$ cup granulated sugar

2 large eggs

$1/4$ cup plus 1 tablespoon heavy cream

$1/4$ cup sour cream

$1/2$ teaspoon kosher salt

$1^1/2$ cups Pumpkin Butter (page 81)

$1^1/2$ tablespoons maple syrup

$1/4$ cup molasses

$1^1/2$ teaspoons bourbon (optional)

1. Preheat the oven to 325°F. Butter a 9 by 13-inch baking pan.

2. To make the crust, in a stand mixer fitted with the paddle attachment, mix together the butter and sugars on low speed until they form a crumbly mixture. Add the flour, salt, and cinnamon and continue to mix on low speed until a dough starts to form. Pat the dough in an even layer in the prepared pan and bake until the top turns a light golden color, 20 to 25 minutes.

3. Meanwhile, to make the filling, in the stand mixer fitted with the paddle attachment, cream together the cream cheese and sugar until smooth. Stir in the eggs, then add the cream, sour cream, and salt. Stir in the pumpkin butter, followed by the maple syrup, molasses, and bourbon, if using, and mix until smooth. Pour the pumpkin mixture over the par-baked crust and bake until the pumpkin has set (the edges will begin to crinkle and the center should no longer look raw), about 30 minutes. Cool completely, and then slice into squares. Store the cookies in the refrigerator or freezer.

AUTUMN CHICKEN DINNER

ROASTED AND PICKLED BEET
SALAD WITH PICKED HERBS • 236

PAN-SEARED CHICKEN WITH
CELERY SAUCE AND TOMATO
JAM–ROASTED POTATOES • 237

BLUE CHEESE WITH PEAR AND
VANILLA AIGRE-DOUX AND
ROASTED HICKORY NUTS • 238

{ this *Menu* serves 4 }

Something changes in September and October, and it involves more than the climate. This menu acknowledges this change of pace. It is a meal to prepare when we want to invite a few friends over but we don't have an afternoon free to baby a roast or painstakingly simmer a sauce. With a few jars of preserves and a couple of sauté pans, we can put together a meal that is thoughtful, balanced, and tastes a lot more complicated than the ingredients may suggest.

Cooking meat or vegetables in a sauté pan over high heat causes sugars to caramelize, imparting sweet nutty flavor. Sautéeing also offers a great way to make a pan sauce. A splash of wine, stock, or water releases bits of caramelized meat or vegetable from the pan, which can then be poured over the finished dish. Meals prepared in sauté pans are best when balanced with acidity. Here, pickled celery augments sweeter celery root, and tomato jam enlivens roasted fingerling potatoes. The smell of roasting chicken and potatoes alone might be just the thing to pry my family away from their projects and draw them to the table.

ROASTED *and* PICKLED BEET SALAD *with* PICKED HERBS

Beets harvested in colder weather have more concentrated sugars, which stand up well to the tang of pickled beets. A handful of herbs added at the end gives the salad a fresh finish. Pictured on pages 234 and 235.

1 pound red beets (about 4)
¼ cup extra-virgin olive oil, plus more
    for drizzling
Kosher salt and freshly ground
    black pepper

1 cup Red Wine–Pickled Beets, in their
    pickling liquid (page 52)
Red wine vinegar (optional)
½ small sweet onion (preferably candy
    or Vidalia), thinly sliced

1 cup loosely packed mixed fresh herbs
    (any combination of picked chervil,
    tarragon leaves, parsley leaves, and
    sliced chives)

1. Preheat the oven to 400°F. Remove the beet greens, if attached, and place the beets in a small baking pan. Drizzle the beets with just enough olive oil to coat and then season them generously with salt and pepper. Cover with foil and bake for 35 minutes to 1 hour, testing occasionally for doneness with a wooden skewer. Once cool enough to handle, slip the skins off with your fingers or a kitchen towel and slice the beets into disks.

2. Drain the pickled beets, saving about 3 ounces pickling liquid. In a small pot over medium heat, simmer the pickling liquid until it has reduced by half. Stir in the ¼ cup olive oil. Taste the vinaigrette, adding a splash of red wine vinegar if it needs more acidity. In a large bowl, dress the roasted and pickled beets with the vinaigrette. Mix in the onion and herbs and serve in a salad bowl or divide between 4 plates.

PAN-SEARED CHICKEN *with* CELERY SAUCE *and* TOMATO JAM–ROASTED POTATOES

Depending on the bird, two breasts can be ample for four people. If you have a large bird, use two instead of the four called for here.

2 tablespoons grapeseed oil

4 skin-on, bone-in chicken breasts, 4–6 ounces each

Kosher salt and freshly ground black pepper

1 tablespoon unsalted butter

1 celery root, peeled and diced (about 2 cups)

1 clove garlic, sliced

1 cup sliced Pickled Celery (page 28)

1/4 cup Crème Fraîche (page 17)

3 green onions, sliced

Tomato Jam–Roasted Potatoes (recipe follows)

1. Preheat the oven to 400°F.

2. Heat the oil in a large sauté pan over medium-high heat. Season the chicken with salt and pepper. In two batches, sear the breasts, skin-side down, until the skin turns golden brown. Transfer to a roasting pan and cook 15 to 20 minutes. Remove from the oven and cover with aluminum foil.

3. In the same sauté pan used to sear the chicken, melt the butter over medium heat. Add the celery root and cook until it begins to caramelize, about 3 minutes. Stir in the garlic and transfer to the oven. Roast until the celery root is cooked through, about 10 minutes. Remove from the oven and stir in the pickled celery, crème fraîche, and green onions. Cook until the crème fraîche thickens slightly, 1 minute more.

4. To serve, bone and slice each breast into 3 to 5 pieces. Divide among 4 plates, topped with the celery root sauce, and serve with the potatoes on the side.

Tomato Jam-Roasted Potatoes

Tomato jam adds sweetness and acidity to the potatoes, a welcome balance next to the rich celery sauce. I favor Russian Banana fingerlings, but any small potato can be used.

1/4 cup grapeseed oil

1 pound fingerling potatoes (about 20)

Kosher salt and freshly ground black pepper

1 rosemary sprig

1/2 cup Tomato Jam (page 48)

3 cloves garlic, sliced

1. Preheat the oven to 400°F.

{continued}

2. In a large, ovenproof sauté pan over medium-high heat, warm the oil. Add the potatoes, season with salt and pepper, and sear until they just begin to brown, about 1 minute. Add the rosemary sprig and transfer the pan to the oven. Roast until the potatoes are tender when pierced with a fork, 30 to 40 minutes.

3. Remove the pan from the oven to the stovetop and remove the rosemary sprig. Stir in the jam and garlic and cook over medium heat, stirring often, until the garlic softens and the jam thickens, about 3 minutes. If the jam becomes too thick, add a splash of water to the pan. Taste for seasoning, adding more salt if needed.

BLUE CHEESE *with* PEAR *and* VANILLA AIGRE-DOUX *and* ROASTED HICKORY NUTS

One of the easiest—and best—ways to serve homemade preserves is as a condiment with cheese. Here, vanilla and pear complement the intrinsic sweetness of a blue cheese like Hook's from Mineral Point, Wisconsin, while wine and vinegar stand up to the cheese's signature tang. After the first frost, hickory nuts begin to fall from the trees, only to be quickly gathered by foragers (and squirrels). While these sweet nuts are tough to crack, they can be purchased already shelled at farmers' markets in the fall. If hickory nuts are unavailable, use walnuts.

$^1/_2$ cup hickory nuts
$^1/_2$ cup Pear and Vanilla Aigre-Doux (page 100)
8 slices fruit-and-nut or sourdough bread
4 (1-ounce) pieces blue cheese

1. Preheat the oven to 300°F. Place the hickory nuts on a baking sheet and bake, checking the nuts often to make sure they don't burn, until lightly toasted, about 15 minutes. Remove the nuts and increase the oven temperature to 400°F.

2. Strain the aigre-doux liquid into a small pot, reserving the pears. (If there is a vanilla bean in the aigre-doux, remove it and save for another use.) Reduce the liquid over medium heat until it reaches a syrupy consistency, coating the back of a spoon. Cool to room temperature. Slice the pears into bite-sized chunks, then stir them into the syrup.

3. Arrange the slices of bread on a baking sheet and bake, turning the pieces over halfway through, until evenly toasted, about 5 minutes. To serve, divide the cheese among 4 plates. Spoon some aigre-doux on each plate and garnish with the hickory nuts and toast.

THANKSGIVING

{ this *Menu* serves 10 to 15 }

It's assumed that if you cook for a living, you would rather someone else did the honors on Thanksgiving. Not so at my house. This is a holiday when a chef should—excuse the Bobby Flay phrase—throw down. Go all out. Show off. On Thanksgiving, I may close the restaurant, but I maintain control of the stove.

When I was growing up outside of St. Louis, Thanksgiving leaned toward tradition. We played football. We ate turkey, stuffing, sweet potatoes, green beans, and cranberry sauce. Through these family feasts I developed a steadfast appreciation for Thanksgiving, but I've made changes to how I celebrate. Some changes have been subtle, like buying a heritage turkey. Some are more significant, such as braising turkey legs separately to make a rich gravy. While I didn't include a recipe for greens here, I often serve a side of spinach and kale along with the feast, simply wilting the greens in olive oil until tender.

Naturally, I also employ preserves. Sides of spiced cranberry aigre-doux and butternut squash aigre-doux augment the turkey as elegant condiments. In serving local foodstuffs supplemented by preserves, I feel as if I've returned to how Thanksgiving was prepared way back, when celebrating the local harvest took the main stage and using out-of-season ingredients was not an option.

Even though I take Thanksgiving seriously, I don't believe it should put you out. The trick is working ahead. I tackle the turkey days in advance. On Monday, I start preparing the turkey. Tuesday I start gathering all of my ingredients for the side dishes. And then I start staggering preparations for both the bird and the sides.

Most of us would never dare to make wholesale changes to family traditions. So pick out a couple of ideas from this menu and let them mingle with your classics. I urge you not to overlook the cranberry aigre-doux as a stand-in for cranberry sauce. The quick-pickled leeks in the stuffing could also dress up braised greens. And if you have a jar of fermented Brussels sprouts, braising them with chestnuts—for Thanksgiving or another winter feast—will be a revelation.

ROASTED TURKEY *with* SMOTHERED GRAVY

I take an unconventional approach to roasting turkey that may infuriate traditionalists who need to see a whole bird being carved ceremoniously at the table. I never wait for the big day to roast turkey. Instead, I butcher the bird into pieces well before Thursday. The neck, backbone, and wings go into stock, the legs are saved for braising, and the breasts are brined and roasted. More important, however, is the technique: by preparing the turkey in pieces, the breast meat isn't dry and the gravy is rich with large pieces of dark meat. Pictured on page 240 and 241.

1 (15-pound) turkey

1. To butcher the turkey, cut away the wings and reserve for the broth. Remove the heart and liver from the cavity and reserve for the Pickled Leek Stuffing (page 246). Remove the gizzards and save for the Smothered Gravy.

2. With the bird breast side up on the cutting board, remove the legs: with a sharp boning knife, make a cut in between the breast and the thigh joint, and then sever the connection between the thigh and the back. Once both legs have been removed, detach the thighs from the drumsticks, then cover and refrigerate. With a sturdy knife or pair of kitchen shears, cut out the backbone and neck, leaving the breast meat on the breastbone. (When propped breast-side up, the turkey will look ready to roast, just without legs.) Reserve the backbone and neck for the stock and refrigerate the breast meat until ready to brine.

Brine

You can make the brine as much as a week in advance. I brine the turkey breasts no later than Tuesday.

makes about 1 gallon

1 gallon water
1/2 cup kosher salt
1/2 cup packed brown sugar
1/4 cup *herbes de Provence*

2 heads garlic, halved crosswise
   (but left unpeeled)
1 onion, sliced

1. In a large pot bring the water, salt, sugar, herbs, garlic, and onion to a boil. Simmer until the salt and sugar have dissolved. Cool and refrigerate.

2. Place the breasts in a large storage container or pot and cover with the chilled brine (the meat should be completely submerged). Cover and refrigerate for at least 1 but no more than 2 days.

Roasted Turkey Breasts

I roast the turkey to a lower internal temperature because they're rewarmed before serving.

Brined turkey breasts
2 tablespoons unsalted butter, melted

1. Remove the breasts from the brine, pat dry, and let come to room temperature.

2. Preheat the oven to 425°F. Place the breasts in a roasting pan fitted with a rack and brush with butter. Roast until the meat reaches an internal temperature of 135°F to 140°F, about 45 minutes. Let the meat rest for about 15 minutes. Alternatively, cool the breasts, cover, and refrigerate overnight.

3. Remove the whole breasts from the breast bone, then slice each breast crosswise. Place the slices in a large casserole and spoon the hot gravy over the top. Place the turkey in a warm oven until ready to serve (if the breasts are still slightly pink, the hot gravy will finish cooking the meat).

Turkey Stock

Make this stock early in the week to have it ready for the smothered gravy and the stuffing.

makes 16 cups

Turkey backbone, neck, and wings	1 gallon water
2 onions, chopped	4 sprigs thyme
2 carrots, chopped	2 bay leaves
2 stalks celery, chopped	5 black peppercorns

Preheat the oven to 400°F. Place the backbone, neck, and wings in a roasting pan and roast until the skin and bones begin to brown, about 15 minutes. Add the onions, carrots, and celery and roast until the vegetables have caramelized, about 15 minutes more. Scrape the bones and vegetables into a stockpot and cover with about 1 gallon of water. Deglaze the roasting pan with a splash of water and scrape the caramelized bits into the pot. Add the thyme, bay leaves, and peppercorns and bring to a boil. Decrease to a simmer and cook for 3 hours. Strain the stock, cool, and refrigerate. Before using, scrape away any fat that has risen to the surface and reserve for the Pickled Leek Stuffing (page 246).

Smothered Gravy

This gravy is made over a couple of days. On Tuesday I braise the legs and let them cool in the braising liquid. The next day I pull apart the meat, discard the bones, and strain the braising liquid. On Thanksgiving, I finish the gravy.

makes about 12 cups

2 tablespoons grapeseed oil
Turkey drumsticks and thighs
Kosher salt and freshly ground
    black pepper
Gizzards (optional)

1 onion, chopped
1 carrot, chopped
2 stalks celery, chopped
5 to 7 cloves garlic, chopped
1 cup white wine

8 cups turkey stock (page 244)
$\frac{1}{2}$ cup unsalted butter
$\frac{1}{2}$ cup all-purpose flour
2 cups whole milk

1. Preheat the oven to 300°F. In a large sauté pan over high heat, warm the oil. Season the legs, thighs, and gizzards with salt and pepper. In batches, sear the turkey pieces and transfer to a large roasting pan. In the same sauté pan, sweat the onion, carrot, celery, and garlic until lightly caramelized, about 6 minutes. Deglaze with the wine and reduce by half. Pour in the stock and bring to a simmer. Spoon the stock and vegetables over the thighs and legs, cover the pan with aluminum foil, and roast until the meat is very tender, about 2 hours. Cool the legs in the braising liquid and refrigerate overnight.

2. Scrape off any fat that has risen to the top of the braising liquid and set aside for the stuffing. Remove the legs and thighs from the braising liquid and pull the meat off the bones. Bring the liquid to a boil, then strain and cool. Refrigerate until ready to make the gravy.

3. In a small saucepan, melt the butter. Stir in the flour and cook the roux until it turns pale gold and smells slightly like browned butter. In a large pot, bring the braising liquid and milk to a boil. Decrease to a simmer and whisk in the roux. Simmer over medium-low heat, stirring often, until the gravy coats the back of a spoon, about 15 minutes. Add the turkey meat and simmer until the meat is hot. Keep warm.

PRESERVED LEMON *and* THYME BUTTER

The best part of a preserved lemon is the rind, but I've found that the pulp, which is typically discarded, also can come in handy. Whenever I use the rinds of preserved citrus, I save the pulp for making compound butters like this one.

makes about ¹/₂ pound

6 wedges Preserved Lemon
  (about 1 lemon), page 115
1 tablespoon grapeseed oil

2 shallots, minced
3 tablespoons chopped fresh thyme
¹/₂ cup white wine

1 cup unsalted butter, cubed, near
  room temperature
Kosher salt and freshly ground
  black pepper

1. Rinse the lemon wedges under cool running water for 20 minutes to rinse off excess salt. Remove the rind from the pulp and reserve for the Scarlet Turnips with Crème Fraîche and Preserved Lemon (page 249). In a food processor, purée the pulp.

2. In a small sauté pan over medium heat, warm the oil. Sweat the shallots until softened, about 1 minute. Stir in the thyme and cook 1 more minute. Stir in the preserved lemon purée, then deglaze the pan with the wine. Simmer until the wine has almost completely evaporated, then transfer the mixture to the food processor.

3. Add the butter to the lemon purée and pulse until well-blended. Season lightly with salt and pepper as needed. Spoon the butter into small ramekins, cover with plastic wrap, and chill in the refrigerator for at least 3 hours or overnight. To serve, unwrap and place ramekins around the table.

PICKLED LEEK STUFFING

For many Americans, stuffing is the most important dish at the Thanksgiving table. I stay relatively classic, with a couple of new additions: quick-pickled leeks and Gruyère cheese. After making turkey broth, I save the fat that rises to the surface to mix into the dressing. This imparts turkey flavor without having to bake the dressing in the bird's cavity.

1 cup unsalted butter
1 turkey liver (optional)
1 turkey heart (optional)
Kosher salt and freshly ground
  black pepper
Turkey fat, if available

2 stalks celery, chopped
1 carrot, diced
1 yellow onion, diced
5 cloves garlic, minced
1 tablespoon chopped fresh thyme
12 cups day-old cubed country bread

8 cups Turkey Stock (page 244)
1 cup Italian parsley leaves, chopped
3 large eggs, lightly beaten
Quick-Pickled Leeks (recipe follows)
2 cups grated Gruyère cheese

1. If using the heart and liver, in a small saucepan over medium heat, melt 1 tablespoon of the butter. Sear the heart and liver for about 30 seconds on each side, and season with salt and pepper. Cool and mince.

2. Butter a large Dutch oven or two smaller casseroles. In a large, wide pot over medium heat, melt ³/₄ cup of the butter and a couple of tablespoons of turkey fat, if available. Stir in the celery, carrot and onion. Cook until slightly softened, about 3 minutes. Mix in the garlic and thyme, cook 1 minute more, then add the bread. Mix until the bread is coated in the butter. Pour in the stock and add the parsley. Season with salt and pepper. Fold in the heart and liver, followed by the eggs. Spoon the dressing into the Dutch oven.

3. Drain the leeks, reserving the pickling liquid to make another batch, if desired. In a large sauté pan, melt the remaining 3 tablespoons butter. Sweat the leeks in the butter until softened. Pour over the dressing, pressing the leeks into the bread. Scatter the Gruyère over the top, then cover with aluminum foil and refrigerate at least 1 hour or overnight.

4. Preheat the oven to 400°F. Bake, covered, until the sides are bubbling and the dressing is hot in the center, about 45 minutes.

Quick-Pickled Leeks

I've tried processing pickled leeks to store on the shelf with other preserves, but I've never been pleased with the results. The processing time seems to compromise their delicate texture. With a quick pickle, however, the leeks retain their shape and integrity. This quick pickle also can accent glazed vegetables, roasted poultry, or grilled fish.

makes about 3 cups

4 leeks	3 bay leaves
1¹/₂ cups champagne vinegar	Juice and grated zest of 1 lemon
1 cup water	1 teaspoon kosher salt
3 sprigs thyme	

1. Slice off the root ends of the leeks, keeping as much of the white end intact as possible. Trim away the dark green tips. Make an incision lengthwise halfway through the leek. Pry the leek open and run under water, fanning it open to remove any residual dirt. Slice the leeks crosswise into ¹/₄-inch pieces.

2. In a pot bring the vinegar, water, thyme, bay leaves, lemon juice and zest, and salt to a boil. Add the leeks, cover, and simmer for 2 minutes. Remove from the heat and cool completely. Refrigerate until needed. (This can be made more than a week ahead.)

SMASHED YUKON GOLD POTATOES

There are all sorts of healthy ways to prepare potatoes. This is not one of them. But potatoes served on Thanksgiving should be dressed up more than usual for a good reason. They will stay creamy and hold heat better if made with plenty of butter and cream. I call this preparation "smashed" because I don't bother with a potato ricer or food mill. Instead, I put the boiled potatoes, skins and all, in a mixer and let the paddle attachment do all of the work.

4¹/₂ pounds Yukon gold potatoes, quartered
Kosher salt

1¹/₂ cups heavy cream.
¹/₂ cup unsalted butter, cubed and at room temperature

Freshly ground black pepper

---

1. Put the potatoes in a large pot with a few generous pinches of salt. Cover with 1 inch of cold water and bring to a boil. Decrease to a simmer and cook until the potatoes are tender. Drain and let stand for a few minutes.

2. In a small sauté pan over medium-high heat, bring the cream to a simmer. Remove from the heat.

3. Preheat the oven to 200°F. Let an ovenproof casserole with a lid warm in the oven while you finish the potatoes. Put half of the potatoes in a stand mixer fitted with the paddle attachment. Add half the butter and mix on low speed until the potatoes turn into a chunky, creamy mixture. While the mixer is still running drizzle in some of the warmed cream and mix briefly, just until the potatoes take on a soft, creamy consistency. Season with salt and pepper. Repeat the same process with the remaining potatoes. You will use all of the butter, but you may not use all the cream. Transfer to the preheated casserole, cover, and keep warm in a low oven until ready to serve.

BRAISED FERMENTED BRUSSELS SPROUTS
with CHESTNUTS

Brussels sprouts sauerkraut is an unexpected treat, at once mild and tangy. Open a jar, give it a good rinse, and braise it with chicken stock for a simple but sophisticated side dish. To make them appropriate for a celebration, however, I add meaty chestnuts which accentuate the sweeter side of the sprouts. Look for shelled, unsweetened French chestnuts, which can be found either frozen or in jars around Thanksgiving. Avoid marrons glacés, which are candied chestnuts.

---

4 ounces bacon, diced
2 tablespoons butter
2 sweet onions (such as candy or Vidalia), sliced

5 cloves garlic, minced
8 cups Brussels Sprouts Sauerkraut (page 111), drained and rinsed
1 pound shelled, unsweetened chestnuts

4 cups chicken stock (page 130) or turkey stock (page 244)
Kosher salt and freshly ground black pepper

---

1. Preheat the oven to 325°F. Make a lid out of parchment paper to fit over the large Dutch oven or pot you plan to use to braise the Brussels sprouts (see Making a Parchment Paper Lid, page 20).

2. In the same pot, render the bacon until it becomes crisp, about 5 minutes. Swirl in the butter and add the onions and garlic. Sweat until the onions become translucent, about 4 minutes. Stir in the Brussels sprouts and chestnuts and cook 1 to 2 minutes more. Pour in the stock and bring to a boil. Place the parchment lid on top and put the pot into the oven. Braise until the chestnuts are tender, about 35 minutes. Taste and season with salt and pepper, if needed.

SCARLET TURNIPS *with* CRÈME FRAÎCHE *and* PRESERVED LEMON

You can use any trunips for this recipe, though my favorite are small scarlet trunips which look like radishes. I like to find small turnips, no bigger than the top half of my thumb. The cooking times for turnips tend to vary so monitor doneness by piercing pieces with a fork. This side dish is best made the day you serve.

6 wedges Preserved Lemon (page 115)
2 tablespoons unsalted butter
1 sweet onion (such as candy or Vidalia), sliced

2 pounds scarlet turnips, trimmed and halved or quartered
Kosher salt

1/2 cup Crème Fraîche (page 17)
1 cup loosely packed Italian parsley leaves, chopped

1. Rinse the lemon wedges under cool running water for 20 minutes to rinse off excess salt. Drain the wedges, remove the pulp, and cut away as much pith as possible without losing any of the rind. (Save the pulp for the lemon butter on page 246.) Mince the rinds; set aside.

2. In a large Dutch oven or heavy-bottomed pot over medium-high heat, melt the butter. Add the onion and cook over medium-low heat until soft and lightly caramelized, 5 to 7 minutes. Increase the heat, stir in the turnips, and season with a couple of pinches of salt. Cook for a few minutes more until the turnips begin to brown. Decrease the heat back to medium-low, cover, and cook until the turnips are nearly done, about 8 minutes.

3. Uncover, stir in the lemon rinds and crème fraîche, and cook until the turnips are cooked through, another 3 to 5 minutes. Stir in the parsley right before serving.

BUTTER ROLLS

With the rich, complex flavors of a Thanksgiving meal, I keep the rolls simple. For a golden-brown crust and a dynamic presentation, I bake them in a large, well-seasoned cast-iron pan. In keeping with the spirit of using preserves, I serve them with a preserved lemon compound butter. For a bread-hungry group, I double the recipe and bake two pans of rolls.

makes 30 small rolls

¹/₂ ounce / 15 grams fresh yeast or 1 teaspoon active dry yeast	1 pound, 1¹/₂ ounces / 500 grams / 4 cups all-purpose flour	3 ounces / 85 grams / 6 tablespoons unsalted butter, cubed and slightly softened, plus extra for glazing the rolls
¹/₃ ounce / 12 grams / 1 tablespoon honey	¹/₄ ounce / 9 grams / 2 teaspoons kosher salt	
13¹/₂ ounces / 380 grams / 1¹/₂ cups whole milk, at room temperature (around 70°F)		

1. In the bowl of a stand mixer, use a spoon stir the fresh yeast and honey into the milk until dissolved. (If using active dry yeast, add the yeast to the milk. Do not stir. Let stand 5 minutes, then stir in the honey.)

2. Attach the dough hook to the mixing bowl. With the mixer running on low speed, gradually add half of the flour to the yeast slurry and continue to mix on low speed until a paste forms, about 1 minute. Stir in the rest of the flour and the salt and mix on medium-low speed until smooth, about 4 minutes.

3. Meanwhile, lightly oil a bowl; set aside. Decrease the mixer speed to low and gradually add cubes of butter to the dough as it mixes. Once all the butter has been added, continue to mix on low speed until the dough is smooth and pulls away from the sides of the mixing bowl, about 5 minutes. Transfer the dough to the oiled bowl and cover with plastic wrap. Let the dough rise at room temperature until doubled in size, 1 to 1¹/₂ hours. Punch down the dough to deflate it, cover it again with plastic wrap, and let it rise again for 30 minutes.

4. Oil a 12-inch cast-iron skillet; set aside. Lightly flour a counter. Transfer the dough to the counter and, using a knife or bench scraper and a scale, portion the dough into thirty 1- to 1¹/₂-ounce pieces about the size of a golf-ball. To form each ball, cup the palm of your hand around the top of the piece of dough and move your hand in circles. Friction from the work surface will help form the dough into a ball. Too much flour on the work surface can interfere with shaping the dough. If this happens, wipe the counter with a damp cloth.

5. In tight concentric circles, arrange the rolls in the prepared skillet. Cover with a slightly damp kitchen towel and let rise at room temperature until the rolls have almost doubled in size, about 35 minutes. (You also can cover the skillet in plastic wrap and refrigerate overnight. Before baking, let them come to room temperature.)

6. Preheat the oven to 350°F. Brush the tops of the rolls with melted butter. Bake, rotating the pans halfway through, until the tops are evenly browned and the bread is baked through, 25 to 30 minutes. Cool the rolls in the skillet for at least 20 minutes before serving.

GLAZED BUTTERNUT SQUASH AIGRE-DOUX

Dressing up thin slices of butternut squash with a sweet-tangy sauce not only shows a different way to present ubiquitous winter squash, but it also makes the meal feel more like a special occasion.

4 cups Butternut Squash Aigre-Doux
(page 98), not drained
2 tablespoons unsalted butter

Kosher salt
1 whole nutmeg, for grating

Pour the aigre-doux into a large sauté pan. Over medium-high heat, simmer the liquid until it begins to coat the squash, about 6 minutes. Swirl in the butter and season with salt to taste. Right before serving, grate nutmeg over the top.

CRANBERRY AIGRE-DOUX RELISH

Star anise, black peppercorns, and vanilla provide a subtle, spicy backdrop for the tart cranberries, making this aigre-doux an ideal holiday condiment. Served in a plain white bowl, they provide striking contrast on the table.

4 cups Cranberry Aigre-Doux (page 99)

Strain the liquid and set aside the cranberries. In a small pot over medium heat, reduce the liquid by half. Stir in the cranberries and serve warm.

CRANBERRY-PEAR CRISP

With a heap of bright Wisconsin cranberries and fall pears, this crisp is well suited for the Thanksgiving table. The best part (according to my family) is the crumbly topping, so I don't skimp. More crumble on top also curbs the tartness of the cranberries.

2 large pears
5 cups fresh cranberries
2 cups sugar
2 cups all-purpose flour

1/4 cup whole wheat flour
1 teaspoon kosher salt
1 cup cold unsalted butter, cubed

1. Place a rack in the middle of the oven and preheat the oven to 350°F.

2. Peel, quarter, and core the pears. Halve each wedge and slice crosswise into small chunks. Spread the pear pieces and cranberries evenly in a 9 by 13-inch baking pan. Sprinkle $^1/_2$ cup of the sugar over the fruit and gently mix to combine.

3. In a stand mixer fitted with the paddle attachment, mix the remaining $1^1/_2$ cups sugar with the flours and salt on low speed. While the mixer is running, gradually add the butter and continue to mix until a coarse crumble forms. Spread the crumble evenly over the fruit, gently pressing it into the fruit (expect it to be a thick layer).

4. Bake until the cranberry juices are bubbling and the topping is golden brown, about 50 minutes.

PUMPKIN BUTTER ICE CREAM

There is no doubt that this ice cream is rich, and a little goes a long way. But if you have a large crowd of ice cream lovers coming over, consider doubling the recipe. If doubling, you will need to freeze the base in two batches.

makes about 1 quart

1 cup whole milk	$^1/_4$ teaspoon kosher salt
1 cup heavy cream	6 large egg yolks
$^1/_2$ cup sugar	1 cup Pumpkin Butter (page 81)

1. In a pot over medium-high heat, whisk together the milk, cream, $^1/_4$ cup of the sugar, and salt. Bring to a boil and remove from the heat.

2. In a medium bowl, whisk together the egg yolks and the remaining $^1/_4$ cup sugar. Slowly ladle about 1 cup of the milk into the eggs, whisking constantly until smooth. Whisk the tempered egg-yolk mixture into the milk and cook the custard over medium-low heat, stirring constantly, until it becomes thick enough to coat the back of a spoon, about 5 minutes. Strain the custard into a clean bowl and whisk in the pumpkin butter. Cool over an ice bath. Refrigerate the base for at least a couple of hours or up to 3 days.

3. To freeze the ice cream, give the base a good stir, then pour it into an ice cream maker. Churn according to the manufacturer's instructions and store in a chilled container in the freezer.

WINTER
WEEKDAYS

ROASTED ROOT VEGETABLE SALAD
WITH PICKLED CARROTS, AGED
CHEDDAR, AND APPLES • 257

PORK MILANESE WITH YELLOW
PLUM AND RIESLING JAM AND
ARUGULA • 258

SALTED CARAMEL ICE CREAM WITH
BRANDIED FIGS • 260

{ this *Menu* serves 4 }

It's easy to talk seasonal and local. Sticking to the mantra, especially on a weeknight in the middle of winter, is something else. But winter cooking doesn't have to mean long-cooked, meat-heavy braises, with few vegetables in between. I advocate eating seasonal vegetables year-round, even in the winter, when rutabagas, parsnips, and kale start to feel repetitive. To stave off root vegetable fatigue, I alter my preparations just enough so that new flavors emerge, yielding surprises.

To enliven root vegetables, for instance, I leverage the power of pickles. A drizzle of brine from preserved carrots can turn standard-issue roasted veggies into a warm winter salad while slices of apple and shavings of aged Cheddar add texture and richness. Meanwhile, a plum and Riesling jam makes a surprisingly successful pair with pan-seared pork Milanese, the jam's sweet tang playing off the buttery bread-crumb coating. With a bit of juggling, both recipes can be prepared relatively easily at home in one evening.

For a treat, though, I've included caramel ice cream served with brandied figs. I don't expect someone to whip up an ice cream from start to finish in an evening, but a quart of ice cream made on a Sunday afternoon can deliver indulgence throughout the week, and an open jar of brandied figs keeps in the refrigerator for at least a month.

The point of these recipes is not to shock and awe your gastronomically competitive friends (for that, turn to the Midwinter Feast, page 281). It is for anyone who wants to eat a delicious, seasonal meal that not only lends itself well to customizing (you can use, for instance, veal or chicken instead of pork, or sweet potatoes instead of turnips) but also showcases the power of a well-stocked pantry. And that alone is worth bragging rights.

ROASTED ROOT VEGETABLE SALAD *with* PICKLED CARROTS, AGED CHEDDAR, *and* APPLES

I preheat a large baking sheet in the oven before roasting the vegetables to ensure they caramelize faster. For a similar reason, I slice the carrots and parsnips with an oblique cut (see page 27). Not only does the cut look cleaner, it also leaves more surface area for browning than blunt-cut vegetables do. Pictured on pages 254 and 255.

---

3 tablespoons grapeseed oil

1 celery root, peeled and diced into small cubes

2 parsnips, peeled and sliced into an oblique cut

1 medium purple-top turnip, diced into small cubes, or 3 white salad turnips, quartered

1 carrot, peeled and sliced into an oblique cut

2 sprigs rosemary

Kosher salt and freshly ground black pepper

1/2 sweet onion (such as candy or Vidalia), sliced

1 cup Pickled Carrots (page 26), sliced thinly crosswise

1/2 cup pickling liquid from Pickled Carrots (page 26)

1 apple (preferably Honeycrisp), cored and sliced

1 tablespoon chopped fresh dill or parsley (optional)

1 block aged Cheddar cheese, for shaving

---

1. Preheat the oven to 400°F. Place a large rimmed baking sheet in the oven. Pour the oil on the baking sheet and return to the oven for 1 minute or until the oil is very hot.

2. Carefully stir the celery root in the oil in the pan, return the baking sheet to the oven, and roast 3 minutes. Stir in the parsnips, turnip, carrot, and rosemary; season with a few pinches of salt and pepper; and roast for another 5 minutes. Scatter the onion on top and continue to roast, stirring periodically, until all the vegetables are cooked through and well browned, about 25 minutes.

3. Transfer the warm vegetables to a large serving bowl and remove the rosemary sprigs. Stir in the pickled carrots and 1/4 cup of the pickling liquid. Mix in the apples just to warm through, and then taste for seasoning, adjusting with more salt, pepper, or pickling liquid, if necessary, until the vegetables are well seasoned and mildly tangy. Mix in the dill. With a vegetable peeler, shave curls of Cheddar over the top before serving.

PORK MILANESE *with* YELLOW PLUM *and* RIESLING JAM *and* ARUGULA

Call it Milanese or schnitzel, breaded meat cutlets are simple but undeniably delicious. We have served Milanese as an appetizer at Vie nearly since we opened, which is when we realized it paired perfectly with plum jam. With a side of roasted root vegetables, the Milanese is certainly satisfying enough as a meal.

A squeeze of lemon is a classic way to brighten the flavor, but I prefer to add acidity in the form of arugula dressed with lemon juice and olive oil. The sweet-tangy plum and Riesling jam acts as a perfect bridge between the salad and the pork. Save yourself the first step in this recipe by asking the butcher to pound out the cutlets for you.

4 (4-ounce) thin pork loin cutlets or boneless pork chops	2 large eggs	2 tablespoons olive oil
$^1/_2$ cup all-purpose flour	$^1/_2$ cup grapeseed oil	Juice from $^1/_2$ lemon
$^1/_2$ cup bread crumbs	2 tablespoons unsalted butter	Freshly ground black pepper
$^1/_2$ cup grated Parmesan cheese	Kosher salt	1 jar Yellow Plum and Riesling Jam
	4 ounces arugula	(page 74)

1. Preheat the oven to 200°F. Place a platter in the oven to warm. Trim any visible sinew off the sides of the cutlets. Place a cutlet on a sheet of parchment paper and cover with an additional sheet. With the flat side of a mallet, pound to $^1/_8$ to $^1/_4$ inch thick. Repeat with the remaining cutlets.

2. Place the flour on a plate. On a separate plate, mix together the bread crumbs and Parmesan. Whisk the eggs in a shallow bowl. Dredge each piece of pork in the flour, followed by egg wash, followed by the bread crumbs.

3. In a large skillet or sauté pan, warm about $^1/_4$ cup of the grapeseed oil. In 2 batches to avoid crowding the pan, pan-fry the pork until golden brown and cooked through, about 2 minutes per side. In between batches, wipe the pan clean and add the remaining grapeseed oil. Once each cutlet is cooked, transfer to the warmed platter in the oven. When all the cutlets are cooked, put them back in the pan with the butter and baste for a minute to finish. Place the cutlets on paper towels and season with salt. Divide among 4 plates.

4. In a bowl, mix together the arugula with the olive oil and lemon juice. Season with salt and pepper. Place a generous pile of arugula salad on each cutlet and finish with a spoonful of jam alongside.

SALTED CARAMEL ICE CREAM *with* BRANDIED FIGS

I can't tell you who was the first to add salt to caramel (probably the French). It doesn't matter. As an ice cream flavor, salted caramel is a new classic, pairing deftly with sweet brandied figs. The keys to success: don't go overboard on the salt and don't undercook the caramel. For tips on making caramel, see Caramel Apple Jam (page 78). Serve the ice cream with a few Whole-Wheat Shortbread cookies (page 153) for crunch, if you'd like.

makes about 5 cups ice cream

2²/₃ cups whole milk

³/₄ cup heavy cream

¹/₃ cup powdered milk

1 teaspoon kosher salt

¹/₂ cup, plus 2 tablespoons sugar

¹/₄ cup light corn syrup

2 large egg yolks

1 pint jar Brandied Black Mission Figs
    (page 69)

1. In a pot over medium-high heat, whisk together the milk, cream, powdered milk, and salt. Bring to a brisk simmer and remove from heat.

2. In a separate pot over medium-high heat, combine the sugar and corn syrup. Cook until the sugars begin to brown. Decrease the heat and swirl the pan. Continue to cook until the sugars reach a deep golden brown color. Remove the pot from the heat and pour in the warm milk mixture. Be cautious: the mixture will splatter and the caramel will seize up and harden. Return the pot to the stove and cook over medium heat, stirring occasionally, until the caramel eventually dissolves.

3. In a medium bowl, whisk the egg yolks. Slowly ladle about 1 cup of the caramel milk into the eggs, whisking constantly until well-blended, then pour the tempered egg-yolk mixture into the rest of the caramel milk. Cook the custard over medium heat, stirring constantly, until the mixture has thickened enough to coat the back of a spoon, about 5 minutes. Strain the caramel milk into a clean bowl and cool over an ice bath. Refrigerate the ice cream base for at least a couple of hours or preferably overnight.

4. To freeze the ice cream, give the base a good stir, then pour it into an ice cream maker. Churn according to the manufacturer's instructions and store in a chilled container in the freezer.

5. Strain the fig brandy syrup into a small pot over medium-high heat. Reduce the syrup until it can coat the back of a spoon, about 5 minutes. Stir in the figs and cool to room temperature.

6. Serve scoops of the ice cream with a spoonful or two of figs (you may have some figs left over).

WINTER: winter weekdays

CHILI NIGHT

BEEF CHILI WITH CHOW CHOW, CHEDDAR, CRÈME FRAÎCHE, AND PICKLED CANDY ONIONS • 265

JENNIFER'S CHOCOLATE CHIP COOKIES • 266

{ this *Menu* serves 10 }

Like real barbecue, chili is one of those foods that sparks arguments among aficiona-dos. Texans eschew beans, vegetarians eschew beef, and residents of Cincinnati inexplicably ladle it over spaghetti. But for most of us, chili means a savory pot of beef and beans, the perfect cold-weather food.

For my family, it's also the perfect food for Halloween, when dinner needs to be simple and sub-stantial, and for the holiday season, when company is in town and the last thing any of us feel like doing is another round of dishes. I'll set up a crock pot to keep it warm as family and friends filter through the house.

My chili could be mistaken for a piquant beef and black bean stew. Instead of ground beef, I opt for cubes of beef chuck or shank augmented with smoky beef bacon, which supplies rich, deep flavor. Like many braises, it tastes better reheated. (Make it the day before to allow the meat to cool in the cooking liquid for the best results.) But what sets my chili apart is the condiment selection—and a bowl of chili is hardly complete without a topping of some sort. I open jars of corn relish and pickled candy onions made the previous summer. I also offer homemade crème fraîche and some grated aged Cheddar. Then I let my guests compose their own idea of what a perfect bowl of chili should look like.

BEEF CHILI *with* CHOW CHOW, CHEDDAR, CRÈME FRAÎCHE, *and* PICKLED CANDY ONIONS

There is nothing wrong with making chili with ground beef, but using beef cubes adds more dimension: unlike ground beef, I can sear the pieces until caramelized, which gives the braise a deeper, more complex flavor. I also cook the chili slowly in the oven so the meat is tender and the pickled hot peppers have mellowed in the sauce.

According to food science expert Harold McGee, soaking beans before cooking them not only allows them to cook better, it also reduces that less-than-comfortable side effect of eating beans. After soaking, I parcook the beans and then add them to the beef to finish cooking. If the chili is too brothy when it comes out of the oven, simmer it on the stove until the sauce thickens. Pictured on pages 262 and 263.

---

2 cups dried black beans

2 tablespoons grapeseed oil

8 ounces Beef Bacon (page 116), diced

2 pounds beef chuck or shank, cut into
    $^1/_2$-inch cubes

1$^1/_2$ teaspoons kosher salt

$^1/_2$ teaspoon freshly ground black pepper

2 onions, diced

1 carrot, diced

7 or 8 cloves garlic, minced

2 tablespoons tomato paste

1 tablespoon cumin seeds, toasted and
    coarsely ground

1 tablespoon sweet smoked paprika

4 cups Canned Tomatoes (page 46)

6 cups beef stock (page 131)

1 cup Grilled and Pickled Hot Peppers
    (page 37), drained and diced

1 pint Chow Chow (page 29)

1 pint Pickled Candy Onions (page 25),
    drained

2 to 3 cups grated Cheddar cheese

1 to 2 cups Crème Fraîche (page 17)

---

1. Soak the beans in water to cover for at least 4 hours or overnight. Drain the beans and place in a pot. Cover the beans with cold water, bring them to a boil, and drain. Cover the beans once again with cold water, bring to a boil, and lower to a simmer. Cook for 30 minutes, then drain. (The beans will be partially cooked.)

2. Meanwhile, preheat the oven to 300°F. In a large, ovenproof 8-quart Dutch oven or heavy-bottomed pot over medium heat, warm the grapeseed oil. Add the bacon and cook until it barely starts to brown, 2 minutes. Season the beef chuck with salt and pepper, add to the pot with the bacon, and sear until browned on all sides, about 5 minutes. Stir in the onions, carrot, and garlic and cook until the vegetables soften, about 5 minutes.

3. Stir in the tomato paste, cumin, and paprika and cook for 1 minute more. Pour in the tomatoes and stock and bring the pot to a boil. Stir in the hot peppers and beans, then cover and place in the oven. Cook the chili for 2$^1/_2$ hours, then remove the lid and continue to cook until the meat is completely tender, another 30 minutes. Taste for seasoning, adding more salt and pepper if needed. You should have about 16 cups. If the chili is too thin, put it on the stove and simmer it (uncovered) until the sauce thickens.

4. To serve, ladle the chili into large bowls. Set out the chow chow, pickled onions, Cheddar, and crème fraîche at the table and let guests to garnish their chili to their liking.

JENNIFER'S CHOCOLATE CHIP COOKIES

The only kind of sweet that I want after a simple bowl of chili is something classic, and these cookies deliver. My wife, Jennifer, makes these cookies so often that she measures ingredients by eye, wielding a mixer with effective speed. Through the years, she has made a couple of notable changes. She upgraded to European-style butter, comprising a high, 82 percent butterfat. And she played around with sugar, finding that so-called vegan sugar has slightly coarser crystals, which gives the cookies a sweet crunch (though granulated works fine, too). For chocolate, she has tried several combinations. I favor bittersweet chips, but the fan favorite is milk chocolate. Jennifer uses a convection oven and bakes them for 8 minutes for a deliciously chewy cookie. Without convection, the cookies may take a couple of minutes more.

makes 5 dozen cookies

1 cup unsalted butter (preferably 82% butterfat), at room temperature

1 cup granulated sugar (preferably vegan sugar)

1 cup packed light brown sugar

2 large eggs

1 teaspoon pure vanilla extract

1 teaspoon kosher salt

1 teaspoon baking powder

1 teaspoon baking soda

2^1/$_4$ cups all-purpose flour

2 cups chocolate chips (your choice)

1. Position the oven racks so that one is in the lower third of the oven and the other is in the upper third. Preheat a convection oven or standard oven to 350°F. Line 2 baking sheets with parchment paper or lightly oil them.

2. In a stand mixer fitted with the paddle attachment, blend the butter and sugars until creamy. Mix in the eggs and vanilla. Gradually add the salt, baking powder, and baking soda, scraping down the sides of the mixer in between additions. Once mixed, gradually mix in the flour. Scrape down the sides, then stir in the chocolate chips until incorporated.

3. Using about 1 heaping tablespoon for each cookie, form 4 rows of 5 on the prepared sheets, leaving at least 1^1/$_2$ inches between each cookie. Bake the cookies, rotating the sheets from top to bottom halfway through, until the edges of the cookies are golden brown and the tops are barely set, 8 minutes in a convection oven or 9 to 10 minutes in a conventional oven. Repeat with the remaining cookie dough until all of the dough is baked. The cookies keep in an airtight container for a week, but they never seem to last that long in our house.

WINTER: *chili night*

A BEER CELEBRATION

{ this *Menu* serves 8 }

When the first big microbrew explosion occurred in the 1990s during my New York City line-cooking days, I became a casual fan. It would take several more years before I began to appreciate how well these handcrafted beers paired with food. In my training grounds—fine-dining, French-inspired restaurants—beer had one place only: the post-shift drink. That is hardly the case now. There has rarely been a better time to feature local beers on the menu.

Brewing has been an integral part of the Midwest since the nineteenth century, when German families such as the Pabsts and Schlitzes set up shop in Milwaukee. In the Great Lakes region today, large craft breweries, like Goose Island, coexist with three-guy operations that make beer in unlikely corners, from residential corridors in Chicago to the far, far suburbs. And that's not even getting into the brewing buzz in Wisconsin, Michigan, Missouri, and Indiana—nor does it tap into the rising gypsy brewing phenomenon, where talented brewers travel from coast to coast making beer in other brewers' facilities. With the range of beers that these inventive brewers produce, from clove-accented wheat beers to unusual sour ales, I rarely find myself in a beer-food pairing rut.

A few times a year we put on beer-pairing dinners, highlighting a different local brewer with each course. We've also opened up the doors to home brewers, hosting a contest in which amateurs can size up the competition. For each event I draft a menu that complement the various beers. It's a different sort of challenge to balance hops and fizz with aged beef or arctic char. I tend to favor rich aromas, such as smoke, or meaty dishes, like braises. Cheese also is inherently complementary, and a piece of aged Cheddar drizzled with beer jam is a slam-dunk with just about any beer. When pairing beer with food, I also borrow a technique from wine pros, starting with light beers and getting progressively more complex as the meal progresses. Or I just start off with a potent Beer Jam Manhattan (page 209)and see where the night takes me.

Even when we get a little fancy, there is still one underlying feature of these dinners that separates them from others: approachability. The most expensive beers are still on the affordable side. And that alone is worth a toast.

SMOKED STURGEON *with* RUTABAGA SAUERKRAUT LATKES *and* CRÈME FRAÎCHE

Smoked sturgeon makes regular appearances on my menus. The mild fish soaks up smoke expertly, lending itself well to appetizer courses. Even when I don't smoke sturgeon outright, I grill it over hardwood so it absorbs a bit of smoke. The fish also shines with lighter-style beers.

I usually set up an outdoor smoker (see The Draw of Smoke, page 197) to smoke fish at Vie. But because my outdoor smoker will go for a few hours, I can smoke a host of other ingredients as well. So if I only need a smoker for twenty minutes, I set up a stovetop smoker. To smoke on a stovetop, you will need a large disposable aluminum pan or a beat-up deep restaurant-style hotel pan with foil (don't waste a good hotel pan on smoking—it will ruin the pan). You also will need hardwood chips (½ cup or so, available at many hardware stores), a wire rack, and some aluminum foil. Before you start, make sure your kitchen's vent is in working order, or at least that you can open a window. If you intend to smoke on a stovetop often, you might want to invest in an inexpensive stainless-steel stovetop smoker.

The key to remember for either the outdoor or the stovetop method is that this is a hot smoke: the fish needs to reach an internal temperature of 135°F to 140°F. If the smoke burns out and the fish still isn't cooked, remove it from the smoker and bake at 300°F until cooked through. Before I smoke any fish, I leave it in the walk-in cooler on a rack, uncovered, to dry out. At home, you can leave it in the refrigerator uncovered. This allows the surface of the fish to form a pellicle, a layer of skin that absorbs smoke. Smoke won't adhere as well to a damp surface. Pictured on page 272.

SMOKED STURGEON
2 pounds sturgeon fillet, skinned
1 teaspoon caraway seeds
1 teaspoon mustard seeds
1 teaspoon coriander seeds
1 teaspoon dill seeds
1 teaspoon fennel seeds

¼ cup kosher salt
2 tablespooons brown sugar
Grated zest of 1 lemon

1 cup Crème Frâiche (page 17)
¼ cup chopped fresh dill
Kosher salt and freshly ground
  black pepper

3 to 4 drops Tabasco Sauce
16 Rutabaga Sauerkraut Latkes
  (recipe follows)
1 or 2 stalks Pickled Celery
  (page 28), diced
Fresh dill or chervil sprigs (optional)

---

1. To prepare the sturgeon, pat the fillet dry with paper towels and place in a storage container. In a dry sauté pan over medium heat, toast the caraway, mustard, coriander, dill, and fennel seeds. Grind in a mortar and pestle or a coffee grinder dedicated to spices. In a small bowl, mix the spices with the salt, sugar, and zest. Coat the sturgeon in the cure, then cover and refrigerate for 4 hours.

2. Remove the sturgeon, rinse lightly, and pat dry. Place on a rack and refrigerate, uncovered, overnight.

3. Prepare a stovetop smoker. Line a deep, disposable aluminum pan large enough to cover two burners with aluminum foil or use a stovetop smoker. Pile about ½ cup of wood chips on one end of the pan and cover with a

{continued}

wire rack. Place the sturgeon on the rack. Put the pan over a pair of front and back burners with the wood-chip end over the front burner. Cover the smoker snugly with aluminum foil. Cut a small slit in the end opposite the wood chips to allow smoke to escape. Ensuring that the ventilation fan is on, turn the front burner to medium. Once smoke begins to escape through the hole in the aluminum foil, turn down the heat and gently smoke until the sturgeon reaches an internal temperature between 135°F to 140°F, about 20 minutes. Remove the sturgeon and cool completely before serving. The fish will keep, wrapped in plastic and refrigerated, for about 1 week.

4. For serving, in a small bowl, mix the crème frâiche with the dill, salt, pepper, and Tabasco. Using a sharp knife, slice the sturgeon into 1/4-inch-thick pieces. Divide the slices between 8 plates. Place two latkes on each plate and garnish with a dollop of crème frâiche, pickled celery, and a sprig of dill or chervil.

Rutabaga Sauerkraut Latkes

At first you may be inclined to turn up your nose at the idea of these latkes. They're actually quite mild, with a subtle sweetness from the rutabaga sauerkraut that balances out the smoky flavor of the fish. They're also good on their own with crème frâiche and applesauce.

makes about 16 latkes

2 pint jars Rutabaga Sauerkraut (page 109)	1/2 teaspoon kosher salt	2 shallots, minced
3/4 cup all-purpose flour	1/2 cup whole milk	Grapeseed oil, for frying
1 teaspoon baking soda	2 tablespoons unsalted butter, melted	
	1 large egg	

1. Drain the sauerkraut and rinse under cold running water. Pat dry. In a bowl, combine the flour, baking soda, and salt. In a smaller bowl, whisk together the milk, butter, and egg. Mix the milk and egg into the flour until well blended, then fold in the sauerkraut and shallots.

2. In a large sauté pan over medium-high heat, warm enough grapeseed oil to coat the bottom of the pan. In batches to avoid crowding the pan, drop 2 tablespoons of the batter per latke into the oil and fry, turning once, until the latkes are evenly brown, about 2 minutes per side. Transfer the latkes to a warmed platter and repeat with the remaining batter. Serve warm.

PORK RILLETTES

The Dordogne in southwestern France is best known for its Périgord truffles and foie gras, but it also is probably the epicenter of meat cooked in duck fat. Every fall, farmers would braise ducks in duck fat to make confit. As long as the meat remained covered with a cap of duck fat inhibiting air from penetrating the mixture, it wouldn't spoil.

My pork rillettes, in which pork shoulder is braised in either pork or duck fat, borrows from this tradition. I make rillettes in large batches then divide the meat into individual containers, capping each portion with a layer of still-warm fat. When it cools, the fat hardens and forms a seal. When it is time to eat, I pop off the fat cap and spread the rillettes on toast, adding a dab of mostarda or savory jam. Pickled vegetables, like giardiniera, add pleasant crunch and acidity to the plate. When eaten together, rillettes and condiments are the perfect match for a brown ale.

Specialty grocery stores and upscale butcher shops occasionally carry duck fat, or they can order it for you. You can also buy it from Amazon.com. We buy it in tubs, which we keep refrigerated between uses. If you have fat left over, which is likely, strain it and save it for cooking vegetables, searing meat, or making more rillettes.

---

5 cloves garlic, minced
2 tablespoons chopped thyme
1 tablespoon kosher salt
1 tablespoon coriander seeds, cracked
1 teaspoon freshly ground black pepper
Grated zest of 1 lemon
3 pounds boneless pork shoulder,
　quartered
10 cups duck fat or rendered pork fat
3 bay leaves, preferably fresh

2 shallots, minced
2 tablespoons chopped tarragon
2 tablespoons chopped Italian parsley

1/2 loaf country bread or baguette
Extra-virgin olive oil
Kosher salt and freshly ground
　black pepper
4 ounces baby mustard greens
　or arugula

Lemon juice
1 half-pint jar Cherry Mostarda
　(page 92)
Pickled vegetables, such as
　Pickled Carrots (page 26),
　Giardiniera (page 34), or
　Dill Pickles (page 30)
Whole-grain mustard (optional)

---

1. In a small bowl, mix together the garlic, thyme, the salt, coriander, pepper, and zest. Coat the shoulder pieces in the seasoning blend, add the bay leaves, cover, and refrigerate at least overnight or up to 2 days.

2. Preheat an oven to 275°F. Pat the shoulder pieces dry and place in a Dutch oven. In a pan, warm the fat just until it turns liquid. Pour the fat over the shoulder, ensuring that each piece of meat is covered with a layer of fat. Place the Dutch oven over medium heat and warm until the fat begins to bubble. Cover, transfer to the oven, and cook until the meat is tender enough to flake apart when pierced with a knife, 3 1/2 to 4 hours. (The meat should stay covered in fat this entire time. Add more fat if necessary.) Cool completely in the fat and refrigerate overnight or up to a week.

3. Over medium-low heat, warm the pork and fat until the fat liquefies. Remove the shoulder pieces and place 2 pieces in a stand mixer fitted with the paddle attachment. On low speed, break up the pork pieces until some of the meat begins to shred (do not overmix). Add half of the shallots, 1 tablespoon of the tarragon, and 1 tablespoon of the parsley and mix on low speed. While the mixer is on, drizzle in just enough fat so that the rillette has a nice sheen, about 7 ounces of fat. It should not look dry but it also should not be soupy. Repeat with the

rest of the pork, mixing in the remaining shallots, tarragon, and parsley and just enough fat so that the meat looks the same as the first batch. Taste each batch and season with more salt if needed. You will have about 5 cups of rillettes and about 8 cups of leftover fat. Strain the fat and refrigerate for another use.

4. Pack about 3 ounces of rillettes into 4-ounce ramekins. You will have more than you need for 8 servings. If you plan on serving the rillettes in a day or so, wrap and refrigerate them until ready to serve. If you plan to store the rillettes for a longer period of time, pour enough fat on top of the rillettes to cover it entirely. Store, covered, in the refrigerator. Remove the rillettes from the refrigerator at least 30 minutes before serving.

5. Preheat the oven to 400°F. Slice the bread into $^1\!/_2$-inch-thick pieces. If the slices are large, cut them in half. Brush each side with olive oil, then arrange on a baking sheet and season with salt and pepper. Bake, turning the pieces over once, until evenly toasted on both sides, about 10 minutes.

6. In a small bowl, mix the greens with a tablespoon or two of olive oil, lemon juice, salt, and pepper to taste. Divide the salad among 8 plates. Place a ramekin on each plate and spoon a dollop of mostarda on top. Serve a few pieces of toast on each plate, along with the pickled vegetables. Bring mustard, extra mostarda, and extra pieces of toast to the table.

BEER JAM–GLAZED BEEF CHEEKS *with* WHOLE-WHEAT SPAETZLE *and* ROASTED BEETS

Often, braised beef comes in a pool of liquid. These cheeks are different, cooked until the braise is almost completely absorbed by the beef cheeks. The beer jam adheres to the cheeks, giving the dish a lacquered finish. Beef cheeks might need to be ordered in advance. Otherwise, you can substitute two pounds of beef stew meat instead. With beef braises, I prefer stout beers, which mirror the richness and sweetness of the braise. Pictured on pages 268 and 269.

8 beef cheeks (about 6 ounces each)	1 onion, diced	$^1\!/_2$ cup Beer Jam (page 60)
Kosher salt and freshly ground black pepper	1 cup dark beer (porter or stout)	Whole-Wheat Spaetzle (recipe follows)
	3 bay leaves, preferably fresh	Roasted Beets with Chives
Grapeseed oil	1 sprig rosemary	(recipe follows)
2 carrots, diced	1 head garlic, halved crosswise	
2 stalks celery, diced	4 cups beef stock (page 131)	

1. Preheat the oven to 300°F. Trim the cheeks of any visible silver skin. Pat dry and season evenly with salt and pepper. Heat a thin layer of grapeseed oil in an ovenproof heavy-bottomed pot or Dutch oven over medium-high heat. Sear the cheeks, turning over once, until evenly caramelized on both sides. Transfer to a plate.

{continued}

2. In the same Dutch oven, stir in the carrots, celery, and onion and cook until lightly caramelized. Deglaze with the beer, using a wooden spoon to dislodge any browned bits of meat and vegetables from the bottom. Stir in the bay leaves, rosemary, and garlic. Simmer until the beer has reduced by half. Return the cheeks to the Dutch oven and pour in the broth. Bring to a boil, then cover and transfer to the oven. Braise until the cheeks feel tender when pierced, about 3¹/₂ hours. Cool completely in the liquid and refrigerate up to 3 days.

3. Bring the braise to a simmer and then remove the cheeks. Strain the braising liquid into a pot and simmer over medium heat until reduced by half, 8 to 10 minutes.

4. Preheat the oven to 400°F. Arrange the cheeks snugly in a tight-fitting baking dish or cast-iron pan and pour the reduced braising liquid over the top. Roast, uncovered, until the cheeks are hot through and the liquid has reduced further, about 15 minutes Brush the cheeks with the beer jam and broil until the jam begins to sizzle and adhere to the cheeks, about 5 minutes. (For a more lacquered effect, repeat this step with more beer jam). Serve family-style with sides of spaetzle and roasted beets.

Whole-Wheat Spaetzle

Thicker than regular spaetzle, whole-wheat spaetzle is sturdy enough to hold up to braised beef cheeks. To make spaetzle, you will need an inexpensive sliding or ricer-style spaetzle maker. If you don't have a spaetzle maker, you can improvise with a colander, pouring in a ladleful of batter at a time and pushing it through the holes into the water. For the alternative to work, the holes should be at least ¹/₄ inch thick.

1³/₄ cups all purpose flour	1²/₃ cups sour cream	Grapeseed oil
1 cup whole wheat flour	3 large eggs	1 or 2 tablespoons unsalted butter
Kosher salt		

1. In a large bowl, combine the flours and ¹/₂ teaspoon salt. In a small bowl, whisk together the sour cream and eggs and fold the mixture into the flour, mixing until smooth. You will have about 4 cups of batter.

2. Oil 2 baking sheets. Bring a large pot of salted water to a boil. Fill the well of the spaetzle maker with a small ladleful of batter, hold the spaetzle maker over the pot, and slide the batter over the holes. It will drip into the water, forming short squiggles. Let the spaetzle bubble to the surface and cook for a minute. Using a wire skimmer or slotted spoon, transfer the spaetzle to the oiled baking sheets. Repeat until all of the batter is used. If using a perforated pan or a colander, push one ladleful of batter at a time through the holes with the base of a ladle or a rubber spatula.

3. In a large sauté pan over medium heat, warm about 1 tablespoon grapeseed oil. In batches to avoid crowding the pan, sear the spaetzle until lightly browned. Swirl in a spoonful of butter, season with salt, and transfer to a warmed serving bowl.

Roasted Beets with Chives

While I was tempted to add pickled beets to this side dish, straightforward roasted beets are a better match for sweetness of the braised beef cheeks.

8 medium red beets	Kosher salt and freshly ground	2 tablespoons unsalted butter
Extra-virgin olive oil	black pepper	2 tablespoons minced fresh chives

1. Preheat the oven to 400°F. Remove the beet greens, if attached, and place the beets in a small baking pan. Drizzle the beets with olive oil and coat with a few generous pinches of salt and pepper. Cover with aluminum foil and bake for 45 minutes to an hour, testing occasionally for doneness with a wooden skewer. (Once the skewer glides easily into the beets, they are done.) Once the beets are cool enough to handle, slip the skins off with your fingers or a kitchen towel and cut into bite-sized chunks.

2. In a sauté pan, melt the butter. Swirl in the chives, followed by the beets. Season to taste with salt and pepper and transfer to a warmed serving bowl.

CHEESE TART *with* APRICOT PRESERVES

This dessert takes full advantage of the natural pairing between cheese and fruit preserves. I prefer fresh sheep or goat cheeses from Prairie Fruits Farm in central Illinois, but any pleasant, soft cheese will work in this recipe. Similarly, while apricot truly complements the cheese filling, other stone fruit preserves are fine stand-ins. A thin layer of lemon curd is another delicious option.

I've included a simple recipe for tart dough. It makes enough for two shells. Though you only need one for this dessert, I find it's easier to make the dough in a larger quantity so I have some extra. Pictured on page 278.

makes 1 tart

¹/₂ recipe Tart Dough (recipe follows)	Grated zest of 1 lemon	¹/₄ cup heavy cream
6 ounces cream cheese, softened	1 teaspoon pure vanilla extract	¹/₂ cup Apricot Jelly (page 65)
6 ounces fresh goat cheese	¹/₄ teaspoon kosher salt	
¹/₂ cup sugar	2 large eggs	

1. On a lightly floured surface, roll the dough into a 13-inch round. Carefully fold the round into quarters and place in a 9- or 10-inch tart pan with a removable bottom. Unfold the round and gently press into the bottom of the

{continued}

pan, trying not to stretch the dough to make it fit. (If the round is too small, remove it from the pan and roll it out a little more.) Fold the overhanging dough into the sides of the pan so the sides are thicker than the bottom. Trim away any excess by running a rolling pin over the edges of the pan, and refrigerate the shell for 20 minutes.

2. Preheat the oven to 400°F. Using a fork, lightly prick the bottom of the shell. Line the shell with aluminum foil, making sure that it covers the sides of the tart as well as the bottom. Bake until the dough is a pale golden color, 15 to 20 minutes. Remove the foil and cool for at least 20 minutes. Decrease the oven temperature to 350°F.

3. In a stand mixer fitted with the paddle attachment, mix the cheeses on medium speed until smooth. Mix in the sugar, zest, vanilla, and salt. Beat in the eggs, 1 at a time, then drizzle in the heavy cream. Pour into the par-baked tart crust and place on the lower rack of the oven. Bake until the top is set and has puffed up slightly, about 30 minutes.

4. While the tart is still warm, heat the jelly in a small saucepan. Pour the jelly evenly over the top of the tart, using an offset spatula to smooth out the top if necessary. Refrigerate the tart for 30 minutes before serving.

Tart Dough

makes two tart shells

1¹/₂ cups all purpose flour	¹/₂ cup cold unsalted butter, cubed
2 tablespoons sugar	1 large egg yolk
¹/₄ teaspoon kosher salt	About 4 tablespoons ice water

1. In a stand mixer fitted with the paddle attachment, mix together the flour, sugar, and salt on low speed. While the mixer is on, gradually add the butter and continue mixing until a coarse crumb forms. Mix in the yolk and 2 tablespoons of the ice water and continue to mix on low speed until the dough starts to come together. If it is still dry and won't stick together, add a tablespoon more of water at a time until the dough can be formed into a ball. (The dough may still be slightly on the crumbly side.)

2. Place the dough on a lightly floured surface and knead a few times until it comes together. Divide the dough in half and shape each half into a flat disc. Wrap in plastic wrap and refrigerate for at least 4 hours or overnight. (If you don't plan on making a second tart within a week, freeze one of the patties.)

A MIDWINTER FEAST

FRIED CHEESE CURDS WITH PICKLED
PEPPER VINAIGRETTE • 283

DUCK FAT–POACHED WHITEFISH
WITH DILL PICKLE VINAIGRETTE
AND BRAISED SAUERKRAUT • 284

POTATO GNOCCHI WITH
SAN MARZANO TOMATO SAUCE
AND PECORINO • 286

SLOW-ROASTED PORK BELLY WITH
GARLIC CONSERVA AND GLAZED
PICKLED SUMMER BEANS • 287

BITTERSWEET CHOCOLATE
MARQUISE WITH SUMMER
BERRY JAM • 288

{ this *Menu* serves 4 to 6 }

Midwesterners are familiar with this habit: winter arrives and we retreat into social hibernation. From what I hear from family and friends from other parts of the country, this isn't just a Midwestern habit. With this menu, I offer a way to break out of that dull rut. Invite a few good friends over for a thoughtful multicourse meal. If the duck fat–poached whitefish doesn't tempt them, then the chocolate marquise is bound to elicit a response. If not, round up a few new friends.

This menu is about much more than entertaining. It demonstrates the reason that I spend several hours each summer putting up jars of pickles and jams. Opening a jar of tomatoes in January that was canned last August transports me back to the fresh flavors of summer. In the middle of winter, a simple sauce made from these tomatoes turns plain potato gnocchi into a special treat. The same goes for fried cheese curds, which instantly become memorable when dressed with sweet pickled peppers, or for the pickled summer beans, which offer needed contrast to a rich slab of pork belly.

And these tips go beyond this menu. Each dish on this menu is a template for how I use preserves year-round on my menus. With this in mind, it's easy to modify some of these recipes to incorporate other preserves. Pickled snow peas are a fine stand-in for summer beans. Round cherry bomb peppers can take the place of pickled sweet peppers, if heat is what you're after. And the dill pickle vinaigrette served with the whitefish can be made with pickled celery, fennel, or even asparagus. (Try spooning it over leafy greens or roast chicken.) The bottom line: when you have a pantry full of preserves, you also have an arsenal of flavors at the ready, no matter the season.

FRIED CHEESE CURDS *with* PICKLED PEPPER VINAIGRETTE

Mild and strangely squeaky, cheese curds are requisite purchases on Wisconsin road trips. The best come directly from good Cheddar makers, like Hook's in Mineral Point, Wisconsin. If you have a favorite cheese maker nearby, look for signs out front proclaiming "Fresh Curd Today." I also make this vinaigrette with spicy Pickled Cherry Bomb Peppers (page 36), though I use fewer peppers. Pictured opposite.

6 cups vegetable oil
1 cup rice flour
1/2 cup all-purpose flour
1 teaspoon baking soda

Kosher salt
1 1/4 cups plus 2 tablespoons chilled
   club soda
1 pound cheese curds

Pickled Pepper Vinaigrette
   (recipe follows)

1. Line a platter with paper towels; set aside. Heat the oil in a 3-quart pot over medium-high heat until a candy or deep-fat fry thermometer reads 350°F, about 7 minutes.

2. In a large bowl, whisk together the flours, baking soda, and a pinch of salt. Whisk in the club soda until the mixture is the consistency of a thin pancake batter. (It should be able to lightly coat your finger.)

3. Mix the curds into the batter until evenly coated. In small batches, remove the curds from the batter, shaking off any excess, and scatter them across the surface of the oil so they don't stick together. (Be careful: the curds will splatter when they hit the oil.) Fry until the batter puffs around the curds and turns golden, about 1 minute. Using a skimmer or slotted spoon, lift the curds out of the oil and drain on the prepared platter. Season with salt (if the curds are already salted, you may not need to add more). Repeat until all the curds are fried.

4. Place the curds on a clean serving platter and spoon the vinaigrette around and on top of them. (You will have extra vinaigrette; it keeps in the refrigerator for at least a week.) Serve immediately.

Pickled Pepper Vinaigrette

makes nearly 2 cups

1 cup Grilled and Pickled Sweet Peppers
   (page 39)
1/2 cup Grilled and Pickled Sweet Peppers
   pickling liquid (page 39)

1 shallot, minced
2 tablespoons sliced fresh chives
1/2 cup extra-virgin olive oil
Kosher salt (optional)

Dice the peppers into small squares. In a small pot over medium heat, reduce the pickling liquid by half. Remove from the heat, stir in the peppers, shallot, and chives, and whisk in the olive oil. Season with salt, if needed.

DUCK FAT–POACHED WHITEFISH *with*
DILL PICKLE VINAIGRETTE *and* BRAISED SAUERKRAUT

There is hardly a more forgiving way to cook fish than to gently poach it in duck fat. As long as you monitor it to ensure the fat doesn't get too hot, the whitefish will turn out tender. Duck fat imparts enough richness to the whitefish to allow it to stand up to sauerkraut. For a slam-dunk wine pairing, pour an Alsatian Riesling with this course.

For best results, make the sauerkraut and vinaigrette before you poach the fish. If you plan to serve six people, add two more portions of fish to the pot. Pictured on pages 280 and 281.

---

4 cups rendered duck fat

4 (3-ounce) portions whitefish

Kosher salt

Braised Sauerkraut (recipe follows)

Dill Pickle Vinaigrette (recipe follows)

1/4 cup loosely packed dill sprigs

2 tablespoons thinly sliced Dill Pickles (page 30)

1 tablespoon olive oil

---

1. In a wide, heavy-bottomed pot over medium heat, warm the fat until it becomes transparent and reads 150°F with a thermometer. Season the fish with salt and nestle the portions into the fat. Gently poach the fish until it becomes firm and opaque, about 15 minutes. It may take some vigilance to maintain a steady, low temperature. If the temperature creeps up too high, turn the burner off for a minute or two.

2. Using a slotted spoon or fish spatula, lift the fish out of the fat and place in the center of 4 warmed plates. (The fat can be strained and cooled for other uses.) Spoon some sauerkraut onto each plate, then drizzle the vinaigrette over the top of the fish and sauerkraut. In a small bowl, mix the dill sprigs and pickle slices with a splash of olive oil and spoon over the fish to garnish.

Braised Sauerkraut

You can apply this recipe to other kinds of sauerkraut. It's especially good with the turnip (page 112) and the rutabaga (page 109) versions.

2 cups Classic Sauerkraut (page 108)
1/2 teaspoon coriander seeds
1/2 teaspoon dill seeds
1/2 teaspoon fennel seeds
1/2 teaspoon caraway seeds

1/4 cup diced bacon
5 to 6 tablespoons unsalted butter
2 stalks celery, thinly sliced at an angle
1 sweet onion (such as candy or
    Vidalia), sliced

1 cup Riesling
1 cup Chicken Stock (page 130)
Kosher salt and freshly ground
    black pepper

1. Preheat the oven to 400°F. Make a lid out of parchment paper to fit over the Dutch oven or pot you plan to braise the sauerkraut in (see Making a Parchment Paper Lid, page 20).

2. Drain the sauerkraut in a colander. Rinse with cold water and let drain. In a dry sauté pan over medium heat, toast the coriander, dill, fennel, and caraway seeds.

3. In a wide, heavy-bottomed pot over medium heat, render the bacon until crisp, about 5 minutes. Swirl in 4 tablespoons of the butter, then add the celery, onion, and spices and cook until the onion is soft and translucent, about 5 minutes. Stir in the sauerkraut and wine and bring to a boil. Pour in the stock, season with a few pinches of salt and pepper, cover with the parchment lid, and transfer to the oven. Braise until the sauerkraut is very tender and the liquid has reduced by more than half, about 45 minutes. Season to taste with more salt and pepper, if needed, and swirl in the remaining 1 to 2 tablespoons of butter.

Dill Pickle Vinaigrette

makes about 1 1/2 cups

1/2 cup Dill Pickle pickling liquid
    (page 30)
1/4 cup diced Dill Pickles (page 30)

1 shallot, minced
2 tablespoons chopped dill
1 teaspoon honey

1/2 cup extra-virgin olive oil
Kosher salt and freshly ground
    black pepper

In a small pot, reduce the pickling liquid by half. Stir in the dill pickles, shallot, dill, and honey, then whisk in the olive oil. Season to taste with salt and pepper.

POTATO GNOCCHI *with* SAN MARZANO TOMATO SAUCE *and* PECORINO

Everyone claims to have a trick to ensure that their potato gnocchi is lighter than the other guy's. It's very simple, actually. Cook the potatoes in their skins, let them steam for a few minutes, then dry them out in the oven. I also like to work with the potatoes while they're still warm. This recipe easily serves six, though extra gnocchi freeze well for up to a month.

1¹/₂ pounds Yukon gold potatoes (about 3 large potatoes)
Kosher salt and freshly ground black pepper

2 tablespoons unsalted butter at room temperature
1 large egg, lightly beaten

¹/₂ cup plus 1 tablespoon all-purpose flour, plus extra for dusting
Tomato Sauce (recipe follows)
Pecorino, for grating

---

1. Preheat the oven to 325°F. Oil a baking sheet or line it with parchment paper.

2. Put the potatoes in a large pot and cover with at least 1 inch of water. Add a generous pinch of salt and bring to a boil. Lower to a simmer and cook until tender, about 40 minutes for large potatoes. Drain the potatoes and let them steam in their skins. Once cool enough to handle (but still quite warm), peel and quarter the potatoes. Spread the pieces on the prepared baking sheet and place in the oven. Bake the potatoes until fairly dry, about 20 minutes.

3. While warm, pass the potatoes through a food mill fitted with a medium plate. Season with about ¹/₂ teaspoon of salt and a few pinches of pepper: the potatoes should taste well-seasoned. Using a spatula, mix in the butter, followed by the egg and the flour. Mix until the dough just starts to come together.

4. Lightly flour 2 baking sheets; set aside. Lightly dust a work surface with flour. Gently knead the dough a few times (do not overwork the dough or the gnocchi will be tough). Using a bench scraper or knife, divide the dough into 6 or 7 equal portions. Using your fingertips, roll each portion of dough out into a long dowel, about 20 inches long and ¹/₂ inch in diameter. With the bench scraper or knife, cut the dowel into 1-inch pieces. Spread the cut gnocchi in a single layer on the floured baking sheets and refrigerate until needed. Alternatively, the gnocchi can be frozen. You will have about 9–10 dozen gnocchi.

5. Bring a large pot of salted water to a boil. Add the gnocchi. After they float to the surface, simmer briefly (the total cooking time will be about 2 minutes). Meanwhile in a wide, shallow pot, bring the tomato sauce to a gentle simmer, thinning with water from the gnocchi if it looks too thick. Using a wire skimmer or slotted spoon, lift the gnocchi out of the water and drop into the tomato sauce. Gently stir and cook until the sauce clings to the gnocchi, about 1 minute more.

6. To serve, divide the gnocchi into warmed bowls and grate pecorino on top.

Tomato Sauce

¹/₄ cup extra-virgin olive oil
1 small yellow onion, diced
7 cloves garlic, minced

¹/₄ teaspoon red pepper flakes
6 cups Canned Tomatoes (page 46)
Kosher salt

3 sprigs thyme
3 sprigs oregano

In a 4- to 6-quart pot over medium heat, warm the olive oil. Stir in the onion and gently sweat until soft, 3 minutes. Stir in the garlic and cook 1 minute more. Add the red pepper flakes, then pour in the tomatoes. Taste the tomatoes to gauge their seasoning, then season with salt as needed. Stir in the thyme and oregano. Gently simmer until the tomatoes have thickened and are no longer watery, about 30 minutes. Remove the sprigs and taste again, adjusting the seasoning if needed.

SLOW-ROASTED PORK BELLY *with* GARLIC CONSERVA *and* GLAZED PICKLED SUMMER BEANS

While braised pork belly is generally delicious, sweet, tangy garlic conserva made from late-summer cloves elevates this dish even higher. Enlivened with fresh tarragon, the pickled summer beans counter the richness of the meat.

1¹/₂ pounds pork belly
Kosher salt and freshly ground
    black pepper
1 cup Garlic Conserva (page 123)

¹/₄ cup extra-virgin olive oil
Glazed Pickled Summer Beans
    (recipe follows)

1. Place the belly on a cutting board with the fat side facing up. Using a sharp knife, score the fat with a crosshatch pattern, making cuts about ¹/₄ inch deep. Season both sides of the belly with salt and pepper. In a small bowl, mix together the garlic conserva and the olive oil and rub onto the belly until both sides are evenly coated. Cover and refrigerate at least overnight or up to 2 days.

2. Preheat the oven to 300°F. Place the belly, fat side up, on a rack in a roasting pan. Roast until a golden-brown crust has started to form, about 1¹/₂ hours. Decrease the temperature to 200°F, cover the belly with foil, and roast until deep brown and tender all the way through when pierced with a fork, about 2 hours more.

3. Remove the foil and let rest for 30 minutes. To serve, slice the belly crosswise into ¹/₂-inch-thick pieces. Serve with the summer beans.

Glazed Pickled Summer Beans

1 pint Pickled Summer Beans (page 42)	Kosher salt
¹/₄ cup Chicken Stock (page 130)	2 tablespoons loosely packed tarragon
2 tablespoons unsalted butter	leaves, chopped

Drain the beans, saving ¹/₄ cup of the pickling liquid. In a medium pot, mix the beans, pickling liquid, stock, butter, and a pinch of salt. Bring to a boil, then decrease to a gentle simmer and cook until the liquid has reduced enough to glaze the beans, about 6 minutes. Stir in the tarragon and taste for seasoning, adding salt if needed.

BITTERSWEET CHOCOLATE MARQUISE
with SUMMER BERRY JAM

This chilled-out chocolate dessert offers a rich backdrop for summer preserves. I reach for dark berry jams, like blackberry, with chocolate, but Rainier cherry or strawberry jams also pair well here. I use a long, 1¹/₂-quart terrine mold to give the marquise a sophisticated shape, but you also could use a standard loaf pan. For best results, make the dessert the day before you intend to serve it. The dessert makes enough to serve 10 people, but extra marquise keeps, wrapped in plastic, in the freezer.

²/₃ cup confectioners' sugar, sifted	8 tablespoons unsalted butter	1 tablespoon granulated sugar
2 tablespoons plus 2 teaspoons unsweetened cocoa powder	4 large egg yolks	1 tablespoon confectioners' sugar
6 ounces bittersweet chocolate (about 72%)	¹/₂ cup heavy cream	¹/₂ cup heavy cream
	2 large egg whites	Blackberry Jam (page 66)

1. Lightly oil a 1¹/₂-quart terrine or a loaf pan. Line smoothly with plastic wrap, allowing a 2-inch overhang on the long sides.

2. Sift together ²/₃ cup of the confectioners' sugar and the cocoa. In the top of a double boiler (or in a heat-proof bowl set over a pot of barely simmering water), melt the chocolate and butter, stirring together until smooth. Remove the bowl from the heat and let cool slightly. Whisk in 1 yolk at a time, then whisk in the cocoa powder mixture until smooth. Remove from the heat.

3. In a stand mixer fitted with the whisk attachment, whip ¹/₂ cup of the cream on high speed until it forms soft peaks. When the whisk attachment is removed it should leave behind soft spikes in the cream.

4. Thoroughly wash and dry the mixer bowl and whisk, then return them to the stand mixer. Whip the egg whites and the granulated sugar on high speed until the meringue forms medium peaks, about 2 minutes. When the whisk attachment is removed, it should leave behind distinct but not stiff spikes in the meringue.

5. Using a rubber spatula fold the meringue into the chocolate. Gently fold in the whipped cream until the batter is evenly blended. Pour into the prepared mold, cover with the overhanging plastic wrap, and refrigerate until firm, at least overnight or up to 5 days.

6. To serve, whip the remaining $^1/_2$ cup whipped cream with the remaining 1 tablespoon confectioners' sugar until it forms soft peaks.

7. To serve, remove the overhanging plastic wrap and invert the terrine onto a cutting board. Fill a pitcher with hot water and place a sharp knife in the water to warm the blade. Peel away the plastic wrap. Dry the knife on a clean kitchen towel, then slice the terrine crosswise into $^1/_2$-inch pieces, periodically dipping the knife back into the water to clean the blade and rewarm it. Place each slice on a chilled plate and garnish with a spoonful of jam and dollop of whipped cream.

INDEX

ACKNOWLEDGMENTS

We offer our deep gratitude to the staff, family, friends, customers, and publishing professionals and who contributed time and support to help us turn a spark of an idea into a fully realized project.

To the crews at my restaurants Vie and Perennial Virant, past and present, for clocking in every day. Special kudos to Nathan Sears, for his development of and dedication to our charcuterie program, and to Jimmy McFarland, for being a unit of support. I'd also like to thank our bartender, Mike Page, who, with Todd Feitl, pioneered the use of preserves in cocktails at Vie.

To Tony Porreca, whose dedication to canning and passion for cooking helped us hone the recipes for the home kitchen.

To the team at Ten Speed Press, especially Jenny Wapner, who enthusiastically polished the story, Toni Tajima for inspired design, Jane Horn for keen copy editing, and Sharron Wood for proofreading.

To our ace photo crew: Jeff and Susie Kauck, their daughter, Dana, and Aaron Corey, all of whom worked to capture the spirit of seasonal preserving on camera.

To Leslie Cooperband and Wes Jarrell of Prairie Fruits Farm and to Bronwyn Weaver and Bob Archibald of Heritage Prairie Farm, for their hospitality at their busy farms during photo shoots.

To Barbara Ingham, for providing professional food-safety advice on canning recipes.

To John Virant, for helping with the fine print.

To Tom Virant, Gary Wiviott, and Craig "Meathead" Goldwyn for smoking expertise.

Several people throughout my career have helped shape my point of view as a chef. I'd like to single out Christine Ferber, for her preserving inspiration, Wayne Nish, for expanding my palate during my line-cook days, and Paul Kahan, for being the first guy to show me that sourcing local produce in Chicago wasn't a fool's errand.

A special thanks to my family, who inspired me to love food and helped me turn Vie—and later this cookbook—into a reality; especially my grandmothers, Rita and Mildred, who taught me the value of preserving; my parents, Mary Ann and John, who instilled an excitement about food into every meal; my in-laws, Gail and Al Tangora, for their ongoing support and steady presence at Vie; and—especially—my amazing wife, Jennifer, and my sons, Lincoln and Zane. Thank you for everything.

Kate would like to thank Barbara Sutton for reading early drafts and for putting up with a refrigerator full of pickling experiments. She would also like to thank Tom and Kathy Leahy for embracing the idea that their daughter was going to spend a year immersed in brine.

Published in the United States by Ten Speed Press,

an imprint of the Crown Publishing Group,

a division of Random House, Inc., New York.

www.crownpublishing.com

www.tenspeed.com

Ten Speed Press and the Ten Speed Press colophon are registered trademarks of Random House, Inc.

Library of Congress Cataloging-in-Publication Data

Virant, Paul, 1970-

The preservation kitchen : the craft of making and cooking with

pickles, preserves, and aigre-doux / by Paul Virant with Kate Leahy ;

photography by Jeff Kauck.

p. cm.

Includes bibliographical references and index.

1. Canning and preserving. 2. Cookbooks. I. Leahy, Kate. II. Title.

TX601.V57 2012

641.4'2—dc23

2011027972

ISBN 978-1-60774-100-8 (print book) — ISBN 978-1-60774-101-5 (ebook)

Cover and text design by Toni Tajima

Prop styling by Susie Kauck

Printed in China

10 9 8 7 6 5 4 3 2 1

First Edition